Aspects of Graeco-Roman Urbanism

Essays on the classical city

edited by
Ronald T. Marchese

BAR International Series 188
1983

B.A.R.

122 Banbury Road, Oxford OX2 7BP, England

GENERAL EDITORS

A.R. Hands, B.Sc., M.A., D.Phil.
D.R. Walker, M.A.

B.A.R.-S188, 1984: 'Aspects of Graeco-Roman Urbanism'.

Price £10.00 post free throughout the world. Payments made in currency other than sterling must be calculated at the current rate of exchange. Cheques should be made payable to B.A.R. and sent to the above address.

ISBN 0 86054 240 8

For details of all BAR publications in print please write to the above address. Information on new titles is sent regularly on request, with no obligation to purchase.

Volumes are distributed direct from the publisher. All BAR prices are inclusive of postage by surface mail anywhere in the world.

Printed in Great Britain

To

My mother and father

Urban studies constitutes a relatively recent field of inquiry which is already marked by a vast body of information on the origins and development of cities in the ancient world. Although a new research concern, cities are among the oldest artifacts of human life. Taken by most social theorists of the past, the city is the image of society and, therefore, a unique form of specialized existence. In the ancient world the city was identified with social and cultural concerns which encouraged individualism and innovation. Variety was the predominant mark of the city in antiquity. The city, after all, was a natural phenomenon suited to human existence. Aristotle argued in the Politics: "men come together in the city to live; they remain in order to live the good life." This quest for the good life was the major concern and feature of the Graeco-Roman city.

If the Graeco-Roman city was a social unit based on personal loyalty, economic pursuit, and political force, it was also a cultural entity which defined the quality of life of its contemporary constituents. It was to be a rational expression of the body politic. At the same time irrational values, conflicting social, cultural, and political ideologies were manifest in the form of municipal organization, both physical and human, tensions between a variety of social and economic classes, and finally wholesale expressions of violence against dominant political regimes. These social pressures were acted out in the physical confines of the Graeco-Roman city. But the city was not a mere physical apparatus of public structures and monuments which provided a locale for social interaction and conflict. The city was civilization itself and, therefore, a dynamic force which established a high standard of sophistication for its constituents.

The articles selected and their positioning conform to a logical chronological sequence. The problem of apportioning space to various issues was especially difficult, given the variety of topics. Most of the selections deal with traditional issues which, on closer examination, become the basis for a radical departure from the ideologies which dominate urban studies today. It is hoped that this re-evaluation will stimulate our colleagues, our students, and the future generation of scholars to explore the ancient world and its urban structures in a more systematic manner.

In a work of this nature much is owed to the labor of others. Directly and indirectly many scholars, colleagues, and friends provided assistance and encouragement during the preparation of the text. I am indebted to my colleagues Ronald Huch and James Gillespie for their comments. I wish to offer my sincere appreciation to Ira M. Lapidus who directed the 1978 N.E.H. seminar on the ancient city. His insights, remarks, and contributions were not only informative, but deeply appreciated. Without his encouragement and assistance this volume would have never reached fruition. To Avis Hedin and Elizabeth Kwapick special thanks are given. Their nimble fingers were a major reason for the completion of the text. Finally, I wish to thank my students at the University of Minnesota. They served as an attentive audience for the papers in this volume.

INTRODUCTION

The growth of cities in particular and the urbanization of life in general have long been a focus of inquiry for social scientists. Class structure, inner city politics, urban locale, population patterns, and the general nature and make-up of the community are among the most frequently discussed issues in urban studies today. To the social scientist, the city is the most prominent feature in world history and an important research locale for interdisciplinary endeavors. A highly visible universal structure, the city reinforces personal commitments and at the same time it creates or should create a sense of civic pride, loyalty, and finally individual responsibility. The city can also be an impersonal entity of interrelated and conflicting institutions which, at times, tends to dehumanize its members. A product and producer of conflicting social values and ideas, the city is to be viewed as a unique combination of good and evil necessary in the fulfillment of man's personal destiny; a destiny which requires man to live in harmony with his own kind and with nature itself. It is this unique dualism which complicates our basic understanding of past city development and organization. At the same time it provides a point of comparison with the social and technological problems modern cities face in today's rapidly changing world.

In an analysis of cities, modern interpretators have realized that the city at one point in time is not the same institution at a different point in time. This has led to the realization that the term city has no universal definition, especially in comparative studies focused on the origins of ancient urban systems. Some writers attend to the physical fact of the city, the commanding presence of a dense concentration of monuments and people fixed in time and space. For those who follow this belief, the word city is used for a dense concentration of people; a shorthand way of referring to defensive functions, economic exchange, patterns of specialization, forms of social stratification, organized politics, and finally a sophistication of culture. The term city is further used as an image of society. This implies civilization and the kinship of men in society and their place in the cosmos. Others offer the view that the economic or technical activities or the political history of cities is the only worthwhile definition of urban life in general and the only means upon which a comparative study can be formulated. Although conceptualized at different times in a rather long historical process, cities, for our purpose, are to be viewed as direct reflections of the prevailing ideologies which define their character and their basic reason for existence. A body of interrelated customs, traditions, attitudes, and finally sentiments, the city, especially the classical city of Greece and Rome, is deeply rooted in the dominant customs and ideals of the people who inhabit it. These bind a city to a specific society, based on shared beliefs, as a living symbol of the social processes of human life.

Cities in the ancient world either established, or were part of, larger established broad based state societies and, as such, were symbols of sophistication, status, and power. The ancient city was administrative, bureaucratic, and finally commercial. All were important in regards to the regal and ritualistic aspects of the societies which produced them. At the same time the ancient city was both homogeneous and heterogeneous in social make-up, political organization, economic pursuit, and finally cultural ideology. Recognized by the political theorists of the classical world, notably Plato and Aristotle, the city was the culmination of the basic desires of man. It became the recognized focus for human groups stripped of their previous family ties and tribal affiliations. Replete with its own sense of destiny, the ancient city was a unique combination of ideals and realities; the former centered in the physical grandeur of public buildings and physical facilities, the latter focused on the harsher realities of daily living.

Although some generalizations on the nature of the ancient city have been attempted in the previous paragraphs, it is evident that the ancient city, as an all embracing recognizable entity within the human landscape, has a detailed and complicated history separated by distinct cultural and historical processes. In actuality two general social and cultural processes are evident: one predominantly confined to the ancient Near East; the second focused in the traditional confines of the classical world of Greece and Rome. Both have been the subject of inquiry in recent years, especially inquiries on the hows and whys necessary in the formation of institutionally defined urban life. To understand the achievements and problems of the city in Greece and Rome it is necessary to place the classical city in its proper historical perspective.

It is safe to conclude that the city was millennia old before the advent of Graeco-Roman culture and its expression within an urban context. The Near East produced dynamic state systems that were urban based in a variety of regions: in Mesopotamia, Syria, Palestine, Anatolia, and finally Egypt. A focus for government and a structure within which all daily activity took place, the Near Eastern city was an awe inspiring physical institution densely populated and extremely complex in its internal and external manifestations. The development of an overall Near Eastern type, although limited by environmental factors, was part of a long historical, cultural, and technological process. This process can be sequentially divided into four basic stages: (1) from the beginnings of time to 10,000 B.C. - an age of hunter-gatherers and intensive hunter-gatherer groups; (2) from 10,000 to approximately 3500 B.C. - a period marked by incipient urban life, the establishment of permanent agricultural villages, and finally proto-urban communities, especially in Mesopotamia; (3) from 3500 to 2400 B.C. - a period marked by dense concentrations of people, monumental architecture, temple cities, theocracies, early city-states, and finally multi-city regimes under the domination of newly formed aristocratic authority: (4) and finally a period from 2400 - 1500 B.C. - a period marked by the creation of empires with regal centers supported by a vast urban hierarchy. Although individual regimes rose and fell, especially in the late third and second millennia B.C., the type of political, social, economic, and cultural development represented by imperial authority was permanently institutionalized. At the same time the formation of Near Eastern empires progressively transformed the structure of city societies from symbols of local authority, power, and sophistication, to those representing the cosmopolitan values of an imperial regime.

The key to the origin of Near Eastern cities lies in the village communities of the fourth millennium B.C. In these small, self-contained and self-sufficient communities, the social, political, and religious relationships were forged. The integration of life between non-related families allowed for larger cooperative efforts, especially in the extensive and intensive exploitation of the environment, to take hold and develop. This appears to have been important in the formation of social hierarchies. The division or specialization of labor increased, and this furthered the rise of stratified societies, levels of dominance and subserviance, and finally institutionalized control mechanisms over larger populations. The implied stratification of society created the basis for a ruling elite which in turn further weakened the family to the point individual effort was transferred away from the family unit and household to the households of powerful men. In the evolution of village life, economic, social, political, and religious changes went hand in hand. Some have seen connections among these various changes as the basis for the formation of early cities. V. Gordon Childe (1960) stressed the centrality of economic change and envisioned a process by which improved technology and divisions of labor, led to the stratification of village life and the formation of the city. Robert Adams (1966) on the other hand stressed the primacy of social and cultural elements in the emergence of cities. From his point of view the dominance of some men over others preceded and promoted economic and technical change. Elites favored the extension of irrigation, the improvement of agricultural production and specialization of labor so that surpluses would be generated to support their households. H. Frankfurt (1956) and T. Jacobsen (1976) stressed the priority of religious ideas and religious commitment of the community. The mark of change was the construction of temples. Commitments to the worship of the gods motivated villagers to build and enlarge temples, to accept the authority of the priestly officials to organize the village economy and to increase production and the division of labor in the interest of service to the temple. In actuality, the interaction between the economic, political, and religious sectors provided the basis for the city in the Near East. All led to new forms of social, economic, and religious organization – from temple theocracies to the political state, territorial defined, under royal authority. Both provided a new concept of community life which transcended the limited specialized interests and loyalties of the family, and the clan, and united a larger segment of the population in the service of the gods or their vicars on earth, be they priest or king. By ordering their lives, by submitting to the will of the gods and their earthly representatives, the efforts of men could help assure the order of nature and the universe. The concentration of managers, priests, craftsmen, and workers brought surrounding villagers into closer contact with these new religious, political, and social centers of life. Centralized activity, especially religious, and concentrated populations marked the formation of city societies.

The evolution of Greek and Roman urban society, although relatively late in the historical processes of urbanization, proceeded along a parallel course with the Near East. This parallel development, especially in the evolutionary processes from village commonwealths to urban centers with subordinant satellite communities, was, however, marked by social and ideological differences. Greek urban values were not defined by an overriding system of sacred symbols or institutions. Belief in the gods did not set a standard for economic, social, or political existence. Religious beliefs or religious dominance of society did not develop an integrated economy or centralized political leadership constructed on religious principles. The gods, although feared and respected did not govern personal behavior. Religion was notably absent in the development of political authority. The attainment of excellence, arete, was the primary social value which legitimized political authority and the right to govern. This right, however, was not absolute. The pursuit of honor was tempered by the possibility of failure and the loss of arete and political authority. Political leadership also brought with it personal commitment; to one's kind, household, and finally to those individuals who defined the social community. This pursuit of excellence had a corresponding impact on the emergence of the Graeco-Roman city. Physically, comparisons with the Near East are obvious: the early physical formation of Graeco-Roman cities featured a dense core of shrines, temples, administrative offices, defensive systems, and a concentration of the local population in a dense urban core. Politically and socially Graeco-Roman urbanism broke new ground. Politically it was characterized by the evolution of governmental organizations from monarchy to aristocracy, to oligarchy, to democracy - or the oscillation between oligarchic and democratic principles, and finally to a return to monarchy within an imperial situation. The evolution of political forms, however, implied a deeper change in society itself. This appears in the realm of citizenship. Citizenship was defined within a civic matrix guaranteed by a civil constitution and laws which allowed participation within the political structure of the state and the shaping of the communities destiny. Not only was a new method of participation created but a new civic ethos established free from the whims of aristocratic rule. Each individual admitted to the civic body as a citizen had the legitimate right to pursue the realization of arete. This personal quest for excellence also benefitted the Graeco-Roman city by defining a new level of civic moral values - agathos politites. Civic pride and loyalty became standard features of the urban value system. Thus, to the classical mind, the city was an expression of order and law, constitutionally defined, and, as such, it had little in common with the sprawling, irrational cities of the Near East. Senseless Nineveh with all its grandeur was to be abhorred. For the pre-Alexandrian world of Greece, the city reached fruition in the logic and value systems of Plato and Aristotle. After all, the city was an expression of the inner virtue of man, individually and collectively. Not only was the good life possible, it was guaranteed.

It is safe to say that well-defined cities did not appear in the Mediterranean basin before the ninth century B.C. Certainly earlier civilizations existed in the Mediterranean that had a quasi-urban base, most notably the Minoan and Mycenanean worlds of the second millennium B.C. Contemporary with the major empires of the Near East, both civilizations featured moderate population clusters which gravitated

4

towards highly specialized palace centers or citadels. Many of the functions of later urban life are evident: political authority, social elites, specialized craft laborers, economic distribution, and religious ideology. However, a concept of civic participation and a sense of belonging was absent. The proto-urban stage attained in the second millennium B.C., however, was interrupted by the collapse of the great palatial centers which had fostered a limited urban format. Mediterranean urban development was arrested and reseeded into a dark age which followed the disappearance of palace elites.

The Greek city was the product of fusion. An idea of the physical community of place and the territorial state survived in the oral traditions of the Greek Dark Ages. The memory of the great palatial centers of second millennium B.C. Greece were attached to the social processes of a far simpler Greek world. Tribal in nature such processes created the nucleus for group solidarity in the ninth and eighth centuries B.C. and became the necessary pre-requisite for the classical urban ideal, the polis. Although diverse societies, notably Etruscan and Latin, advanced along an urban road, it was left to the Greeks to create the polis. It was this concept that was slightly altered and adapted by the Romans which allowed them to govern a uniform cultural and social world far greater in size and complexity than the narrower confines of the Near East. A unique fusion of people and historical events made the polis a different institution than its Near Eastern counterpart. Greek poets and natural philosophers maintained that the polis was built on justice which guaranteed the traditional rights of all social classes. This created a unified world view for the members of the polis. To Plato and Aristotle, such unity could be achieved only by limited numbers of citizens, numbers large enough to insure self-sufficiency but small enough to make total participation possible. The smallness of the polis made it a better place to live.

Classical urbanism was centered in the polis and its Roman manifestation, the civitas. Much has been written about the classical conceptions of the city, by both contemporary authorities such as Plato, Aristotle, and Cicero, and by modern scholars, most notably Victor Ehrenberg (1968) and A.H.M. Jones (1940). All tend to agree that the classical city was a natural outgrowth of human needs and desires. A physical manifestation in the same tradition as the Near Eastern city, the polis/civitas tended to transcend the limits of its physical bonds in a way that others failed to do. It was the social forces of the classical city that made it unique. It was a living, breathing entity of citizens and their families.

The Greek polis originated in the pre-political period of the early first milennium B.C. Although clouded in the distant past and the confusion of a dying social system, the Greeks of later generations were quick and articulate enough to comprehend, chronicle, and explain the processes of urbanization and the confrontation between the city-dweller and his rustic counterpart (Lloyd). This process of encounter and the overall definition of quality living was an essentially Greek concern. Evident in the Iliad and Odyssey, the Greek polis crystallized in the great age of Greek enlightenment (seventh and sixth centuries B.C.). The polis was no longer to be viewed as a mere place of refuge. Men

5

were the _polis_. It became a spiritual structure rather than a physical
entity. A sense of belonging emerged which distinguished the _polis_ from
all contemporary forms of association (Anderson). Defined in terms of
the mind but based on the traditional notions of the family, the _polis_
became the focus of the good life and, as such, a natural creation
rather than the product of chance or human caprice. Evident in the
Platonic and Aristotelian _polis_ of the fourth century B.C., the good
life was an integral part of the Greek urban experience. The good of
the _polis_, which encompassed the good of the individual and the life of
the family, were inseparable. Indeed the _polis_ existed for the sake of
the good. Unity within the _polis_ was a rational unity and the goal of
the _polis_ was integrally attached to the whole as well as to the
individual part. As Plato argued, the _polis_ was a natural phenomenon
based on virtue. It is this underlying concept which created the
foundation for the classical city; the attainment of the good life but
not divorced from civic participation.

Thus, the _polis_ was unique and its early historical development
uniform. Between 800 and 400 B.C. the transformation of Greek urban
society was complete. The _polis_ had begun as a society of small clans
and tribes with aristocratic leadership and a coalition of aristocratic
heads of families in which citizenship was defined according to kinship.
It was transformed into a unitary political society, the corporate body
of all who were admitted to the citizen class, with citizenship defined
by a combination of membership in descent organizations, territorial
residence, and by the legal notions of the relations of citizens to the
state. The values of the _polis_ played an equally large part in the
transformation of society. Greek values favored the formation of
voluntary associations for political and religious purposes. The Greek
respect for _arete_ legitimized the struggle for power and wealth and
allowed men to channel opportunities generated by political and economic
change into the struggle for individual gains. At the same time
religious concepts were far too weak to inhibit institutional changes as
a solution to the struggle for power. However, the _polis_ was a spent
force by the close of the fifth century B.C. Although idealized in the
fourth century, the _polis_ was to be superseded by the world state.
Greek uniformity gave way to a broad expression of Greek pragmatism in
the post-Alexandrian world of the third and second centuries B.C. As
with everything else Alexander drastically altered the _polis_. Platonic
and Aristotelian conservatism, a reflection of the homogeneous nature of
Greek society from the sixth to the fourth centuries was shattered
forever by Greek advancement and the establishment of Greek urban life
into the far reaches of the Near East. A transformation took place, a
transformation evident as early as the late fifth century. Greek
society had always maintained a pan-Hellenic ethnic, cultural, and
linguistic identity which transcended the boundaries of the individual
polis. These undercurrents were reinforced in the fourth century by a
more cosmopolitan cultural consciousness. The breakup of traditional
kinship and household ties not only led to new forms of city polites but
also to a broadening of Greek moral and social ideas. Evident in the
growth of universal philosophies and religions, typical Greek concepts
of the city were combined with those in the Near East millennia earlier.
A combination of Hellenic ideals and Near Eastern control mechanisms
centered in a variety of administrative, commercial, and culture

functions created the foundation for a new urban consciousness, a new comprehension of order, and finally a new ethos. The Hellenistic city drew its heritage from the best of both worlds. Fusion led to uniformity which was consciously pursued by the Seleucids and Romans. The creation of a cosmopolitan spirit with sprawling civic centers was clearly tied to the uniformity in social, political, and cultural makeup of the Hellenistic city.

With the unification of the eastern and western Mediterranean worlds by Rome at the close of her Republican existence in the first century B.C., the western conception of the urban ideal had materialized. Rome continued the process of urbanization on the Greek model in the Near East. At the same time classical culture was extended, through the establishment of cities based on the Roman model, to the very frontiers of the western Roman world. By the second century A.D., imperial Rome stood at the apex of a vast league of cities and their associate urban hierarchies. As the focus of a world state, Rome's own image was impressive. Densely inhabited, overcrowded and congested, the city of Rome was the direct heir of an imperial ideal. As a world capital, Rome was the focus of sophistication which was, in turn, exported in the form of Graeco-Roman culture (Ramage). In essence, Rome was the world and a world unto itself. She suffered immense problems based on an inadequate environment, bad sewage and fool control, disease, and finally noise pollution. This negative impression was countered by a sense of excitement and a grandeur never attained before in the long history of urban development. Imperial fora, public baths, theaters, and its overall vastness made Rome stand out as a jewel amongst jewels. As a city and imperial capital, Rome established conceptions of taste and fashion which were imitated by the provincial cities of her empire (Orr). Rome became the archtype of cities. She inspired morality and a sense of religious conviction. At the same time Rome was the axis of a vast realm of differing cultures all of which looked to her for political leadership. Rome effectively and powerfully fused the Hellenic, Hellenistic, and Near Eastern worlds into a rich cultural unit. This was expressed through one common vehicle, the individual provincial city (Miller). Stretching from the far reaches of the German frontiers to Mesopotamia and the traditional heart of the classical world, the Graeco-Roman city literally unified the ancient world into a homogeneous entity which was predominantly city based.

By the second century A.D. the Roman world had the appearance of a broad-based federal structure with Rome, the common town, at the apex of a vast league of city-states. Technically equal in their political and social make-up, this legal fiction of equality quickly broke down by the end of the second century. Rome increasingly interfered in the local organization of the classical city and assumed direct responsibilities for their administration. The collection of taxes, maintaining agricultural production, highways, aqueducts, and commercial routes, previously perrogatives of local governments, were taken over by imperial agents in the third century. Compared with the first and second centuries, in which the ancient world saw the finest flowering of cities as radiant symbols of the age, the third century was one of desperation. Inflation, declining physical prosperity, and finally external conflict and internal civil war took a drastic toll on the city. In this climate, the classical city stagnated. Its civic spirit, an integral part of its social character and cultural idealism, was sapped. Economic collapse furthered social tensions and civic patriotisms, once a responsibility, had become a crushing burden.

If the classical city atrophied in the third century, alterations in imperial authority also are evident. The first two centuries saw the princeps, the first citizen of the state, become an absolute monarch who ruled by military authority. Thus, imperial authority became a personal concern rather than an expression of civic power-sharing. Such a transformation obviously was detrimental to the old ideals of the city, ideals which guaranteed asemblance of civic responsibility at the local level and participation at the provincial and federal levels. Conflict along the imperial frontiers, civil strife, social tensions, and economic and political collapse caused a re-evaluation of the older concepts of life. Certain communities weathered the storm, especially in the East where a vigorous economic and social life was maintained to a fairly late date. As the city changed due to external pressure and internal readjustment by the imperial administration, so too changed the relationship between religion and society. Classical municipal organization was integrately associated with pre-Christian ideologies. A break with old religious concepts also meant a break with a rich classical past. Pagan worship was part of the city heritage, a heritage not fully accepted by Christianity which had its own means of organization. Not wholly compatible, municipal structures eventually were absorbed into a new ecclesiastical framework.

In general, municipalities suffered greatly in the third century. Institutionally the city-state changed. Physically the unwalled beauty of the typical second century community was replaced by a smaller, walled redoubt with a lower standard of prosperity and a shrinking population. Such losses, essential factors in the declining revenues of the Roman state were met by edicts of compulsion which tied individuals to social rank, administrative office, and occupational pursuit. What was once a free spirit, the life blood of the Graeco-Roman city, had now become a compulsory burden.

In conclusion, differences in the late Roman world stemmed from the relatively recent urbanization of the west in comparison with the long processes of development in the Near East. Traditions that were deep seated allowed for a limited municipal revival in the East in the fifth and sixth centuries A.D. Such was not the case in the West where city life stagnated and disappeared by the seventh century A.D. The institutional and emotional factors which fostered the classical city literally ebbed away in the West. In the Byzantine East, the city remained the focus of intellectual life despite its diminished importance as an economic and political center. The old urban ideals of Greece and Roman, however, found a new direction with the advent of Christianity and its acceptance as a favored religion after Constantine. This new direction was not without problems, problems which fueled social unrest and violence (Gregory). Public disorder based on conflicting religious ideologies, the lack of the daily necessities of life, and personal and group frustration were common features and easily vented within the new urban order. Although conflict was common,

Byzantine cities maintained contact with the deep cultural traditions of the past. Clinging to an older tradition that was, at times compatible with the new religious order, the Byzantine city survived well into the medieval period.

In this brief and rather general introduction of the ancient city certain features are evident which pertain directly to the formation of the Graeco-Roman city and the inherent problems these communities faced. Cities have to be understood not only as physical expressions of society itself in which they serve as foci for economic, political, and cultural activities but also as a value system with a well-defined ethos. In this manner the Graeco-Roman city, be it a typical example of local authority or the seat for an all embracing imperial state, was a symbol of the human condition of the classical and late classical age. The Greeks and their Latin successors did not consider their urban constructs as cold fact but as living beings, symbols of order, and as arenas of moral and personal fulfillment. The city was life itself with a well-defined ideology, culture, physical layout, and finally problems. Within the context of the city social organization and cultural ideologies were forged. At the same time social tensions, conflict, and the daily problems of living were part and parcel of the urban scheme. The classical city of Greece and Rome was a symbol of the society which produced it. Shared beliefs, customs, and traditions set the stage for a unique urban attitude. It is our purpose to offer insights on the cultural ideals, social attitudes, and finally the urban problems and tensions within the Graeco-Roman city during its existence on center stage in the history of the city.

Bibliography

Adams, Robert, 1966: *The Evolution of Urban Society*, Chicago.

Childe, V. Gordon, 1960: *What Happened in History*, London.

Ehrenberg, Victor, 1960: *The Greek State*, London.

Frankford, Henri, 1956: *The Birth of Near Eastern Civilization*,
New York.

Jacobsen, T., 1976: *The Treasures of Darkness: A History of
Mesopotamian Religion*, New Haven.

Jones, A.H.M., 1940: *The Greek City from Alexander to Justinian*,
Oxford.

Greek Urbanity and the Polis

Charles Lloyd

"THE LAW-ABIDING TOWN (POLIS) . . . OUTRANKS SENSELESS NINEVEH"
(Phocylides)

In a valuable modern assessment of the history of theories on the city, M.I. Finley (1977:305-327) is disparaging about the current trend in the historiography of the ancient city. He finds fault with the increasing number of histories of individual cities: "With scarcely an exception . . . they lack a conceptual focus or scheme: everything known about the place under examination appears to have equal claim . . . The city qua city is flooded out" (Finley 1977:324).

This same criticism would hardly apply to Victor Ehrenberg's The Greek State, first published in 1932 but revised and reissued several times since, for this book still remains the point of departure for any discussion of the Greek polis. At the time it was written it filled a "distressing gap" (Schaefer 1960:422) in the modern historical treatment of the polis. It is still hailed as "concise, original, distinctive," a "lasting panorama" (Meier 1969:366), and so thought-provoking as to spark controversy. As one of the most comprehensive and accessible works on the Greek polis, Ehrenberg's book deals both with the Hellenic polis and its permutations during the Hellenistic era. But throughout, the "ideal type" (Idealtypus) of Max Weber underlies Ehrenberg's treatment: realizing that the term polis implies a process of abstraction, "we must recognize the unity that underlies the plurality . . . it will be our task to describe what is typical" (Ehrenberg 1964:3). It has been this approach that has drawn criticism from recent scholars in the field: "Ehrenberg's purpose in the 'ideal type' is the starting point (for all criticism) . . . Whether one . . . can consider the most noteworthy and really significant form of communities to be also the typical form for that time period appears doubtful to me when a very great number of important communities exist in an entirely different form of government" (Meier 1969:368). Meier expresses what is probably a typical misgiving about Ehrenberg's dependence on undated political and sociological evidence and about his almost static approach to the polis which obscures its constant evolution: "we have the choice, simply on the grounds of certain characteristics applicable, certainly, since the eighth century, of accepting the polis as a state in the most time-worn and practically meaningless sense of the word or of distinguishing in a more precise sense the polis of a prepolitical or early political form from that of a more or less complete nationality . . . " (Meier 1969:374). Finley in his survey is quite sensitive to the problems that Ehrenberg's method presents (Finley 1977:324), but finds even in the "ideal type" a way out from the "cul de sac" of modern histories of individual ancient towns in which broad questions and purposes are overshadowed or ignored. His suggestion may provide a workable compromise: "the variations within each type, the changes and developments, the implications over the whole range of human thinking

11

and acting require detailed, concrete exposition--an exposition which would at the same time be a test of the ideal type" (Finley 1977:324).

The extensive evidence about the polis with its multiple and almost protean shapes makes it difficult to treat in a unified yet accurate way. Modern historians and archaeologists, relying on the ancient written records as a basis, have done much to uncover the facts about many Greek poleis but for several reasons an overall view of the Greek polis is still, in large part, elusive. In terms of citizen population and area, great divergencies exist between the populations of Syracuse, Acragas, and Athens, all over 20,000, and that of Mycenae with a total army of eighty men fighting at the battle of Plateia, and between Sparta's 3,200 square miles of territory and, say, Corinth's 330. Neither of Hellas' two greatest poleis can be considered really typical. Athens with its total population in the fifth century at over 300,000 had complex and diverse commerce and industry and an exceptionally vital and articulate culture, unsurpassed in the ancient world and, perhaps even in the modern era; its traditions were staunchly democratic. But Sparta, with its vast territory farmed by serfs, was essentially rural; it preserved an almost archaic form of habitation and a conservative militarism. One binding characteristic of the polis, it would seem, is self-sufficiency, political and economic, yet in some areas, notably Arcadia and Boeotia, poleis either develop very late or are overshadowed by a confederacy with a common council and dual citizenship.

But the ancient Greeks themselves write on the topic of the polis and understand its uniqueness. Though the purposes of the sixth-century Phocylides from Miletus are not those, certainly, of an Ehrenberg or even of an analytical Aristotle, his cultural comparison of the Greek polis with the Mesopotamian Nineveh is compelling if only for its acute perceptiveness: "The law-abiding town (polis), though small and set on a lofty rock, outranks senseless Nineveh" (Phocylides, Diehl 1949-52:4; translated and cited by Chester Starr 1961:344). Phocylides' law-abiding polis brings to mind both the justice (dike) and "the maintenance of traditional right" for all social classes (eunomia), two components of the polis that bind its disparate elements into a unity (Starr 1961:342-343). Aristotle conceives of the polis as having a limited number of citizens--large enough to insure self-sufficiency but small enough to make total participation possible (Politics 1957:1325b-1326b). So also Phocylides thinks that the smallness of the Greek polis may make it a better place to live than an expansive Mesopotamian city like Nineveh. The modern reader is likely to assume that observations of this sort are ordinary among the ancients, but Oppenheim, writing on the Mesopotamian city, is struck by the completeness of the written record of Greek urbanization. He stresses the uniqueness of a people who were both quick and articulate enough to comprehend, chronicle and explain the process of urbanization: "Nowhere in the literary records from Mesopotamia will we find such insight and readiness to appraise one's own characteristic ways" (Oppenheim 1977:126).

But literary evidence for Greek urban attitudes and urban outlook-- the frame of mind and stereotypes that derive from living in the polis-- is much more indirect and much less incisive than Greek perceptions of

what the polis is. Whether the evidence comes from the Homeric epics of
the eighth century or from the late fifth-century comedies of
Aristophanes, confrontations of the city dweller and his rustic
counterpart provide an evolving picture of Greek urban sophistication.
These data consist of words, phrases and statements that the careful
observer must sift and evaluate in order to arrive at some understanding
of the nature of this urban outlook and its outward manifestations. The
fifth century presents a special difficulty since virtually all
attitudes isolated and discussed are drawn from Athenian sources. But
the position of Athens as the only ancient Greek city in the modern
sense of the word makes this limitation less severe. Since the Greek
literary evidence for urban sophistication is scattered and appears in
quite different literary sources, the clearest kind of organization,
perhaps, is chronological, and unless otherwise noted, all dates refer
to the pre-Christian era.

HOMER AND THE CITY

Detailed evidence for the existence of the polis is not to be found
in the Iliad and Odyssey, yet the framework of the later polis can be
detected and with it attitudes that characterize an organized city life.
The Homeric epics are the products of a long oral tradition, and even
the rudimentary town life which is discernible in them cannot be linked
definitively to anything more specific than a broad period of
archaeological time. Data concerning institutions and values in the
poems may, in fact, pertain equally to the poet's own time (late eighth
century) and to the last centuries of the Dark Age; in many instances
the latter is more likely true.[1]

Though faint and monochrome, the image of the fifth-century polis is
visible in epic. Like our knowledge of the beginnings of Greek town
life during the late Dark Age and early archaic period, the Homeric
picture of the city is still inchoate and incomplete. In fact, whether
the word "city" should be used as a description of the Homeric polis is
doubtful since it is no way equivalent to the classical polis or any
conventional, contemporary notion of what a city is, but it appears here
for want of a better term. Just the same, certain attitudes toward the
physical city emerge as important. The mad flight of the Trojans from
Achilleus' onslaught to the safety inside the walls of Troy's citadel
(Iliad 1966:21.606-607), points up an obvious attraction and necessary
function of the city--safety and protection. Most eighth-century Greek
cities on the mainland were unwalled (Kirsten 1956:52), but Mycenae as
well as other late Bronze citadel sites had walls. Even so, the
population of Troy does not customarily live within the walls but only
when the city was under seige (Thomas 1966:7). And with its
concentration of goods the city begins to have an effect even on
outlying areas. At Patroclus' funeral games Achilleus offers an iron
throwing-weight as a prize in the discus contest which will supply the
victor with iron for five years: "Nor indeed will his shepherd or
ploughman (have to) go to town (polis) because they need iron, but he
(the victor) will provide it" (Iliad 1966:23.834-835). Thus,
inhabitants of regions far away from the city begin to show a grudging
dependence on the concentration of goods and wealth the city possesses.

Either because of travel expenses or the untimely interruption of their work, Achilleus assumes that these rural folk resent the dependence the city forces on them.

The _Odyssey_ provides a fuller picture of the city than does the _Iliad_. In it a new feeling of community can be detected which the town assembly (_agora_) typifies. Though this communal gathering requires the king or a member of his family to initiate it (for example, _Odyssey_ 1979:2.1-14, 8.1-10, but at _Odyssey_ 1975:24.420 it is spontaneous), in the _Odyssey_ a consciousness can be seen for the first time of the distinction between the private and the public. In speculating about the purpose for which Telemachus calls the assembly in book two (32), Aegyptius asks whether news of an invading army or "some other public matter" (_ti demion allo_) has necessitated the gathering. Again, Telemachus informs Nestor that he has come on a private matter not a public one when he arrives at Nestor's palace seeking news of his father (_Odyssey_ 1979:3.82). When he goes on to Sparta, Menelaus asks him whether he comes on public or private business (_demion e idion_, _Odyssey_ 1979:4.314).[2]

Townpeople in the _Odyssey_ often put the assembly place also called _agora_ to other uses which suggest some growing sense of community. For Ithaca the _agora_ is the town center where Telemachus logically expects to find Peiraeus and the stranger Theoclymenes (_Odyssey_ 1975:17.52-53). Syrie, Eumaeus' former home, had an _agora_ that was the "people's place for sitting and talking" (_Odyssey_ 1975:15.468). The _agora_ of the Phaeacians has permanent seats (_Odyssey_ 1979:6.267). What is more, these areas, both in the _Iliad_ and in the _Odyssey_, are centers where justice for the community is carried out; the trial scene in the second city of Achilleus' shield is a good example (_Iliad_ 1966:18.497-508; also: _Iliad_ 1966:16.387, _Odyssey_ 1979:12.439-440).

These communal activities, moreover, taking place in the city-center, the _agora_, reinforce an assumption made in the _Odyssey_ that living in a city is the usual and expected form of human habitation. The greeting formula, for instance, establishes city as a means of identification: "where is your city (_polis_) and where your parents'?" (for example, _Odyssey_ 1979:1.170, 10.325, _Odyssey_ 1975:15.264). Hermes resents his mission to Calypso's desolate island, so far removed from the mainstream of human life: "and no city of men (_broton polis_) is nearby" (_Odyssey_ 1979:5.701). Similarly the poet of the _Odyssey_ finds the Cyclopes remarkable because of their atypical sort of existence (_Odyssey_ 1979:9.105-115). They do not live in cities and have no assemblies either deliberative or legislative (_boulephoroi oute themistes_). Special notice is also taken of Laertes who stays on his farm and no longer travels to the city. For a man of his station, he is the exception to the rule (_Odyssey_ 1979:11.187-188). At the other extreme, Eumaeus chides Telemachus because his trips to the country are all too infrequent--he spends most of his time in the city (_epidemeuo_; _Odyssey_ 1975:16.28). These examples corroborate well the point that Adolf Fanta makes: The city is "the central point, the focus (_Mittelpunkt_) of the _demos_" (1882:43).

It follows, then, that as the focus of human activity and the normal form of human habitation, the city is beginning to affect those who dwell in it by shaping their attitudes. Conversely, people living beyond the city's influence do not experience the normative force that close habitation and common interest create but have their attitudes shaped by other forces and conditions. In the _Odyssey_ just such a distinction, or perhaps it should be called an antithesis, exists between town and country. Much of the action of the last books of the _Odyssey_ shows just how distinct town and country are in the mind of the poet. Movement on Ithaca (and elsewhere) is always stated in these terms, as if such a division is usual and established. Odysseus and the swineherd, for example, proceed from the country to the town (ex agroio polinde, _Odyssey_ 1975, 17.182), for, as Odysseus remarks, "it is better for a beggar to beg his dinner in the city (kata ptolin) than in the country" (kat' agrous) (_Odyssey_ 1975, 17.18-19). The city is the hub of human activity, the only place where Odysseus can find men together in sufficient numbers to provide for his needs. Telemachus visits the fields (agroi) and then returns also to the town (eis asty)[3] (_Odyssey_ 1975:15.504-505). In asking Odysseus his identity Alcinoos the Phaeacian king establishes the fact that in terms of town life there are two distinct groups of people: "people living in the city (asty) and those living around it" (hoi perinaietaousin) (_Odyssey_ 1979:8.551).

Interaction between these two groups sparks a realization, especially in town dwellers, of the differences that separate them as a body from their rural counterparts. The communal life of the Odyssean town, though incomplete as compared with that of the classical _polis_, is sufficiently full to engender in townsmen some sense of common values and shared roles. Conflict between these two groups, city and country, erupts infrequently in the _Odyssey_, yet, when it does, it reveals the extent to which townspeople have been affected by their life together. While Eumaeus is taking Odysseus to the city to begin his begging, they encounter Melantheus the unfaithful farm worker of Odysseus who now serves the suitors exclusively. His close association with the suitors and with the town, the center of their activities, affects his behavior. Putting on airs, he reviles and abuses Eumaeus and Odysseus, calling them both kakoi ("base"), a term signifying the moral and social opposite of the suitors and their kind (agathoi, a term for "aristocratic") (Adkins 1972:12-14). Part of his disdain and animosity stems undoubtedly from his hostility to any supporter of Odysseus such as Eumaeus; the converse is true of Eumaeus' display of temper to follow.

Eumaeus does not consider the suitors the only cause of Melantheus' rude abuse (_Odyssey_ 1975:17.244-246):

> He (Odysseus) would, then, scatter away all the
> glories (aglaia)[13] that you now wear so haughtily
> (hybrisdo)--always roving all over the town (asty)
> while no-good (kakoi) herdsmen wreck the flocks.

Eumaeus' retort implies that Melantheus has not only assumed the suitors' habit of insulting rural servants but that he also now has acquired some of the affectations and mannerisms (aglaia; cf. _Odyssey_

1975:17.310) bred by town life--whether attitudinal or actual--that the suitors also manifest. His reply reveals besides the rural point of view that the city represents a mode of living characterized by idleness and waste as compared with the hard work of the fields. Eumaeus apparently equates the idle luxury of the suitors and their class with town life and, therefore, fears the possibility of a dangerous lack of customary rural restraint that goes along with city living.

A second encounter presents the conflict of town and country values from the point of view of the city dweller. When Penelope bids Eumaeus set up Odysseus' bow for the contest among the suitors, he and the herdsman Philoetius start to weep at the sight of their lost master's bow. The reaction of Antinous, the foremost suitor, is the first direct evidence of an emerging urban sophistication in the Odyssey:

> The stupid rustics! They can't see further than their
> noses! (nepioi agroiotai, ephemeria phroneontes: trans-
> lation by Rieu 1945, 318) A pitiful pair! Why do you
> release your tears now and disturb the heart in the lady's
> breast? As it is, her heart is sunk in pain since she
> has lost her dear husband. Be quiet, sit down and eat,
> or go outside and cry! (Odyssey 1975:21.85-90)

The city dweller's attitude toward the rustic is clearly a stereotype already--he is boorish, unattuned to the constraints of the more refined society of the city. That Antinous' response is that of a young nobleman to dull farmhands (Ribbeck 1888:4) cannot be ruled out, but the poet could well have used another term of abuse like those hurled at Eumaeus elsewhere (for example, Odyssey 1975:17.218, 17.375, 18.327) had that been the case. Instead Antinous calls them dull rustics.

Just how differently city dwellers perceive themselves to be from rustics becomes apparent here. Before confronting the rustics with their rudeness, Antinous speaks momentarily to the members of his own group in Ithaca, suitors, and townsmen, who alone because of their common background in the city share his attitude toward rustics. As he implies, Eumaeus and Philoetius show the lack of restraint and the narrow-minded outlook usually thought of as countrified. The rustic is condemned here because he is, as an outsider, completely unaware of the social intricacies of a city code of behavior.

URBAN ATTITUDES IN THE EMERGING POLIS OF THE LYRIC AGE

As was seen, the Greek outlook on the city appears first in the slowly evolving, fluid oral epic tradition of the Iliad and the Odyssey. As products of this popular tradition and, therefore, more intimately connected with the life of the revolutionary era in which the polis came into being, the Homeric epics have a formative influence on later Greek attitudes that is easy to under-estimate; so also, Homeric notions of an emergent polis are important antecedents of attitudes to come in the polis full-blown.

In the mere century between the appearance of the _Iliad_ and _Odyssey_ in written form (750-700 B.C.) and the poetry of Archilochus (Diehl 1949-52:74 dates with certainty to 648 B.C.), revolutionary changes take place in the Greek world which culminate in the formation of the historical _polis_. Rapid increases in commerce have a loosening effect on society: those who reap its rewards both directly and indirectly feel a new independence and control over their own lives and dealings. In many areas a waning kingship fades into a form of government largely dominated by a full-fledged aristocracy. The continuing popularity of local hero cults under its tutelage engenders a new solidarity.

But the real significance of these changes is psychological, for the emerging _polis_ is little different physically from its antecedent. Throughout the epoch of the _polis_' evolution a thoroughly agricultural economy prevails. The usual configuration of the city with its fortified upper town surrounded by the sprawling habitation of the _asty_ does not change much either--the _agora_ as city-center, for instance, appears later--despite a substantial increase in population.

Furthermore, the advent of the hoplite phalanx brings about a psychological transformation of irreversible and lasting consequence-- the creation of "a new sense of unity and common interest and a new feeling of importance among what (are,) in the mass, fairly ordinary men" (Forrest 1966:96-97).[4] No longer is the army made up of a ragtag band of farmers with makeshift arms and armor giving ineffectual support to a smaller cadre of armed aristocrats engaged in the real fighting, "heroic" single combat. The security of the commonweal now depends on the serried ranks of individuals, aristocrats and non-aristocrats, whose new hoplite shields and thrusting spears make ordered fighting en masse a most effective weapon for personal and communal protection. A sense of belonging results but there is a subordination of individual will and effort to the purposes of the larger community, the _polis_.

This shared experience of protecting the city, more than any other probably, forges the feeling of _polis_ which the Greek lyric poets express. To the early Greeks, in fact, even to those who, in the latter part of the fifth century, listen to Pericles' Funeral Oration as Thucydides records it, it is this feeling of communality and this subordination of individual will to the common purpose that constitutes the _polis_ and not its physical manifestations. Writing early in the sixth century the Lesbian poet Alcaeus is the first to express this idea: "Not stones nor wood nor the carpenters' art make a _polis_, but wherever men are who know how to keep themselves safe, there both walls and _polis_ are" (Lobel-Page 1963:Z103; cf. Lobel-Page 1963:E1). To conceive of the _polis_ in such a way characterizes the men who inhabited the _polis_ while it still possessed its independence as a vital political force. That the Athenians, for instance, rely entirely upon the collective courage of their citizen-soldiers aboard the ships at Salamis and decide to forsake entirely the physical _polis_ in which they lived reveals something important about what they understand to be the feeling that makes the _polis_. Thucydides has Nicias at Syracuse express it more succinctly than Alcaeus: "Men are the _polis_" (Thucydides 1970:7.77.7).[5]

17

But for status-conscious aristocrats subordination to the common interests of the early polis, however necessary they conceived it to be, is still hard to swallow. To them (as well as to those who would emulate them) the Spartan poet Tyrtaeus tries to make more palatable the role which the aristocrat (ho agathos) must play in the common defense of the polis. Writing in terms of mid-seventh century values, Tyrtaeus reveals the tension between the individual and the collective which is typical of the closed society of the polis. Excluding from mind and song other prestigious pursuits and qualities, the poet concentrates on the most traditional aristocratic excellence (arete), bravery in battle, but only in so far as it is important to the polis--"this is a common good (xynon esthlon) for the city and the whole demos." (Diehl 1949-52:12.15). If the agathos possesses this "best prize among men,"[6] the grim courage of the hoplite line rooted against the enemy's onslaught, he wins the grateful response of his peers in the polis. The polis is both the means and the theatre for the bestowing of the warrior's awards. Tyrtaeus emphasizes the high degree of individual esteem and aggrandizement the polis has to offer. If the warrior returns victorious, the men of the polis, both young and old (Tyrtaeus twice stresses the diversity of support), will honor him and not just at the time of his victory. Even as an old man everyone will yield place to him at public meetings. The dead hero receives immortality from the polis in the common lamentation of all citizens and the conspicuous reverence the polis will have for his grave, his children and all his descendants.

In another poem (Diehl 1949-52:6) Tyrtaeus reveals the unhappy alternative of the agathos who, disgraced by cowardice, has no city. The polis does not receive him at all, but, as an outcast from holdings and polis, he is forced with parents, wife and children to a life of begging. Even outside and beyond the polis he is still shamed in the eyes of his absent comperes: abominable (ekhthros) to all he meets, he disgraces (aiskhyno) his lineage and travels with loss of status and property (atimia) and the evil of failure (kakotes; Adkins 1972:12-14, 35-37).

While reminding his listeners of the necessity of fighting for the polis (the devastating effect of the fall of the whole city on the individual is obvious), Tyrtaeus offers the aristocratic element what it most wants to hear in the only terms the shame culture[7] understands: fighting in the common hoplite defense will bring the greatest prestige the polis can give. Thus, to be successful the polis must provide for the safety and well-being of the community as well as satisfy the social needs and aspirations of its individual members. As Starr puts it, "From the seventh century on--even from the Homeric world onward--the Hellenic outlook was stamped by a complex, fructifying tension between human egotism and communal ties." (Starr 1961:300).

Obviously Tyrtaeus writes to exhort his fellow-citizens to fight bravely in the second Messenian conflict; no less perceptible are the rewards he offers in behalf of the other inhabitants of the polis. Tyrtaeus is really expressing the new influence the polis has on the individual. Regretably virtually all the evidence of this new awareness has a strong aristocratic bias, but individuals for the first time voice varying degrees of comprehension that the attitudes of their fellow-citizens, the rest of the _polis_, can affect them--Starr's fructifying tension. The sixth-century poet Simonides of Ceos may have had in mind this interaction in a tantalizingly brief fragment: "the _polis_ teaches a man" (Diehl 1949-52:53).

The _polis_, then, is a corrective or directive force which continually maintains the communal ties that hold the individual in its midst. Archilochus, for example, is forced to admit this pressure: "No one who pays any attention to the criticism of the people (_demos_) would ever get very much pleasure out of life" (Diehl 1949-52:9). So also Mimnermos of Kolophon (_fl. ca._ 600 B.C.): "You may as well be happy--one of your griefmongering fellow-citizens will speak badly of you, another little better" (Diehl 1949-52:7). The sixth-century Phocylides is also well aware of the power of public opinion: "Friend ought to take thought with friend about whatever their fellow-citizens mutter around" (Diehl 1949-52, 5). Theognis of Megara, writing also in the sixth century, cynically despairs of ever satisfying the men of his _polis_: "But I am not yet able to please all the townsmen. Don't be surprised, Cyrnus, for even Zeus doesn't satisfy everyone either when he rains or when he doesn't" (Young 1971:24-26). A contemporary of Theognis, Xenophanes, does not display any concern about whether he pleases his fellow-townsmen or not--he complains, rather, that their attitudes are ill-advised and injudicious. Boldly asserting his independence from them, he tries to reorder their priorities by suggesting that wisdom (_sophia_) which he claims to possess will go much further toward establishing a well-ordered _polis_ than his fellow-citizens' misplaced devotion to athletic prowess (Diehl 1949-52:2). So also the sixth-century proponent of refined behavior at the symposium, Anacreon, shows little tolerance for his fellow-citizens: "I am not easy nor am I pleasant with my fellow-townsmen" (Page 1962:371).

Just how much the city teaches now becomes clear. In the lyric age the communal feeling of the _polis_ and at the same time the interaction among its citizens are taken for granted--a remarkable transformation from the attitudes reflected in the _Odyssey_. That the poet weighs himself against the collective opinion of his fellow-citizens marks the beginning of a new social awareness. Townsmen begin to realize that their attitudes often derive from the shared life of the _polis_. And at the same time the lyric poets with the emerging _polis_ as the center and scope of their activity become the first to exhibit some sense of the refinement which the city engenders.

The seventh-century Alcman, from the city dweller's point of view, expresses the already clear dichotomy of rustic and urban values:

> He was not a country bumpkin (_agreios_), not gauche
> (_skaios_), not from the unaccomplished (_par' asophoisin_),
> not of Thessalian stock and not a Erysichaean sheep keeper
> but a man from high Sardis (Page 1962:16).

If Alcman is speaking of himself in the poem as Bowra believes (1961:17-19), the Spartans may have questioned the credentials of this poet who had immigrated to their _polis_ apparently from Lydian Sardis located inland from the Ionian coast. But Alcman reveals much more in his defense about what he is not than about what he is, and by implication he may be applying these pejorative terms for rustics to the residents of his new city Sparta, a far cry from the Sardis he once knew. His catalog of rustic epithets is quite full even in this short fragment--from the general "bumpkin" to the occupational "sheep keeper" of a specific rural area--and includes terms which suggest the awkwardness of manner, slow wittedness and ignorance that townsmen often associate with country folk. Presumably, then, Alcman thinks that he owns certain standards of comportment, wit and perhaps poetic skill that place him far out of reach from any imputation of rusticity--all because he comes from "high Sardis."

Under Mermnadic rule from about 650 on, this wealthy Lydian city of Sardis was of special interest to the Greeks of the seventh century. Intercourse with the Greek world had been established at an early date, so that it becomes a model to the Greeks for what a real city looked like: "Sardis, an active and prosperous city, may have shown the Greeks what in material terms a city could be" (Hammond 1972:146). Though Alcman's urban outlook and sophistication may derive from Lydian rather than Greek origins, he undeniably expects his Spartan listeners to understand (as undoubtedly they did) the difference he sees between country and city modes of life.

This difference is something the seventh-century Alcaeus of Lesbos experiences firsthand. Forced to live in the country for some time during his exile from Mytilene, he finds his separation from the _polis_ a painful thing: "I, poor wretch, live a rustic's life (_moira_ . . . _agroiotike_), yearning to hear Assembly summoned, O Agesilaides, and Council . . . " (Lobel-Page 1963:130.16-20; translation: Page 1965:199). Alcaeus' complaint is surely that of an aristocrat out of his element, the give-and-take of _polis_ politics, but he also is a city dweller who misses the ordered social encounter and exchange which the city's political routine calls to mind. However he is classified, the culture of the city is such an important part of his existence that life outside the hubbub of its social activities is scarcely tolerable.

For Sappho, another seventh-century poet of Lesbos, the _polis_ is no less a creator and controller of attitudes than for Alcman and Alcaeus. But in Sappho this city-bred sophistication appears for the first time in an outward manifestation. Gibing at a rival through a lover once her own, she makes fun of the girl's dress: "And what countrified (_agroiotis_) girl holds your senses spell-bound, dressed in countrified (_agroiotis_) clothes? She doesn't even know enough to pull her skirt over her ankles" (Lobel-Page 1963:57). That certain elegance, hard to define, yet exhibited no doubt by Sappho's own clothing, is lacking in the haphazard manner in which this young woman's skirt is draped. Sappho perceives this inelegance entirely in terms of country and city. This recognition by outward appearance, by externals, reflects the degree to which Sappho's participation in the social life of the _polis_ and her close association with the other women of the _polis_ have influenced her perceptions.

In another fragment (Lobel-Page 1963:98) she reflects upon past styles in hair dress from her mother's time to the present. After mentioning the red headband of her mother's era and a wreath of blooming flowers (her choice for her daughter), she turns to current fashion: "recently an embroidered headband from Sardis . . . cities" (Lobel-Page 1963:98.10-11). Hardly unexpected is the possibility that urban society, the society of the polis, set current fashion patterns. And Mytilene with its proximity to the Ionian coast falls, to be sure, under the cultural sway of its important eastern neighbor Sardis. The fragment breaks off with the tantalizing word cities (poleis), and suggests that, in light of the growth of the polis and its attitudes, an urban concept of dress may be quite natural now. Sappho's comment, then, belongs to a larger picture of sophisticated dress that can no longer be seen.

Just as with dress, the polis also gives rise to urbane forms of speech. As Phocylides points out, noble birth does not necessarily insure elegance of expression: "What use is high birth for those whom grace (kharis) accompanies neither in words nor in counsel?" (Diehl 1949-52:3). But the poet implies that aristocratic upbringing and graceful speech normally go together. Clearly again, though it is impossible to separate entirely what is aristocratic and what is urban about their outlook, aristocrats do set the mode of urbanity. But the kind of elegance that Phocylides speaks of is really the product of the verbal intercourse--commercial, intellectual, political, social--which the polis alone nourishes and provides in great measure.

But this elegance of speech and counsel is an outward manifestation of an inner quality which, because it is born out of varied social experiences and encounters, is also the product of city living. In the poems of Theognis the first understanding of the individual's interrelations with the group and of the dynamics of social behavior comes to light. Undeniably urban and undeniably aristocratic, the mark of the sophisticated man is both restraint and versatility, the part of social propriety that allows the individual to adapt outlook and actions to fit the outlook of his associates and the needs of a particular social situation. As Theognis says, "We must never laugh, happy at our own good advantage, Kyrnos, when we sit beside someone crying" (Young 1971:1217-1218).

What appears here to be restraint alone reveals itself in fuller treatment as an adaptability to the requirements of every social situation:

> Kyrnos, turn toward all friends an ever-varying disposi-
> tion, suiting your temperament to that of each. Take on
> the temperament of the manifold octopus, which appears to
> be of the same substance as the rock it lives with: now
> follow along this path, now be a different color. Savoir-
> faire (sophia)[8] is better, indeed, than inflexibility
> (atropia; Young 1971:213-218).

Suaveness and an easy composure belong to the man who adapts his moods and behavior to those of his friends. The friends he speaks of belong,

21

no doubt, to an aristocratic circle that has the city as the focus of its activities. Just as there is a certain dress code which separates the rustic from the city-dweller, so also a tactful versatility exists, a poise, born of the sociableness of the city, which distinguishes the sophisticated man from the unadaptive rustic. Theognis' comparison with an octopus emphasizes the completeness and effectiveness that the adaptation must have. As if by camouflage, the individual who exhibits this social savoir-faire appears as one with the group, and his mood becomes identical to his friends'. Like the subtle octopus that assimilates itself to its rocky environment, he is lost to sight. That Theognis sees this adaptability as a skill (sophia) suggests that it is something acquired, learned, as it happens, from the continuous social interchange of the city. Yet the poet has no specific name for the quality and so must resort to a term of more general application like sophia. Whatever its designation, this kind of social ease and self-awareness becomes an essential component of the refinement that the city nurtures.

THE SYMPOSIUM

The polis alone with its confluence of human activities creates a social matrix for Greek social institution most influential upon Greek society as a whole yet one rarely understood as such--the symposium. Evidence from a group of sixth-century Greek lyricists supports the view that the Greek dinner party provided a setting where men of like minds and interests could acquire and practice the poise and social savoir-faire which mark them as both urban and aristocratic. Aware, it seems, of the acculturation that is occurring in their own times, these poets approach the symposium not only as a laboratory of refined urban behavior but also as the showcase for it.

Xenophanes, for instance, describes the elaborate preparations necessary for the symposium. He stresses the cleanliness, order and subtle provisions that make for a decorous and cheerful atmosphere: floors, cups and guests' hands are clean; wreaths and perfume are ready; wine and food have been tastefully arranged; the sweet smell of frankincense and flowers awaits the hymn to the god that opens the festivities (Diehl 1949-52:1). Theognis also mentions music as an expected part of a symposium. In a poem praising Cyrnus (Young 1971:241-242) young men "attractive in a seemly way" (eukosmos eratoi) sing beautiful songs to flute accompaniment.

Such seemly, ordered and tasteful surroundings set a tone for the occasion which does not comport with the boisterousness and even violence which usually results from heavy drinking. To avoid such consequences, Anacreon has his slave mix the wine with water "so that I may again celebrate Bacchus in the decorous way" (anhybristos, "without causing insult"; Page 1962:356a.5). In the same vein he condemns Scythian drinking habits for their lack of the propriety so essential to the refined atmosphere of the symposium:

22

> Come again, let us practice no longer the Scythian
> drinking style with its noise and shouting, but let's
> drink moderately (hypopino) amid beautiful songs (Page
> 1962:356b).

Restraint and the quiet beauty of song have replaced what Anacreon cites
as the non-Greek uncouthness of the Scythians who are to become
proverbial for this kind of behavior.

Xenophanes also urges some standard of moderation in the enjoyment
of wine (Diehl 1949-52:1.17-24). He praises the symposiast who loses
neither his memory nor his striving after excellence while imbibing. In
place of songs about violent behavior of any sort, including some old
standbys about the Titanomachy or Giantomachy, he prefers a quiet
respect for the gods.

Theognis has a much more subtle understanding of the social dynamics
of the symposium. To him the successful symposium is an elusive and
fragile thing; everything must move naturally and smoothly, yet the
proper moderation and restraint must be reached with precision. Though
he uses pointed admonitions later, Theognis begins tactfully to show how
nothing elegant is forced or contrived. No one wishing to leave the
symposium should be required to stay nor should the one person wanting
to stay be made to go. And the symposiast sleepy with wine ought not to
be roused nor the wakeful urged to sleep. If a man wants another cup,
he should have it (Young 1971:467-474). In the freedom of this easy
social setting, Theognis unobtrusively offers his own idea of elegant
behavior at the symposium:

> But as for me--for I hold to a proper measure (metron) of
> honey-sweet wine-- . . . and I will reach that goal
> when wine is most gracefully (khariestatos) drunk by
> a man, when I am neither entirely sober nor too drunk
> (Young 1971:475, 477-478).

The adjective kharieis is used later also in fifth-century symposium
literature to describe elegance and gracefulness of both dress and
speech (Lloyd 1976:107-109). Theognis strives here for that degree of
intoxication which promotes conversation easily and makes wit and humor
most enjoyable. Theognis adds that, if the banqueter goes beyond this
point, he resembles the "no-account day-laborer" whose appetite for wine
knows no bounds. Theognis makes one final suggestion, a remarkable one
in that it shows to what extent the spirit of communality which pervades
the polis makes its way into this more exclusive group: "Speak to the
middle (mesos) of the group, at the same time to one and all, and in
this way, the symposium does not lack elegance" (gignetai ouk akhari;
Young 1971:495-496). Theognis here asserts the important balance that
must exist even at the symposium between the individual and the group.
Not unlike the polis, the symposium is primarily a group activity but
one in which the individual is not barred from the attention he
deserves.

Conversation at the symposium is of a special sort. It is pleasant
but also enlightening. As Theognis says,

> when invited for dinner, you ought to sit next to a
> good man (esthlos) who knows all learning (sophia);
> try to catch what he says whenever he says something
> learned (sophon) so that you may be instructed and go
> home taking this acquisition with you (Young 1971:
> 563-566).

This kind of sophia is not equivalent to that which Theognis uses to describe poise and social savoir-faire (Young 1971:213-218) yet it probably shares with it that acquired skill of cleverly fitting each remark not only to the mood of the group but also to the subject of conversation. Theognis may possibly mean that this sophia is the refined art of dinner conversation.

Theognis also has something to say about the opposite of this refined man--the frivolous, talkative guest whose constant chatter, empty and tedious, makes him boorish and intolerable to the rest of the company:

> It is a very harsh burden for a garrulous man (kotilos)
> to be quiet, and when he opens his mouth he appears
> ignorant (adaes) to those near him and they despise
> him. Only out of necessity should this man mix with
> the others at the symposium (Young 1971:295-298).

The garrulous guest gives the impression of being not only socially ignorant and inept but also egocentric, since his constant chatter violates the delicate balance between group and individual. In a negative way Theognis emphasizes the poise and awareness of social nuances necessary for this elegant occasion.

But the master of sympotic conversation and behavior is that man who possesses enough self-knowledge to enable him to see himself as others see him. Again, this rounding out of the individual personality can only result from the constant congress of human communication in the polis and the intimate association of men at the symposium:

> The tactful man (pepnymenos) seems to be a member of
> the dinner company but everything appears to pass by
> him as if he weren't there. Let him toss in his jokes--
> let him keep a poker face--till he finds out what tempera-
> ment each person has (Young 1971:309-312).

This tactful man wears a facade of cool nonchalance--the conversation appears to go right past him as if he were somewhere else entirely. To create this effect, the symposiast must be aware of the way his fellow banqueters perceive him and must exhibit a composure both patient and restrained. He tries his jokes on the group, remaining reserved until he can gauge accurately the temperament of those around him. In this way he will be able to fit better his remarks and his witicisms to the mood and make-up of the group. The masking and control of his emotions require some knowledge of himself and how the group looks on him; they are vital components of the social adaptability, savoir-faire, sophia (pepnymenos connotes a similar shrewdness) which Theognis establishes as a basis of the refined behavior of the symposium.

The symposium's intimate social exchange plays a part in creating the growing self-awareness of the individual in Greek society.[9] Both it and the social savoir-faire which typify the refined behavior of this urban gathering derive ultimately from the closely-knit, shared life of the polis and mark the coming of age of Greek society.

URBAN ATTITUDES IN THUCYDIDES

In Thucydides' history of the Peloponnesian War a picture of the full-blown polis emerges, and the social differences between city and country modes of life affect attitudes more than ever before. To provide a proper background for his treatment of the Pelopponesian conflict Thucydides shows in the case of Mycenae and the Trojan War that a city's physical appearance is no valid indicator of its actual political vitality or military might:

> . . . if the city[10] of the Lacedaemonians should be aban-
> doned and only the temples and foundations of buildings
> were left, people of a time far in the future would, I
> believe, be quite hesitant to put much credence in the
> Spartans' power as compared with their reputation . . .
> (and) since they do not concentrate their habitation in
> the city nor enjoy expensive temples or buildings and
> since they still live in villages (komai) in the ancient
> Hellenic fashion, their city would appear to be inferior
> (to what it really is). But were the same thing to hap-
> pen to Athens, its power, I think, would be guessed at
> twice what it is, just from the city's outward appearance
> (Thucydides 1970:1.10.2).

He chooses Sparta and Athens for this comparison deliberately, for it is his plan throughout the first two books of his history of the Peloponnesian War to create what Finley terms an "elaborate study" (Finley 1942:112), contrastive in nature, of these two poleis. As Thucydides points out, Sparta's scattered and anachronistic, if not reactionary, mode of habitation with no public buildings of any magnificence makes a bleak showing against the city Athens had become by the end of the fifth century. The new post-bellum Athens, now a true urban center, dazzles the visitor's eye with its sheer size, the bustle of its industry and commerce and the extravagance of the Periclean building program.

Thucydides examines these two poleis from several perspectives, highlighting particular differences between the two cultures so that the immediate causes of the conflict fit logically into a larger framework. That Thucydides is an Athenian is especially significant in this undertaking. Athens has the singular distinction in the classical era of being "the only polis of Hellas which has become a city in the sense of the modern development" (Kirsten 1956:109). Thucydides himself observes early in Athens' history the urban course of its development: "The Athenians were the first to lay down the sword and take up a less restrained and more luxurious way of life" (Thucydides 1970:1.6.3). This rather recent urbanization of Athens and its growth during the fifth century only accentuate for the Athenians the differences between the urban outlook and the rural. Not every _polis_, in fact, is by nature the sort that can engender truly urban attitudes and prejudices. And so for Thucydides and his readers to weigh Athens and Sparta on a scale of urbanism or ruralism would be quite natural.

In Pericles' first speech (Thucydides 1970:1.140-144), the Athenians are characterized as a _polis_ possessing an urban frame of mind. Pericles describes their opponents, the Peloponnesians (including the Spartans), as farmers (_autourgoi_, Thucydides 1970:1.141.5; _andres georgoi_, Thucydides 1970:1.142.7) and implies that they possess other rural traits. Thucydides does not distinguish the Spartans who use the helots to cultivate their fields from the other Peloponnesians whose armies are, in fact, composed of men who till their own soil (_autourgoi_) apparently because he thinks that the Spartans, although freed from the limitations of planting, harvesting and protecting the crops, do share the same rural frame of mind with their allies and neighbors.

In this Periclean speech Thucydides emphasizes the importance that land has in the rural mind (Thucydides 1970:141.3-7, 142.7), an importance which the urbanite might feel is excessive. Along with the comparative poverty and the isolation of being shut off from the sea, almost total dependence on the land affects the development of social values in the _polis_. From the superior Athenian standpoint, because the Peloponnesians are _autourgoi_, they are better prepared to expend human lives in battle than their material resources and more afraid of losing what wealth they have in wartime than of risking their personal safety (Thucydides 1970:1.145.5). To the Athenians who a half century before abandoned the entire physical city to the Persians to save the real city, the human one, this rustic set of priorities would appear foreign indeed. Later on in the speech Pericles urges the Athenians to consider themselves islanders and forsake their land and houses so as to protect the city and access to the sea. These material possessions are negligible; the men who make up the city are not: "We ought to lament the loss not of houses and land but men's lives, for these things do not own men but men own them" (Thucydides 1970:1.143.5).

If the dependence of the Peloponnesians on the land dictates their perception of the importance of human life, they as allies also fail to understand the functioning of common will and action. The individual's concerns outweigh the common good, a lesson learned not from the common feeling that makes the city but from a rural preoccupation with the land that shoves communal human social relations into second place. Pericles points out that the Peloponnesians do not act in concert, "with one deliberating body" (_bouleuterion_), but each state, having equal voting privileges, is eager to work only for its own interests (Thucydides 1970:1.141.7). They have no comprehension, he suggests, of what is necessary for common intent and unified action--they lack the communal feeling of the _polis_:

26

Once in a great while they come together for a short
interval to consider matters of common interest (<u>ti</u>
<u>ton koinon</u>), but (even then) they take up for the most
part local issues (<u>ta oikeia</u>), and each state thinks
that no harm results on account of its own lack of
concern but that it is the concern of someone else,
in fact, in its stead to make provision for the future,
so that when the common effort (<u>to koinon</u>) as a whole
fares poorly, even though the opinion is held by all
in private, it escapes the notice of the group (Thucydides 1970:1.141.7).

In the famous Funeral Oration Pericles describes a striking contrast
within the Athenian <u>polis</u> to this state of affairs: "Each citizen
concerns himself with both private (<u>ta oikeia</u>) and <u>polis</u> (<u>ta politika</u>)
matters . . . we (Athenians) are unique in regarding the man who does
not take part in the affairs of the <u>polis</u> not as a person who tends to
his own affairs but as someone useless to the <u>polis</u>" (Thucydides
1970:2.40.2).   So for the Athenian assembly listening to Pericles in
both instances, the deliberative process that they are a part of proves
to be an expression of Athenian common will and purpose. They are led
to contemplate both Athens' varied magnitude and its common feeling of
<u>polis</u>, and contrasted with Peloponnesian isolationism (see Thucydides
1970:1.68.1) and parochial frame of mind, this communality of the <u>polis</u>
seems in Hellas' only true urban center a city virtue as well.

The Funeral Oration of Pericles is hardly an irrelevant rhetorical
piece, for it captures in high relief the contrast in attitudes and
institutions of Athens and Sparta. But more to the point, it embodies
the ultimate expression of the Athenian urban outlook. In every day
personal relations an Athenian urban sophistication is clearly present.
As Pericles says, "we conduct the affairs of the city in a liberal
fashion, so also the way we regard each other in our daily pursuits: we
do not hold a grudge against a neighbor for doing what he wants every
day, nor do we give him vexing looks which are not entirely harmless but
can hurt" (Thucydides 1970:2.37.2). The tolerance for which Pericles
praises the Athenians in this speech derives from the close contact of
city life.   Although Thucydides connects this tolerance with the
liberality which characterizes the Athenian management of public
affairs, both originate at least in part from the close living quarters
in a city Athens' size, the highly social milieu of the democratic <u>polis</u>
and the manifold cosmopolitanism of a commercial and industrial center
like Athens. By implication Sparta, a product of a rural outlook and a
<u>polis</u> firmly rooted in the land without the varied social intercourse of
real city life, lacks the forbearance and openness Pericles speaks of.
Neither the callous disregard of a neighbor's affairs nor the nosiness
of a meddling busybody, the quality Pericles describes preserves the
proper decorum, a balance between open interference and complete
disinterest, and reflects a certain social flexibility and restraint.

As the Corinthians pointed out previously (Thucydides 1970:1.70.2-4),
the Spartans lack this urban adaptability. After deriding the Spartan
failure even to perceive any difference between themselves and the
Athenians, they as Spartan allies describe the urban Athenians as "doers

of new things," "innovators" (neoteropoioi), and not hesitators (aoknoi), whereas the Spartan way of life they represent as "old-fashioned" (arkhaiotropos, Thucydides 1970:1.71.2). Again the rural conservatism of the Spartans is betrayed in their old-fashioned and traditional approach to the threat Athens poses, their eagerness to maintain the status quo (Thucydides 1970:1.70.2). But the epithets the Corinthians ascribe to the Athenians suggest the bustle and commercial adventurism of the Athenian city as well as its military aggressiveness.

The flexibility which gives rise to Athenian innovativeness is so deepseated a social characteristic that it becomes a keynote in Pericles' Funeral Oration: "In brief, I assert that our whole city is an education to Greece and that, as I see it, every man among us can in his own right maintain his self-sufficiency in the most varied situations with the utmost grace (meta khariton) and the utmost versatility" (eutrapelos, Thucydides 1970:241.1). The tacit comparison with Sparta's old-fashioned (arkhaiotropos) ways, rigid and graceless, is hardly lost on Pericles' audience. Here Pericles not only defines the Athenian polis in terms of self-sufficient individuals but he also makes clear that for the Athenians this urban adaptability is a frame of mind.

Just as Thucydides regards being adaptable (eutrapelos) as "easily turning," changing one's temperament (turn) to fit the situation, so contrariwise Theognis seems to view its opposite as the inability to adjust, to change, to turn (atropia; Young 1971:218). And many of the glowing remarks pericles makes about the Athenians bear out the significance of this parallel. Though the social situations vary considerably in scope and import, one point remains unalterable: fluidity and mutability of mind and behavior derive from the give-and-take of urban intercourse and is characterisitic of it.

Examples that Pericles cites show the interrelationships of this adaptable Athenian frame of mind and the urban polis Athens has become. The cosmopolitan atmosphere Athens enjoys as a trade center has created a populace atypical of Greece in its need for variety, mental diversion and recreation. The monotony of life (to lyperon) is staved off by games and religious festivals for all classes and tasteful (euprepes) houses and furnishings for individual citizens; Athenians have just as easy access to imported goods as to those locally produced (Thucydides 1970:2.38). Again for Pericles' audience the picture of an isolated Sparta, hard-working, single-minded and rural, comes to mind. Athens, in addition, is an open city, having no restrictions upon visitors (Thucydides 1970:2.39.1), whereas Spartan xenophobia is almost proverbial. In discussing military training and education Pericles breaks away from veiled comparison and condemns outright the lopsidedness of the Spartan system with its painful and severe discipline even for the young. Athenians are just as successful in battle even if theirs is an "easy (unrestricted) way of life" (Thucydides 1970:2.39.1). In fact, Pericles argues that only those who have tasted both pleasures and pains in their lifetime are the most courageous (Thucydides 1970:2.40.3). Again, he appears to be connecting enjoyment of life with the Athenians' multifaceted approach to living. He well perceives, in addition, the waste of time-consuming and *loathesome military drill if Athenians can face danger just as effectively as Spartans but unlike them independently, "with ease of mind" and with a courage, not forced by the state but gotten from the Athenian mode of living (tropoi, Thucydides 1970:2.39.4).*

The restful pauses in the Athenian year, the openness of the city, the multiplicity of Athenian education express more than just versatility; these Athenian attributes are also what Pericles meant by the phrase "with the graces of life" (meta khariton, Thucydides 1970:2.41.1), that is, "grace" in the sense of "charm" or "delight" (see Lloyd 1976:107-109). But coupled with these urban attitudes is another, the restraint (discussed above) that Pericles says the Athenian shows toward his neighbor's private life (Thucydides 1970:2.37.2). As a contrast with Spartan pragmatism and rural conservatism Thucydides formulates in the Funeral Oration the balance of versatility, gracefulness and restraint that earmarks Athenian urban culture: "For we love what is beautiful with simplicity and we love the cultivation of the mind without becoming soft" (Thucydides 1970:2.40.1). Spartan wisdom, on the other hand, stems from "being educated too boorishly (amathesteron) to show contempt for the law and being too harshly trained not to obey it" (Thucydides 1970:1.84.3), as the Spartan king Archidamus puts it. Against this stark Spartan background, the innovativeness and pliability of the city dwellers of Athens stand out--in full view of the rest of Hellas Athens embraces beauty and pursuits of the mind.

In its form and restraint, this Periclean statement displays both subtlety and refinement, measured largely in rhetoric, which Athenian comic writers also connect with urban life as will be seen later. To be lovers of beauty and intellectual pursuits approaches the daring when viewed against Spartan austerity, yet both claims are tempered by qualifying phrases of opposite sorts that create balance with variety. The restraint thus shown clearly avoids what detractors might regard as decadence, moral laxity or a slackening of military discipline. But it represents as well the habit of speech and mind of a man who is urbane in the radical sense of the word and a product of city culture, one who possesses the sophistication that exists only at its core. This restraint, for instance, leads to the use of language (the emphatic an, "in my opinion," Thucydides 1970:2.41.2) which tempers the otherwise almost hybristic claim of Athens as the education of Hellas and makes Pericles very much like Socrates whose refined manners and speech have been carefully documented as an urban phenomenon (Lammerman 1935:26-80). The self-control of Pericles is manifest throughout the Funeral Oration in his modesty and a social awareness of the various kinds of people that make up his audience (see Lloyd 1976:63-66).

Lest, nevertheless, all historic perspective be lost, it must be said that the Funeral Oration is a most idealistic expression of Athenian achievement. During the middle years of the Peloponnesian War the Melian debacle and the disastrous Sicilian expedition only point up their tyranny and rashness, and these extremes do not fit with Pericles' lofty words. Even Pericles' statement "we love what is beautiful with simplicity" can be seen as an attempt by Thucydides to answer the critics of Periclean extravagance (Kakridis 1961:47-48). But, if viewed

in the broader brushstrokes Thucydides intends, the first two books of
his history portray in contrasting silhouettes the thoroughly urban
outlook of the city Athens with its attendant sensibilities set against
the parochialism and conservatism of a rural Sparta. Whether this
urban/rural criterion for comparison withstands the test of historicity
is not so important as Thucydides' seemingly natural proclivity to see
things this way.

RURAL ATTITUDES AND URBAN REFINEMENTS IN ATHENIAN COMEDY

We know that the Athenians, won over to the military policies of
Pericles, did not go out to meet the Peloponnesians when they were about
to ravage Attic farmland in 431 but readied the navy instead. In
subsequent evacuation of farmers from their homesteads to safety within
the city walls severe hardship resulted for the rustic population since
many were leaving long-established homes and shrines to take up crowded,
makeshift lodgings as well as a new and unfamiliar way of life in the
city (Thucydides 1970:2.14.2, 16.1-2).

Although he may be over-simplifying somewhat, Ribbeck (1888:6-7) is
right, nevertheless, to point out that "only just then (when the farming
population moved inside the city), on account of the close habitation
did the realization quickly come about of the difference between city
and country habits and manners." Yet, as has been shown, this awareness
is present much earlier also and grows as the polis develops. It is in
the polis that confrontations between rustics and urbanites usually
occur since the city is the political and economic as well as social
focus of the larger outlying area. During the long confinement of the
rural populace within the city, the constant collision of the two groups
makes them both more aware of themselves as social groupings, separate
and distinct from one another. It may be of some importance that the
word for "refined," asteios, that is "citified" (from asty, "city"),
makes its first appearance in Greek literature in Aristophanes during
this era.

But urban Athenians and rural Athenians are interdependent to a very
great extent and forms a society "much more homogeneous than our own"
(Forrest 1966:26).[11] Distinctions between various social groupings--
aristocrats and lowborn, wealthy and poor, rustic and urbanite--are all
important politically from time to time but permanent political
groupings are not composed of any one of these social groups or of
coalitions of them (Forrest 1966:26-28). And merely as social groups
the lines of separation are hard to determine, especially, for instance,
the kinds of people who are urban or rural dwellers. The good breeding
which the aristocratic urbanite displays doubtless plays a very
important role in the creation of a refined man by Athenian standards,
but the lowborn shopkeeper, also a city dweller, would be expected as
well to have prejudices and attitudes different from farmers who spend
most of their time outside the city. More obvious is the economic
interdependence of these two groups, each relying to some extent on the
other for a market, but again distinctions are not always clear-cut

since the more wealthy urbanite often manages a farm outside the city, like Pericles, for instance (Thucydides 1970:2.13.1).

Strepsiades in Aristophanes' Clouds reveals how closely these two groups are linked. That he is a farmer living some distance from the city and wed to the daughter of a well-to-do noble family from the city needs no special explanation from the playwright since the situation is of common enough occurrence that the audience understands and accepts it. Besides his marriage, Strepsiades' ties with the city are sufficiently strong that he can freely get loans from townsmen he knows (Clouds 1970:1219), although his wife's connections may help (Dover 1968:xxvii, xxix). Above all, like his counterparts in other plays, Philocleon in the Wasps and Dikaiopolis in the Acharnians, Strepsiades' presence in the city seems in no way unusual and points toward the conclusion that country folk spend considerable time in the city.

Presumably, then, many of Aristophanes' spectators are farmers, and he often plays to their sensibilities. Aristophanes' subtle knowledge of rural flora and fauna, in fact, along with his often sympathetic treatment of the farmer's wartime plight and strong advocacy of peace betrays most likely his own rural origins (Youman 1974:73-77). Yet he often portrays rural dwellers mockingly and creates humor from stereotypes of rustics. Whether of rustics or townspeople, the varied evidence from the Greek comedies of Aristophanes and his contemporaries of the late fifth and early fourth centuries offers a much more complete composite than in any other literary genre of the outlooks and attitudes not only of city dwellers but also of their counterparts in the outlying Attic farms.

Presumably passages in Aristophanes describing the delights of country life[12] were enjoyed by rustics and townsmen alike though for different reasons, but of compelling interest are the attitudes rustics have toward the city and the people who live there. As Aristophanes' Acharnians begins, Dicaeopolis muses, as he awaits the beginning of the ecclesia, both about the bliss of rural life and the disrupting spectacle of city life: "I look to the fields and hanker for peace. I hate the city and yearn for my village which never said 'Buy charcoal!' or 'Buy wine!' or 'Buy olive-oil'--it didn't know the word 'buy' but of itself presented us with everything and without that 'buy-word'" (Acharnians 1970:32-36; 'buy-word' is Rogers' rendering, 1960:9). Dicaeopolis surely dislikes the city's noise and confusion, its violation of privacy, but what bothers him more is the irksome necessity of buying needed commodities in the city, a necessity signalled by the den of the vendors' cries. The contrast with his quiet village evokes strong feeling: he hates (stygeo) the city.

The sellers are hardly the only annoyance the agora has in store for the rustic. After Dicaeopolis easily drives away an informer (of contraband trade items), the chorus from the rural deme of Acarnae ruminates aloud on what it would be like to do away with all the pests of the agora so easily (Acharnians 1970, 836-859). The list is impressive. Besides informers, underhanded buyers beat out the legitimate customer. The rustic might be inconvenienced by the unwanted amorous invitations of homosexuals or bored to distraction by advocates like Hyperbolus who "fills passers-by full of his cases." The <u>agora</u> has its resident jester as well, a certain Pauson who jeers and loudly ridicules everyone he sees. Not only does Aristophanes take pot shots at some well-known figures in this catalog, as is usual in Greek Old Comedy, but he describes humorously yet not unsympathetically the predicament of the simple person venturing into such a varied and hostile environment. Aristophanes certainly exaggerates, but the point is not lost that the rustic might find the <u>agora</u> at best distasteful and bothersome, at worst frightening.

In a fragment (Kock 1880-88:387) from a lost play, <u>Islands</u>, Aristophanes describes the happy prospects of a man who gives up the pursuits of the <u>agora</u> to take up farming in the country. The speaker's attitude toward both city and country is captured by the phrase "freed from (rid of) (<u>apallagenta</u>) the affairs of the <u>agora</u>." The pleasures, both auditory and gustatory, of farm life--the bleating of sheep and mooing of cattle, the drip of new wine being strained into a pan, a simple meal of country fowl--are contrasted with the fairly common occurrence, evidently, in the <u>agora</u>, of waiting around for the "fresh" fish to come. When it is brought, three days old and exorbitantly priced, it is subjected to an illegal pawing at the hands of the fish-dealer. This example of the problems of urban living, so unfavorably compared to the easy life of the country, carries some suggestion of the impropriety or underhandedness that the unscrupulous townsman might perpetrate on the unsuspecting farmer.

In fact, the stereotype of the gullible rustic easily duped by the city sophisticate appears fairly often in comedy. The sausage-seller in Aristophanes' <u>Knights</u> (1340-1344) is speaking of this sort of gullibility when he reminds Demus, with metaphors of naive joy borrowed from the barnyard or the fields, that if any speaker promises to care for the people and be their lover (<u>erastes</u>), "you flap your wings and toss your horns." If the import of this remark is that country folk in the <u>ecclesia</u> are swept off their feet by glib promises and smooth rhetoric, Dicaeopolis himself (<u>Acharnians</u> 1970:370-374) characterizes rustics in much the same way: "I know the way rustics (<u>hoi agroikoi</u>) are, how they are so happy if someone says nice things about them and the city, someone spreading it on thick both true and false, and that's where they don't catch on they're being sold down the river." This example along with the instances of unscrupulous business practices in the city like those of the Paphlagonian (<u>Knights</u> 1970:315-319) who rooked rustics (<u>agroikoi</u>) by selling them cheaply made shoes reinforces the not entirely amusing stereotype of the credulous yokel inexperienced in city ways and thus falling victim to them.

Understandably, then, the rustic is depicted as being aware of his inadequacies, so much so, in fact, that he has something of an inferiority complex. The farmer chorus in Aristophanes' <u>Peace</u> (618) admits the extent of its own ignorance of civic matters when it learns from Hermes how Peace disappeared: "Many things indeed slip right by us." Being deceived by the cobbler and by the fishdealer as well as by the smooth-tongued oratory at the <u>ecclesia</u> has led the rustic to consider himself inferior to those who live in the city, especially when he finds himself on their turf. Strepsiades, for instance, attempting to enroll at Socrates' school, knocks at the door only to have the students within revile him for nearly kicking down the door. Strepsiades is apparently so humiliated that he apologizes: "Please forgive me--I live away off in the country" (Clouds 1970:138). As Dover points out (1968:111), the students' accusation is contrived for humorous effect; for such abuse to follow such politeness is a ready source of humor. Anything but stupid, Strepsiades cites his rural origins as the reason for the boorish behavior he is accused of, hoping to deflect further abuse. But his admission is a telling one. Even in this contrived situation the audience understands that the reason for his self-revelation is the stereotype of the rural man who is out of touch with the more sophisticated and more polite patterns of city behavior because of his rural upbringing and separation from urban society. And this stereotype is surely reinforced later on when Socrates reproaches Strepsiades for his slowwittedness and hopeless coarseness: "I've never seen any man so boorish (agroilos[13]), so impossible, so gauche (skaios, "left-handed"), so forgetful--whatever little bits of subtlety he has learned he's forgotten before he learns them" (Clouds 1970:628-631).

This response, typical of the urbanite's attitude toward rustics (Lloyd 1976:33.41, 70-77), reveals an awareness of the great gulf that exists between the city bred and their rural counterparts. The stereotype of the rustic boor is the creation of city dwellers, and Aristophanes employs it primarily for their enjoyment. The other side of the coin, urban refinement, is hinted at in this fragment of Alcaeus, a comedy writer contemporary with Aristophanes: "Now may he become refined (asteios) by living in a city" (polis; Kock 1880-88:26). This tantalizing fragment reveals little about the nature of urban sophistication but it does make it clear that refinement derives from city life. The men who possess this urban refinement and perpetuate the rustic stereotype also (understandably) see the city as the center of their existence and are not very tolerant of those who do not share their adulation of it: "If you have not seen Athens, you're a blockhead. But if you have seen it yet were not captured by it, you're an ass. If you're content to go away from it, you're a packass" (Lysippus, a late fifth-century comic writer, Kock 1880-88:7). The almost hypnotic attraction which, visually, if not socially the city of Athens possesses clearly eclipses any patriotic feeling which may in part prompt this statement. The rustic as he is presented in comedy could hardly be expected to share this admiration for the city. And so, it is not surprising that at least one writer finds it incongruous, even in jest, to conceive of a country boor inside the city: "Then will you bring this hayseed (ononis, "restharrow," a weed troublesome to farmers) into town?" (anonymous, Kock 1880-88:adesp. 438).

The refinement of the city in the late fifth-century goes far beyond just admiration for the city and the realization of the uniqueness of urban life although feelings like these may be a part of it. As was seen in previous eras, the urban frame of mind is reflected in various outward signs such as dress, behavior and speech. During the last half of the fifth century, speech especially begins to bear the mark of refinement as the Sophists and the art of rhetoric become increasingly important in Athenian life. Such Greek adjectives as asteios, kompsos and _leptos_, all denoting "refined" in some sense, are used most often to describe refinement in speech (Lloyd 1976:78-89, 93-101, 103-107). And when the Acharnian chorus, both rural and conservative, begins its invective against the sophisticated young prosecutors with their "succinct phrases," there is no doubt about where they see this refined language originating: "We old men and ancient blame the city" (_polis_; _Acharnians_ 1970:676).

Just as the Acharnian chorus recognizes certain refinements and niceties which they consider specious and over-subtle, so also the father in Aristophanes' earliest play, _Banqueters_, to his chagrin discerns in the speech of his wayward young son a certain vocabulary and diction borrowed from the rhetors and lawyers and can identify by name each learned source (Kock 1880-88, 198). The older generation, rural in outlook and background, condemns this overly citified manner of expression, but another group of Athenians, mostly the young, the _jeunesse doree_ of the aristocratic and wealthy classes are very much taken with these same refinements and flaunt them as a mark of a new distinction and sophistication. Since this refinement is verbal, it lends itself to easy mocking on the stage:

> Demus: I'm speaking of these lads in the perfume stores who
> sit and chatter like this:
>
>   'Phaeax[14] was ingenious (_sophos_) and adroitly (_dexios_)
>   saved himself from death--for he is coercivistic (_synertikos_)
>   and conclusivistic (_perantikos_) and aphoristic (_gnomotypikos_)
>   and precise and impressivistic (_kroustikos_); he's quite
>   restrictivistic (_kataleptikos_) of the disruptivistic
>   (_thorybetikos_).'
>
> Sausage-seller: You aren't being sensitivistic (_katadaktylikos_) to the
>   periphrastic (_laletikos_), are you?

The point of Aristophanes' ridicule is the affectation of the group's language, namely their overuse of adjectives ending in _-kos_. Although the formation of adjectives in this manner is evidenced as early as Homer, nevertheless the use of them increases when Athens experiences the full impact of the rhetors and the Sophists (Peppler 1910:428-432). As Peppler points out, the erudite sound of these formations provided a way for these young men to show off their "new culture" and so these adjectives became "very much in vogue in fashionable society" (Peppler 1910:432). Aristophanes consistently employs them to suggest far-reaching differences in people's education, age, background and upbringing. Throughout _Clouds_, for instance, Socrates and his group employ them and represent, then, the learned men, city-bred, who speak in a refined way (_Clouds_ 1970:476, 728), whereas Strepsiades (_Clouds_ 1970:484, 730) makes use of more traditional and old-fashioned language as would befit a man of rural upbringing.

As in lyric poetry, so also on the fifth-century comic stage the showcase for urbanity is the symposium, and in the "acculturation" of Philocleon in Aristophanes' _Wasps_, urban refinement is exhibited in all its forms--as social virtue, dress, proper comportment, language, wit, conversation and as a trait of the young. Bdelycleon, Philocleon's son, does his best throughout the play to convert his father from the inveterate jurist he is to a more respectable citizen, and as is expected the rustic stubbornness and coarseness of the old man is too much for the son.

In the language of Athens' refined youth Bdelycleon promises (1209) to make his father "a good symposium guest" (sympotikos) and "good company" (synousiastikos). Bdelycleon, in fact, uses nearly twice as many of such -kos adjectives as these in the 400-line parody of the symposium than in the rest of the play (Peppler 1910:436). Teaching his father how to dress for the cultured event is the first task (Wasps 1970:1122-1167), but the old man mistakes the elegant Persian dinner coat for a rough goat-hide cloak. Learning to walk "opulently" and to "mince in a dignified and luxurious way" (Wasps 1970:1168-1169) proves too much for him also. Nor is he able to recline at table by "gymnastically pouring himself like a liquid" onto the couch (Wasps 1970:1212-1213). In matters of table conversation and wit, Philocleon is told to tell "dignified tales" since the other guests will be quite learned and clever" (Wasps 1970:1174-1175). At this point the bathos of the rustic's vulgar stories steals the scene from the tolerant sophisticate with his elegant suggestions.

CONCLUSION

Philocleon in Aristophanes' Wasps fails to acquire the traits of the refined symposiast and brings chaos to the symposium he attends, all to the horror of the dignified guests and the delight of the Athenian audience. And for its humorous effect Aristophanes not only satirizes the uncouth and boorish behavior of the father Philocleon but also the sophisticated society of the symposium itself including the old man's cultivated young son and teacher. Even though Bdelycleon becomes the butt of humor designed to amuse rustic theatre-goers and members of refined Athenian society who might also enjoy this ridicule of themselves, the picture that Aristophanes creates of that urbane young man remains intact. That Philocleon cannot learn even a veneer of sophistication from a series of intensive lessons points up something basic about urban/rural relations that is true even of the two rustics in the Odyssey who violate urban propriety by crying at the sight of Odysseus' bow: the traits of both rustics and urbanites are not only conflicting but deeply ingrained because of their close, almost symbiotic relationship to their respective environments. As Aristophanes brings out in Clouds, Wasps and, perhaps, in the fragmentary Banqueters, the differences separating city and country as well as those separating generations cannot be brushed off lightly.

By the last quarter of the fifth century in Aristophanes' and Thucydides' own time, rapid changes in the Athenian polis are brought on by its rise to preeminence in Greece and by the Peloponnesian conflict which forces farmers to move to the city. This rapid flow of events aggravates and intensifies the differences that separate rustics and city dwellers. The increasing use of rhetoric in the law courts and

35

elsewhere creates feelings of mistrust and inferiority among the uneducated rural population. As Athenian comedy reveals, just the hustle and bustle of a thriving commercial and industrial center can create an environment foreign, confusing, even frightening to rustics who are used to a simpler, quieter setting. And for many rustics, this urban environment is one that, because of war, they are unable to escape.

The close contact of wartime living conditions makes life trying for both urbanites and rustics, and the values of the two groups are in constant conflict. As a result city dwellers become more acutely aware than ever before of shared interests and attitudes, and in numbers they begin to isolate their culture and to think of themselves as urban. Thucydides makes clear that this urban frame of reference is natural and at the same time inescapable as he leads his readers to follow the fortunes of the two antagonists, Sparta and Athens. And by early fourth century thinkers like Plato and Aristotle in their vision of the polis are able to give expression to that Greek self-awareness that Oppenheim finds so rare.

Notes

1. M.I. Finley clearly points out the problems of isolating and interpreting political and sociological evidence in the Homeric epics in Appendix I of the second revised edition of his The World of Odysseus (1979:142-158).

2. Certainly Telemachus' presumed role as a royal representative of Ithaca's interests does not argue for strong civic cooperation and communal action. Hoffmann (1956:155-157; see also Adkins 1960:35, 75-76) has pointed out that heroes of the Iliad and the Odyssey are not preoccupied or even motivated by any attachment or sense of belonging to the city, but their first allegiance is to their household (oikia).

3. D.R. Cole has carefully worked out the distinction between polis (ptolis) and asty in Homer (1976:25-26). Polis is used to describe a fortified town in a public relationship to its people usually as it is viewed from the outside, whereas asty represents "the personal and intimate side of man's life," his home and family. Archaeological evidence and Linear B decipherments are supportive of this interpretation (Cole 1976:143-165). See also Dunmore (1961:174).

4. P.A.L. Greenhalge (1973:150-155) tries to minimize the political implications of what Aristotle (Politics 1957:1297 b. 16-28) also saw as the importance of this military innovation.

5. Cf. Aeschylus, Persians 1955:347-350; Herodotus 1966:8.61; Sophocles, Oedipus the King 1964:56-57; see Stambaugh (1974:309-312).

6. Tyrtaeus' use of aethlon (prize) calls to mind the many athletic contests among the Greeks including the Olympic games where aristocratic competitors could excel. As F.E. Adcock (1962:4-5) points out, "(Hoplite combat) was not the place for single-handed exploits, for the Epic aristeia of champions. The desire for personal distinction must be subordinate: it must find its satisfaction elsewhere, as in the great athletic festivals, where men won honor before all the Greeks."

7. "A shame culture is one whose sanction is overtly 'what people will say'." (Adkins 1972:12). See also Dodds (1966:1-63) and Gouldner (1967:81-86).

8. The Attic forms of sophia and atropia have been substituted for the sophie and atropie of Theognis.

9. Frederic Will (1958:301-311) has shown that the archon-arbitrater Solon of early sixth-century Athens gained a similar self-awareness simply becuase he was "caught between cross-fires of opposing batteries" (305) within the polis and forced to take stock of himself and what he stood for.

10. Here _polis_ means the physical city; see Cole (1976:270).

11. See also Ehrenberg (1943:63-69) whose focus for rural and urban attitudes in Greek comedy is by necessity very broad since he is attempting a complete sociology of Aristophanes' comedies.

12. For example, _Acharnians_ 1970:29-36, 263-276, 988-998; _Knights_ 1970:41-43; _Clouds_ 1970:43-50, 187-190, 1005-1008, 1115-1122; _Wasps_ 1970:259-265, 634, 850. See Crosby (1927:180-184).

13. On the language of rusticity and sophistication in Greek literature see Lloyd (1976:68-110).

14. Phaeax is most likely a rival of Alcibiades whom Plutarch (_Alcibiades_ 1960-64:13) mentions.

Bibliography

Adcock, F.E., 1962: *The Greek and Macedonian Art of War*, Berkeley.

Adkins, Arthur W.H., 1960: *Merit and Responsibility*. Oxford.

_____, 1972: *Moral Values and Political Behaviour in Ancient Greece*, New York.

Aeschylus, 1964: *Aeschyli Septem Quae Supersunt Tragoediae*, Ed. Gilbert Murray. 2nd ed. Oxford.

Aristophanes, 1970: *Aristophanis Comoediae*, 2 vols. Eds. F.W. Hall and W.M. Geldart. Oxford.

Aristotle, 1967: *Aristotelis Politica*, Ed. W.D. Ross. Oxford.

Bowra, C.M., 1961: *Greek Lyric Poetry from Alcman to Simonides*, 2nd ed. Oxford.

Cole, David Russell, 1976: *Asty and Polis: "City" in Early Greek*, Diss. Stanford (Palo Alto).

Crosby, H.L., 1927: "Aristophanes and the Country," *Classical World* 180-184.

Diehl, E., ed., 1949-1952: *Anthologia Lyrica Graeca*, 3 vols. 3rd ed. Leipzig.

Dodds, E.R., 1966: *The Greeks and the Irrational*, Berkeley. Univ. of California Press, 1966.

Dover, K.J., ed., 1968: *Aristophanes: Clouds*, Oxford.

Dunmore, C.W., 1961: *The Meaning of Polis*. Diss. New York University (New York).

Ehrenberg, Victor, 1964: *The Greek State*, New York.

_____, 1943: *The People of Aristophanes*, Oxford.

Fanta, Adolf, 1882: *Der Staat in der Ilias und Odyssee*, Innsbruck.

Finley, John H., Jr., 1942: *Thucydides*, Cambridge.

Finley, M.I., 1977: "The Ancient City: From Fustel de Coulanges to Max Weber and Beyond," *Comparative Studies in Society and History*, 19:305-327.

_____, 1979: *The World of Odysseus*. 2nd ed. Middlesex.

Forrest, W.G., 1966: *The Emergence of Greek Democracy 800-400 B.C.*, New York.

Gouldner, A.W., 1965: _Enter Plato_, New York.

Greenhalge, P.A.L., 1973: _Early Greek Warfare_, Cambridge.

Hammond, Mason, 1972: _The City in the Ancient World_, Cambridge.

Herodotus, 1966: _Herodoti Historiae_, Ed. Carol Hude. Oxford.

Hoffman, Wilhelm, 1956: "Die Polis bei Homer." In _Festschrift Bruno Snell_, Munich.

Homer, 1966: _Homeri Opera (Iliad)_, 2 vols. Edd. David B. Monro and Thomas W. Allen. 3rd ed. Oxford.

_____, 1979: _Homeri Opera (Odyssey)_, Ed. Thomas W. Allen. 2nd ed. Oxford.

_____, 1975: _Homeri Opera (Odyssey)_, Ed. Thomas W. Allen. 2nd ed. Oxford.

Kakridis, I.T., 1961: _Der Thukydideische Epitaphios: ein stilistischer Kommentar_, Munich.

Kirsten, Ernst, 1956: _Die griechische Polis als historisch-geographisches Problem des Mittelmeerraumes_, Bonn.

Kock, Theodorus, Ed., 1880-88: _Comicorum Atticorum Fragmenta_, 3 vols. Leipzig.

Lammermann, Karl, 1935: _Von der attischen Urbanitat und ihrer Auswirkung in der Sprache_, Diss. Gottingen.

Lloyd, Charles O., 1976: _Sophistication and Refinement in Greek Literature from Homer to Aristophanes_, Diss. Indiana University.

Lobel, E., and D. Page, eds., 1963: _Poetarum Lesbiorum Fragmenta_, Oxford.

Meier, Christian, 1969: Rev. of _Polis und Imperium_ and _Der Staat der Griechen_ (2nd ed.) by Victor Ehrenberg. _Gnomon_, 41:365-379.

Oppenheim, A. Leo, 1977: _Ancient Mesopotamia: Portrait of a Dead Civilization_, Chicago.

Page, D.L., ed., 1962: _Boetae Melici Graeci_, Oxford.

Page, D.L., 1965: _Sapphr and Alcaeus: An Introduction to the Study of Ancient Lesbian Poetry_, Oxford.

Peppler, C.W., 1910: "The Termination -kos, as Used by Aristophanes for Comic Effect," _American Journal of Philology_, 31:428-444.

Plutarch, 1960-64: _Vitae Parallelae_. Edd. Cl. Lindskog and K. Ziegler, Leipzig.

Ribbeck, Otto, 1888: _Agroikos, eine ethologische Studie in Abhandlungen der philologisch-historischen Klasse der königlich sächischen Gesellschaft der Wissenschaften_, 10:1-68.

Rieu, E.V., trans., 1945: _The Odyssey_, New York.

Rogers, B.B., trans., 1960: _Aristophanes_, Loeb Classical Library. Cambridge.

Schaefer, Hans., 1960: Rev. of _Der Staat der Griechen_ (2 vols.) by Victor Ehrenberg, _Zeitschrift der Savigny-Stiftung fur Rechtsegeschichte_ (Romanistische Abteilung), 77:422-435.

Sophocles, 1964: _Sophoclis Fabulae_, Ed. A.C. Pearson. Oxford.

Stambaugh, John E., 1974: "The Idea of the City: Three Views of Athens," _Classical Journal_ 69:309-321.

Starr, Chester, 1961: _The Origins of Greek Civilization_, New York.

Thomas, C.G., 1966: "Homer and the Polis," _La Parola del Passato_, 21:5-14.

Thucydides, 1970: _Thucydidis Historiae_, Edd. Henry Stuart Jones and Johann Enoch Powell. Oxford.

Will, Frederic, 1958: "Solon's Consciousness of Himself," _Transactions and Proceedings of the American Philological Association_, 89:301-311.

Youman, A. Eliot, 1974: "Aristophanes: Country Man or City Man?" _Classical Bulletin_, 50:73-76.

Young, Douglas, ed., 1971: _Theognis_, Leipzig.

The Culture of the Greek <u>Polis</u>:

The Unified View of Plato and Aristotle

Albert A. Anderson

> Practically every era of Western civilization has at one
> time or another tried to liberate itself from the Greeks,
> in deep dissatisfaction because whatever they themselves
> achieved, seemingly quite original and sincerely admired,
> lost color and life when held against the Greek model and
> shrank to a botched copy, a caricature (Nietzsche 1956:91).

Why has the Greek <u>polis</u> played so great a role in shaping Western culture? The answer to this question can best be understood by considering the concept of the <u>polis</u> as it was manifested in fifth and fourth century Greece and as it was articulated by the intellectuals of that period. In this paper I shall consider what I believe to be the best formulation of the concept: the unified vision of Plato and Aristotle.

It is frequently believed that Plato and Aristotle disagreed about fundamental matters. Much is made of Plato's alleged concern with eternal essences and Aristotle's critiuqe of that view of the nature of things. It is also asserted that Aristotle and his teacher diverge in their basic attitude toward things. W.T. Jones presents a typical version of this approach:

> The root of all the differences between Plato and
> Aristotle, one may be tempted to say, lies in Aristotle's
> struggle to correct Plato's theory of knowledge. This
> is true, but it is only a part of the truth. Aristotle's
> reformulation of the theory of forms was the result, in
> part, of a purely intellectual struggle to solve the
> epistemological problem; but it was also rooted in a
> temperamental difference. . . .It has been remarked that
> everyone is born either a Platonist or an Aristotelian.
> Plato and Aristotle, that is, represent two different
> attitudes toward the world. Plato was a perfectionist
> whose inclination, even in discussing the problems of
> practical politics, was always toward a utopian solution
> that was impractical precisely because the perfect
> is never realized in this world. Where Plato was other-
> worldly and idealistic, Aristotle was practical and
> empirical(1952:217-218).

In spite of the widespread nature of this understanding of the two central figures of Greek philosophy, I believe that it is wrong on both counts.

Plato's theory of knowledge and reality and his attitude toward the world differs little from that of Aristotle. Jones offers a misreading of both thinkers. What is needed is a fresh approach, one which allows the substance of Greek philosophy to appear. The way for any reader to be convinced about the superiority of one interpretation or another is to read the primary sources and see what is there. But the attitude and expectations we bring to the reading makes a crucial difference. For that reason I wish to suggest a way of reading Plato and Aristotle on the subject of the _polis_ which reveals the unity of their vision.

Plato and Aristotle present a new concept of the _polis_ which must be distinguished (a) from the reactionary desire to return to the old gods and thus traditional ways of life and (b) from the Sophistic vision of the good life which dominated the latter half of the fifth century in Athens. Whatever their differences, they are united by a common vision of the _polis_ both in concept and in attitude. First, I wish to consider the traditional notion of the _polis_ and to discuss its breakdown during the fifth century. Secondly, I shall develop three aspects of the unified philosophy of Plato and Aristotle, showing how this accounts for the lasting nature of their concept of the _polis_.

The origins of the Greek _polis_ can be traced to the family and the _phratria_ (Fustel de Coulanges 1873:118). Its development was indigenous, not the product of diffusion from older civilizations (Hammond 1972:172-173).[1] What is important about the _polis_, however, is not its original form but the unique character it developed in the fifth century. The Greek _polis_ had much in common with the form of the city which began to develop in Summer around the year 3200 B.C.,[2] but its distinctive nature clearly separates it from earlier urban centers. The Greek _polis_ is unique because of its _raison de'etre_. Even though any city, to be a city, requires economic, legal, military, and other such functions, the Greek _polis_ distinguished itself by its spiritual character rather than by its material achievements.

Being a member of the _polis_ was not a matter of birth but a quality of mind. Isocrates, who disagreed with Plato and Aristotle on many issues, was in accord with them on the essential nature of the _polis_:

> So far has our city left the rest of mankind behind her
> in thought and expression that our citizens have become
> the teachers of others, and have made the name Helene a
> mark no longer of birth but of intellect, and have caused
> those to be called Helenes who share in our culture rather
> than our descent (1964:x).

It was during the fifth century that this "enlightenment" vision of the nature of the _polis_ developed. It contrasts radically with the traditional form of the _polis_ which was based upon family membership and which derived its being from religious and paternal authority.[3]

The Religious Roots of the POLIS

The religious character of the family, the _phratria_, and the traditional notion of the _polis_ is of central importance. It extended through both Greek and the Roman civilization, maintaining its strength and influence alongside of other, more sophisticated, cultural forms. Not only did the family religion bind all who were born into the family but it included women who married into the family as well. It even extended to slaves.[4] Contemporary notions of slavery differ from this aspect of Greek and Roman life. The slave lost his freedom, but he derived dignity from his participation in the worship. He took the name of the family and was considered to be a member of it by adoption (Fustel de Coulanges 1873:115). The law was quite clear about the worth of the slave (or "client"):

> If a patron has done his client wrong, let him be
> accursed . . . let him die. The patron was obliged
> to protect his client by all means and with all the
> power of which he was master. . . . One might testify
> in court against a cognate, but not against a client;
> and men continued long to consider their duties towards
> clients as far above those toward cognates. Why?
> Because a cognate, connected solely through women, was
> not a relative, and had no part in the family religion.
> The client, on the contrary, had a community of worship;
> he had, inferior though he was, a real relationship,
> which consisted, according to the expression of Plato,
> in adoring the same domestic gods (Fuestel de Coulanges
> 1873:116).

Thus, the bond between religious worship and political and social association was fundamental.[5]

This is the background against which we must consider the ideas of the polis articulated by Plato and Aristotle. It is customary when discussing Plato's notion of the polis to focus the discussion upon the Republic. Although it is impossible to ignore the Republic when dealing with the topic of the polis, it is difficult to do justice to it because of its ironic and indirect nature.[6] For the purposes of the present essay other dialogues are equally instructive about Plato's notion of the polis.

Of particular interest is the Euthyphro. In that work we see two points: (a) the concept of the polis, which rests upon the religious consciousness described by Fustel de Coulanges, is a strong force in Plato's Athens and (b) Socrates, as a child of the Greek Enlightenment, one who launches devastating logical attacks upon the traditional religious idea of the polis.

Euthyphro meets Socrates at court. He is there to prosecute his own father for murder. Euthyphro says:

> The man who was killed was a hired workman of mine, and
> when we were farming at Naxos, he was working there on
> our land. Now he got drunk, got angry with one of our
> house slaves, and butchered him. So my father bound him
> hand and foot, threw him into a ditch, and sent a man here
> to Athens to ask the religious adviser what he ought to
> do. In the meantime he paid no attention to the man as

he lay there bound, and neglected him, thinking that he
was a murderer and it did not matter if he were to die.
And that is just what happened to him. For he died of
hunger and cold and his bonds before the messenger came
back from the adviser (1971:4C).

Euthyphro is presented here as someone who is an authority on "divine
laws" and he is contrasted with the members of his family who cannot
understand why he is prosecuting his father under these circumstances.
They claim that it is "unholy for a son to prosecute his father for
murder" (1971:4D). But Euthyphro knows that it is equally wrong for his
father to treat a slave as he treats him. What Plato presents in this
encounter is a dramatic example of the conflict which arises when
religious duty demands two opposing actions. Euthyphro, fearing moral
"pollution" of the entire house, chooses to prosecute his father and
cites "religious law" as his justification. This accords exactly with
the picture of traditional religion as developed by Fustel de Coulanges.

There is an even more important aspect of the Euthyphro which should
be noted here. As Socrates presses his examination of Euthyphro's
understanding of religious law and the rational ground which supports
it, it turns out that Euthyphro has little grasp of the rational
foundations of his position. But he is well aware of the connection
between his religious convictions and the polis:

Euthyphro: I told you a while ago, Socrates, that it is
a long task to learn accurately all about these things.
However, I say simply that when one knows how to say and
do what is gratifying to the gods, in praying and sacrificing, that is holiness, and such things bring salvation
to individual families and to states; and the opposite of
what is gratifying to the gods is impious, and that over-
turns and destroys everything (1971:4B).

This passage contains the essence of the struggle which developed in the
fifth century in Greece and resulted, at the end of the century, in
Socrates' execution. If the traditional notion of holiness is
overturned, Euthyphro says, everything will be undermined. That means
that the very foundations of Greek values will be torn up just because
the family and the polis rest upon the notion of holiness, i.e., on the
religious consciousness which nurtured them. Impiety cannot be
tolerated because it destroys everything. Socrates, the symbol of
impiety, must die.

Readers of the Apology, Crito, and similar dialogues are well aware
that in a deeper sense Socrates was not guilty of impiety. In fact, he
may have been far more "religious" in a modern sense of the term than
his accusers. He was, however, guilty of undermining the traditional
notion of piety as articulated by Euthyphro. His devastating attack
upon the foundations of that position are read today by almost every
beginning student of philosophy for the simple reason that it is a
splendid articulation of the problem of establishing foundations for
value judgments. But Socrates did not invent this mode of thinking.
Both he and Plato inherited it from the Greek philosophers of the sixth

and fifth centuries.[7] Socrates was dedicated to the same intellectual
quest as the other great thinkers of the fifth century, but he carried
on his activities in public. His attacks upon popular religion, no
matter how logical and justified to thinking people, were <u>destructive</u>
from the standpoint of Euthyphro and others who relied on <u>traditional</u>
religious consciousness as the basis for making value judgments. The
notion of the <u>polis</u> was at the crossroads: either the questioning of
traditional beliefs had to be abandoned or an entirely new basis for the
<u>polis</u> must be sought. They killed Socrates, but that was not
sufficient.[8]   Plato and Aristotle, realizing the need for new
foundations, picked up where Socrates left off.

The Greek Enlightenment

It is impossible to account for the appearance of philosophy as
presented by Plato and Aristotle without the Greek enlightenment.[9] But
it is equally important to take account of where they differed from the
Sophists. The central point of divergence was over the problem of the
ground or foundation values. Both they and the Sophists considered
value questions to be primary, so this difference is crucial for
understanding their idea of the <u>polis</u>. What is common to the Sophists
is skepticism, the "theoretical centre of Sophistry" (Windelband
1970:116). Both Plato and Aristotle took the quest for knowledge to be
not only essential to the good life but possible to achieve, especially
in questions of value. The Sophist position is best expressed by
Protagoras: "Of all things the measure is Man, of the things that are,
that they are, and of the things that are not, that they are not"
(Freeman 1977:125).

This position is subjected to attack in the dialogues of Plato and
in the writings of Aristotle. Aristotle deals with it tersely:

> The saying of Protagoras is like the views we have
> mentioned; he said that man is the measure of all things,
> meaning simply that that which seems to each man also
> assuredly is. If this is so, it follows that the same
> thing both is and is not, and is bad and good, and that
> the contents of all other opposite statements are true,
> because often a particular thing appears beautiful to
> some and the contrary of beautiful to others, and that
> which appears to each man is the measure (1908:1062b).

The problem with this position is the problem with any contradiction,
and Aristotle's critique is simple and devastating:

> There are some who . . . assert that it is possible
> for the same thing to be and not to be, and say that
> people can judge this to be the case. . . .
> We can, however, demonstrate negatively even that
> this view is impossible, if our opponent will only say
> something; and if he says nothing, it is absurd to seek
> to give an account of our views to one who cannot give
> an account of anything, in so far as he cannot do so.

> For such a man, as such, is from the start no better
> than a vegetable (1908:1006b-1006a).

Plato's analysis is much more exhaustive, but it rests upon the same logic (1967:170cff). Entailed in Protagoras' view is the position that

> in affairs of state, the honorable and the disgraceful, the
> just and the unjust, the pious and its opposite are in truth
> to each state such as it thinks they are and as it enacts
> into law for itself, and in these matters no citizen and no
> state is wiser than another (1967:172).

Protagoras' approach leads to skepticism, and, in the end, to silence. One who believes such a thing is no better than a vegetable.

Plato and Aristotle are at least unified by what they reject. Both join in the enlightenment critique of the traditional religious consciousness symbolized by Euthphro. However, they part company with the Sophists and show the absurdity of the notion that "man is the measure of all things." In seeking to establish new foundations for the polis they avoid both religious authoritarianism and skepticism. But their agreement is much deeper. They are also united by their positive account of the polis and the conceptual foundations upon which it rests.

Three fundamental points of agreement can be distinguished: (1) rational deliberation is the only means of justifying political authority; (2) the good life is the telos (goal) of the polis; and (3) the polis is a natural creation rather than the product of chance or of human caprice, and, for that reason, its essential nature can be known. I believe that a careful reading of Aristotle's works and a proper explication of the meaning of Plato's dialogues support these three points. It is easier to find support for this claim in Aristotle's writing than in Plato's because Aristotle wrote straight prose and Plato wrote a kind of poetry.[10] Both writers must be interpreted to be properly understood, but the interpretation of Plato is much more difficult than that of Aristotle. For that reason I shall concentrate upon Aristotle's elaboration of these three points and refer to those dialogues which I believe show the same thing.

The Primacy of Rational Deliberation

The goal of philosophy is to know the truth. This proposition is fundamental to both Plato and Aristotle. Aristotle says it explicitly:

> It is right, too, that philosophy should be called the
> science of truth: for a theoretical science ends in truth,
> as a practical science ends in action; though practical
> men occasionally indulge in theoretical science, they
> have in view not its eternal truth, but some practical
> and present objective (1960:993b).

When the philosopher turns his attention to the polis, he does so in a way different from that of the practical person (the one who is more concerned about acting than about knowing). This does not mean that philosophers are uninterested in action or that practical people are able to proceed without knowing. But the focus of attention is different. The philosopher is interested in what is "eternal." There is a primacy and an ultimacy which characterize the concerns of the philosopher.

> What is most true is the reason why other things are derivatively true. Hence, the principles of eternal things are necessarily most true; for they are true always and not merely sometimes; and there is nothing which explains their being what they are, for it is they that explain the being of other things. Consequently, status in being governs status in truth (1960:993b).

In spite of the difference in focus, both the theoretical and the practical depend upon rational deliberation, the former directly and the latter indirectly.[11]

The deliberation of the political leader takes the form of what Aristotle calls "practical wisdom."[12] This is related to theoretical deliberation in an intimate way. Ruling in the polis is a function of deliberation, and it is informed by the truth to the extent that it achieves its fundamental purpose. Even though there are other elements which help to nurture the polis (nature and habit), they must be in harmony with rational deliberation and must submit to it.[13] Hence, the priority of rational deliberation for Aristotle is clear.

The temptation with Plato is to go to various dialogues and cite passages which sound similar to those just quoted from Aristotle. There is no difficulty in doing that, since his characters frequently say just this sort of thing. But it is a mistake to equate what Socrates says and what Plato means in the dialogue. Often Socrates' statements and Plato's meaning are close, but not always. The difficulty is in knowing when it is the case and when it is not. We must consider the overall movement of the dialogue in question and determine the meaning of the work as a whole. When we do so we find that there are several dialogues which display the primacy of rational deliberation in justifying political authority.

The most obvious examples are Apology and Crito. In those works Socrates is presented as something of a tragic hero who consciously chooses rational deliberation over the temptations of begging for his life in court and of bribing the guards and escaping from prison. He is presented as the "gadfly" who serves the Athenian polis by stinging it with his penetrating questions. In the Crito the alternative is clear: either Socrates must be persuaded with good reasons to escape, or he will remain and die. Reason is clearly on the side of remaining, so he chooses to drink the hemlock.

But even when the discussion is more subtle and analytical (as in Theaetetus, Sophist, and Statesman), Plato is still working away at the proper connection between rational deliberation and the nature and nurture of the _polis_. In the _Republic_ such analytical distinctions are blended with dramatic exchange and poetic articulation. Many of the dialogues leave us in a state of _aporia_ (rational difficulty), but the problem is still the same. We find ourselves placed between the unacceptable alternatives of being ruled by some kind of irrational authority (whether a tyrant or our own uncontrolled passions) or left with no authority at all (as happens when man becomes "the measure of all things"). For both Plato and Aristotle rational deliberation is offered as the only viable alternative.

The Good Life as the TELOS of the POLIS

The priority of rational deliberation in determining political authority leads naturally to the centrality of the good in the _polis_. Aristotle shows why:

> Every state is a community of some kind, and every
> community is established with a view to some good; for
> mankind always act in order to obtain that which they
> think good. But, if all communities aim at some good,
> the state or political community, which is the highest
> of all, and which embraces all the rest, aims at good
> in greater degree than any other, and at the highest
> good (1972:1252a).

Just as philosophy comprehends the truth of eternal things, so too the good of the _polis_ encompasses all of the other goods because it is the highest good. Human life is political by nature.[14] If one cannot live in the _polis_ or is self-sufficient, then he is simply not human.[15] In direct opposition to the traditional concept of the _polis_, Aristotle argues for the priority of the _polis_ over the family:

> The state is by nature clearly prior to the family and
> to the individual, since the whole is of necessity prior
> to the part; for example, if the whole body be destroyed,
> there will be no foot or hand. . . . The proof that the
> state is a creation of nature and prior to the individual
> is that the individual, when isolated, is not self-sufficing;
> and therefore he is like a part in relation to the whole
> (1972:1253a).

It is the good of the _polis_ which encompasses the good of the individual and the life of the family.

Aristotle is postulating an ideal situation, one in which there is no contradiction between the _polis_ and the family or between the family and the individual. The _polis_ exists for the sake of the good life, "not for the sake of life only: if life only were the object . . . brute animals might form a state, but they cannot, for they have no share in happiness or in a life of free choice" (1972:1280a). What holds the state together is the rational unity provided by education.[16] It is in this way that the happiness and welfare of the individual and that of the _polis_ are united. "There remains to be discussed the question whether the happiness of the individual is the same as that of the state, or different. Here again there can be no doubt--no one denies that they are the same" (1972:1324a).

There is a danger of misunderstanding here. Aristotle does not conceive of a totalitarian state in which unity becomes a monochrome organism with no diversity. He specifically attacks the sort of society which Socrates imagines in the Republic:

> The error of Socrates must be attributed to the false
> notion of unity from which he starts. Unity there should
> be, both of the family and of the state, but in some
> respects only. For there is a point at which a state
> may attain such a degree of unity as to be no longer a
> state, or at which, without actually ceasing to exist,
> it will become an inferior state, like harmony passing
> into unison, or rhythm which has been reduced to a single
> foot. The state, as I was saying, is a plurality, which
> should be united and made into a community by education;
> and it is strange that the author of a system of educa-
> tion which he thinks will make the state virtuous, should
> expect to improve his citizens by regulation of this
> sort, and not by philosophy or by customs and laws. . . .
> (1972:1263b).

The unity of the state is a rational unity. The goal of the state is to achieve the good life both for the whole and for the part. The part, while integrated into the whole by education, is a plurality, not a mindless and monotonous unit.

It is important to note that Aristotle's attack is upon Socrates, not Plato. The "ideal state" which is painted in the Republic is contrary to Aristotle's concept of the good polis. It is also contrary to the philosophy of Plato. As Aristotle says, it would be "strange" to believe that people could be improved by regulations of the sort outlined by Socrates. But the overall conclusion from reading Plato's dialogues (including the Republic) is just the opposite: it is philosophy, not rigid regulations, which promotes the good life both for individuals and for the polis.

In the Crito, for example, Plato presents Socrates remaining in Athens to die rather than escaping. But why? Not just because he has been told to stay. He has often acted contrary to what he was told. What Socrates refuses to abandon is the practice of philosophy. It is not regulations but "the law" which he refuses to undermine, and this law is something divine. Aristotle is opposed to Socrates' totalitarian state in the Republic, but so is Plato. What the Republic shows is the deficiency of such a state, not its desirability. What separates the philosopher from other people is that he keeps his attention fixed upon the ideal polis, not some distorted and mistaken version of it.

Readers of the Republic are faced with a crucial dilemma at just this point. Socrates and Glaucon have arrived at the point where the philosopher is confronted with the difficulty of living in the polis:

In the matter of honors and office too this will be
his guiding principle. He will gladly take part in and
enjoy those which he thinks will make him a better man,
but in public and private life he will shun those that
may overthrow the established habit of his soul.
Then, if that is his chief concern, he (Glaucon)
said, he will not part in politics.
Yes, by the dog, said I (Socrates), in his own city
he certainly will, yet perhaps not in the city of his
birth, except in some providential conjuncture.
I understand, he said. You mean the city whose
establishment we have described, the city whose home is
in the ideal, for I think that it can be found nowhere
on earth.
Well, said I, perhaps there is a pattern of it laid
up in heaven for him who wishes to contemplate it and so
beholding to constitute himself its citizen. But it
makes no difference whether it exists now or ever will
come into being. The politics of this city only will
be his and of none other (1970:592).

This passage contains a paradox, especially if one takes Socrates' words
literally and equates them with Plato's meaning. What is said here is
that the philosopher will stay out of the politics of the polis. But if
that is so, then the entire picture of the so-called "ideal" state which
has been developed in the Republic, the one with the guardians, the
communal living, and the philosopher kings, will be impossible. In this
case it would be absurd to think that Plato offers this as his
prescription for the polis.

One way out of the dilemma is to interpret the "ideal" as referring
literally to something in heaven. That is, of course, what the passage
says. Those who think Plato was a "Platonist" (especially a Christian
one) favor this interpretation.[17] The position which develops from this
line of interpretation is one which can best be termed "supernatural."
The polis, at least the good one, is not a natural development within
the world. It is impossible to achieve it in the world, so the
philosopher must look elsewhere. There is much in Plato's dialogues to
support this interpretation. But the reason for that is the presence in
the dialogues of Pythagorean philosophy and Orphic religious belief
which pervaded Greek culture in the sixth and fifth centuries. I
believe that Plato included that material (especially in the Phaedo) not
to propagate it but to refute it through philosophical examination (much
the same way that he presents Euthyphro's position to show its
weakness). The Platonist "solution" of the tension between the ideal
polis and the historical one leads immediately to an even greater
difficulty, i.e., that of the radical separation between the City of God
and the City of Man.

A better approach is to explore the unity between Plato's philosophy
and that of Aristotle. Rather than seeking the good in a literal
heaven, Plato agrees with Aristotle that it is to be found in this world
if it is to be found at all. The ideal is fundamental to both

philosophers, but it is not a supernatural, mystical essence laid up in heaven. It is natural and knowable. It is the _telos_ of the _polis_.

The _POLIS_ _is_ _a_ _Natural_ _Creation_

Few would question the importance of the good as the goal of the _polis_ for either Aristotle or Plato. But it is much more difficult to convince even the most serious readers of Plato that he and Aristotle agree on the problem of the fundamental nature of knowledge and reality. What W.T. Jones calls "Aristotle's struggle to correct Plato's theory of knowledge" (1952:217-218) is the subject of considerable discussion among scholars. As difficult as this problem is, it must be faced if we are to grasp the unity of the vision of the _polis_ held by Plato and Aristotle. In fact, it is on the level of the ideal, properly understood, that this unity is manifested.

Aristotle's view of the _polis_ as a natural creation is easy to locate. He says: "Hence it is evident that the state is a creation of nature, and that man is by nature a political animal" (1972:1253a). What is especially interesting is the justification he develops for holding that point of view. It is man's possession of speech which gives rise to his political nature:

> Now, that man is more of a political animal than
> bees or any other gregarious animals is evident. Nature,
> as we often say, makes nothing in vain, and man is the
> only animal whom she endowed with the gift of speech
> (1972:1253a).

Other animals have the power to express pleasure and pain through their possession of "mere voice," but the power of speech in man allows him to "set forth the expedient and the inexpedient, and therefore likewise the just and the unjust" (1972:1253a). Man's political nature, therefore, grows out of the natural capacity he has to speak, especially his ability to discriminate good and evil. It is natural for man to use language, and especially for him to use language to make value judgments. This is the foundation for the formulation of the _polis_:

> It is a character of man that he alone has any sense of
> good and evil, of just and unjust, and the like, and the
> association of living beings who have this sense makes a
> family and a state (1972:1325b).

If the _polis_ were not natural, then it could not be good. "Nothing which is contrary to nature is good" (1972:1325b).

Human well-being is a function of (a) the choice of the proper end and aim of action and (b) the discovery of the actions which lead to such ends (1972:1331b). But this would be impossible if there were no order and all were the product of chance. The _polis_ must have a nature and that nature must be knowable. Otherwise human action would be impossible and the good could never be achieved.

> Virtue and goodness in the state are not a matter
> of chance but the result of knowledge and purpose. A
> city can be virtuous only when the citizens who have a
> share in the government are virtuous, and in our state
> all the citizens share in the government; let us then
> inquire how a man becomes virtuous (1972:1332a).

The _polis_ is created, not something eternal. But the rational principles upon which it rests _are_ the object of philosophical inquiry. The _polis_ arises naturally and it is knowable by human beings. The _polis_ is, above all, "the work of education" (1972:1332b). The ideal state, according to Aristotle, is not a product of prescriptions and regulations. On the contrary, it is the achievement of rational deliberation and free choice. This is made possible only by education and intellectual nurture. The _polis_ is created in the natural world by human beings who know what they are doing. This is not a mystical or supernatural venture but the sort of thing human beings do "by nature." It is meaningful, for Aristotle, to speak of an ideal _polis_, but that simply means the one which is determined to be best on the basis of rational inquiry. This is the task of the philosopher, the person who seeks "knowledge of the truth." The writings of Aristotle serve as a splendid example of such inquiry.

Plato, I believe, would differ little from this position. The distortions of his thought which have become popular in our day arise from the tendency of people to take what is said in the dialogues by some character or other as what Plato meant. But this is not what should be done. Plato's meaning is available to us only after careful participation in the dialectical process which emerges from reading and re-reading the dialogues. Plato wrote dialogues for a reason: they are the best way to articulate what he thinks. If he could have said what he had in mind by simple, univocal prose, he would have done so. Aristotle does offer something like the truth in straight prose, but the history of thought since his day is filled with dialectical responses to his statements of "the truth." As desirable as it seems to offer true propositions in clear language, that goal keeps slipping away just when we seem about to achieve it.

To the extent that Plato's vision of the _polis_ can be stated, Aristotle has done so. But Plato's works offer more than a set of propositions. They offer not only excellent formulation on a particular problem, concept, or theory; but, in addition, he also offers severe questioning and opposition to that idea. It is not the dialogues but the reader who is responsible for arriving at the truth of the matter under consideration. For this reason it is folly to try to "state" what Plato thought about any topic in a final and univocal way. The only hope is to read the dialogues and try to grasp the truth through the process of interpreting and evaluating what is said there.

For example, the passage quoted from the Republic dealing with the "ideal" _polis_ is ambiguous. It may be that the Christian Platonists are correct in their reading of that crucial passage. I think not. Plato uses Socrates and Glaucon to pose one of the classic dilemmas of human existence, one which cannot be easily resolved. When Socrates says that there is "a pattern . . . laid up in heaven" we should not take him literally but seriously. This pattern is <u>not</u> to be found "on earth" in the way that Athens can. Its home is "in the ideal." But the ideal is not a supernatural realm, "subsisting" beyond the City of Man. It is the real of the mind, the domain of what Aristotle would call "rational principles," the "eternal things" which the philosopher seeks to know. This vision runs through all of the dialogues. In fact, it is just the purpose of the dialogues to allow the reader to participate in this realm. Those dialogues which seek to understand the nature and good of the <u>polis</u> (which includes almost all of them to some degree) have as their purpose the investigation of the "eternal principles" which manifest themselves in the <u>polis</u>.

This is the <u>polis</u> of which Socrates speaks in the passage from the <u>Republic</u>. It is an ideal <u>polis</u>; and it is only in the politics of that <u>polis</u> that the genuine philosopher will participate. This <u>polis</u> is not "on earth," but it is, as Aristotle says, that which accounts for the being of those contingent cities which do appear on earth. It is not, I repeat, the "republic" which Socrates has painted in the course of the dialogue. That city has been shown to be just the sort of city a philosopher would avoid. It was a mere "wind egg," to borrow a phrase from the <u>Theaetetus</u>.

The ideal <u>polis</u> of the <u>Republic</u> is just the same one that Aristotle had in mind, the one which is not a matter of chance but is the result of knowledge and purpose. It is the one composed of virtuous citizens who have a share in the government. This <u>polis</u> has never existed. It never will. But all cities which exist do so only to the extent that they arise from that ideal <u>polis</u>. It makes no difference whether that city has ever existed or ever will exist on earth. The philosopher, the lover of the true and the good, will participate in that <u>polis</u> and no other. Any other city, when held up against that model, will shrink "to a botched copy, a caricature."

> And so people have continued to be both ashamed and fearful
> of the Greeks--though now and again someone has come along
> who has acknowledged the full truth: that the Greeks are
> the chariot drivers of every subsequent culture, but that,
> almost always, chariot and horses are of too poor a quality
> for the drivers, who then make sport of driving the
> chariot into the abyss--which they themselves clear with
> the bold leap of Achilles (Nietzsche 1956:91-92).

1. Although this issue is a complex one involving a number of difficult historical problems, Hammond's (1972) account is convincing. He concludes: "It is a reasonable, if not more so, to regard the city-state as gradually developed by the Greeks themselves, and as conditioned both by their own genius and by the circumstances in which their cities arose" (1972:173).

2. Hammond's discussion of the "urban revolution" is summarized as follows: "The continuous history of the city began in Sumer sometime around 3200. The Sumerian cities were closely built up and thickly inhabited communities; they had an organized government for the exploitation of the surrounding agricultural territory; they accumulated surpluses and developed specializations in both crafts and in religious and administrative functions; and they extended by commerce or by war their influence beyond their own frontiers" (1972:148). There is a strong resemblance between this account of what is essential to a city and Aristotle's summary of the "necessary offices" of the polis: "To sum up therefore, the necessary offices of superintendence deal with the following matters: institutions of religion, military institutions, revenue and expenditure, control of the market, citadel, harbours and country, also the arrangements of the law-courts, registration of contracts, collection of fines, custody of prisoners, supervision of accounts and inspections, and auditing of officials, and lastly the offices connected with the body that deliberates about public affairs" (Aristotle 1972:1322b30).

    Both of these discussions come close to the most influential contemporary attempt to define the nature of the city: "To constitute a full urban community a settlement must display a relative predominance of trade-commercial relations with the settlement as a whole displaying the following features: 1. a fortification; 2. a market; 3. a court of its own and at least partially autonomous law; 4. a related form of association; and 5. at least partial autonomy and autocephaly, thus also an administration by authorities in the election of whom the burghers participated" (Weber 1958:80-81).

3. Fustel de Coulanges characterizes the primordial form of the family this way: "Each family has its religion, its gods, its priesthood. Religious isolation is a law with it; its ceremonies are secret. In death even, or in the existence that follows it, families do not mingle; each one continues to live apart in the tomb, from which the stranger is excluded. Every family has also its property, that is to say, its lot of land, which is inseparably attached to it by its religion . . . . Finally, every family has its chief, as a nation would have its king. It has its laws, which, doubtless, are unwritten, but which religious faith engraves in the heart of every man. It has its court of justice, above which there is no other that one can appeal to. Whatever man really needs for his material or moral life the family possesses within itself. It needs nothing

from without; it is an organized state, a society that suffices for itself: (1973:113-114).

4. The initiation of slaves into the worship of the family is instructive: "A curious usage, that subsisted for a long time in Athenian house, shows us how the slave entered the family. They made him approach the fire, placed him in the presence of the domestic divinity, and poured lustral water upon his head. He then shared with the family some cakes and fruit. This ceremony bore a certain analogy to those of marriage and adoption. It doubtless signified that the new comer, a stranger the day before, should henceforth be a member of the family, and share in its religion. And thus the slave joined in the prayers, and took part in the festivals. The fire protected him; the religion of the Lares belonged to him as well as to his master. This is why the slave was buried in the burial-place of the family.

But by the very act of acquiring this worship, the right to pray, he lost his liberty. Religion was a chain that held him. He was bound to the family for his whole life and after his death" (Fustel de Coulanges 1873:114-115).

5. Fustel de Coulanges conceived of the relationship as a series of layers of participation. "Thus the city was not an assemblage of individuals; it was a confederation of several groups, which were established before it, and which it permitted to remain. We see, in the Athenian orators, that every Athenian formed a portion of four distinct societies at the same time; he was a member of the family, of a phratry, of a tribe, and of a city . . . . A man enters at different times into these four societies, and ascends, so to speak, from one to the other. First, the child is admitted into the family by the religious ceremony, which takes place six days after his birth. Some years later he enters the phratry by a new ceremony . . . . . Finally, at the age of sixteen or eighteen, he is presented for admission into the city. On that day, in the presence of an altar, and before the smoking flesh of a victim, he pronounces an oath, by which he binds himself, among other things, always to respect the religion of the city. From that day he is initiated into the public worship, and becomes a citizen" (1873:128-29). He concludes: "There seem to be two truths equally manifest: the one is, that the city was a confederation of groups that had been established before it; and the other is, that society developed only so fast as religion enlarged its sphere" (1873:131).

6. The indirect and ironic nature of the Republic has been discussed by various scholars. Leo Strauss (1964, Chapter II) provides one such discussion. However, the most persuasive and provocative inter- pretation I know appears in an article by J.N. Uemura (1965:42-52). Uemura concludes that "Plato is quite badly misinterpreted in the Republic if taken to be outlining a utopian society. Rather, it was Plato's aim to offer an antidote to, and show the complete stupidity of, the construction of any possible utopia built upon wealth or honor, reputation or political power" (1965:52).

7. This full story is much too long to be recounted here. The critique of traditional religion began to surface already in the thought of Xenophanes of Colophon (who was in his prime around 530 B.C.). He says that "Homer and Hesoid have attributed to the gods all things that are shameful and a reproach among mankind: theft, adultery, and mutual deception" (Freeman 1977:22). It was developed by Heraclitus of Ephesus (who flourished around 500 B.C.). The "universal law" (logos) is "common to all. But although the Law is universal, the majority live as if they had understanding peculiar to themselves" (Freeman 1977:24-25). The universal source of wisdom "is willing and unwilling to be called by the name of Zeus" (Freeman 1977:27). Anaxagoras of Clazomenae (in his prime around 460 B.C.) wrote a book which could be bought in Athens at the end of the fifth century (though few could read). Socrates claims (Apology, 26D) that he is wrongly confused with such thinkers who replace the divine and spiritual explanation of things with materialistic accounts (cf. Phaedo, 97 B ff.). He was also confused with the Sophists (Apology, 19 C). The Sophists were known for their skepticism, especially in religious matters. Protagoras of Abdera (who lived during the latter half of the fifth century B.C.) said: "About the gods, I am not able to know whether they exist, nor what they are like in form; for the factors preventing knowledge are many: the obscurity of the subject, and the shortness of human life" (1977:126). Socrates took this kind of questioning to the streets of Athens and in that way "currupted" the young men who came from the "best families.

8. It should be pointed out there that even though important Greek intellectuals were aware of the inadequacy of the traditional religious foundations for the polis, the popular mind continued to be dominated by such notions for some time. For this reason Fuestel de Coulanges is able to continue his analysis through the Roman period. The new concept of the polis existed alongside the older notion. E.R. Dodds explains this process as follows: "I have tried to illustrate . . . the slow, age-long building-up, out of the deposit left by successive religious movements, of what Gilbert Murray . . . has called 'the Inherited Conglomerate.' The geological metaphor is apt, for the religious growth is, on the whole and with exceptions, agglomeration, not substitution. A new belief-pattern very seldom effaces completely the pattern that was there before--sometimes an unconfessed and half-conscious element-- or else the two persist side by side, logically incompatible, but contemporaneously accepted by different individuals or even by the same individual" (1971:179). The genius of Plato's kind of writing is that he is able to display these layers of consciousness. Euthyphro is juxtaposed with Socrates, allowing both approaches to be presented and compared in one unbroken process. In the Republic several layers are presented, with Cephalus, Polemarchus, and Thrasymachus operating on very different levels from Glaucon, Adeimantus, and Socrates. The reader, standing outside all of these positions, has a remarkable view of an entire spectrum of beliefs.

9. I use the term "enlightenment" here in the same sense as does Wilhelm Windelband who claims that "the Sophists are . . . first and

foremost the bearers of the Greek Enlightenment. The period of their activity is that of the expansion of scientific culture. With less ability in independent creation, the Sophists devoted their energies to revising and popularizing existing theories" (Windelband 1970:111).

10. It is Aristotle himself who so designates Plato's work. He says: "There is another art which imitates by means of language alone, and that either in prose or in verse--which verse, again, may either combine different metres or consist of but one kind--but this has hitherto been without a name. For there is no common term we could apply to the mimes of Sophron and Xenarchus and the Socratic dialogues on one hand; and on the other, to poetic imitations in iambic, elegiac, or any similar metre" (1951:1447b). The important assertion here is that Socratic dialogues are an "art" which "imitates by means of language alone." That, for Aristotle, means that Socratic dialogues are "poetry" in the important sense of the term, i.e., they are mimetic. Plato, of course, was the most important maker of Socratic dialogues. Therefore, Plato wrote a kind of poetry.

11. In the Ethics, one of the "practical" sciences, Aristotle makes the connection between practical thinking and deliberation about ultimate matters: "The object of deliberation and the object of choice are identical, except that the object of choice has already been determined, since it has been decided upon on the basis of deliberation. For every man stops inquiring how he is to act when he has traced the initiative of action back to himself and to the dominant part of himself: it is this part that exercises choice. . . . Since, then, the object of choice is something within our power which we desire as the result of deliberation, we may define choice as a deliberative desire for things that are within our power; we arrive at a decision on the basis of deliberation, and then let the deliberation guide our desire" (1962:1113a).

12. "Practical wisdom . . . is characteristic of the ruler" (1972:1277b).

13. "Nature, habit, rational principle must be in harmony with one another; for they do not always agree; men do many things against habit and nature, if rational principle persuades them that they ought" (1972:1332b).

14. "Man is by nature a political animal" (1972:1278b).

15. "He who is unable to live in a society, or who has no need because he is sufficient for himself, must be either a beast or a god; he is no part of the state" (1972:1253a).

16. "No one will doubt that the legislator should direct his attention above all to the education of youth; for the neglect of education does harm to the constitution" (1972:1337a).

17. Paul Shorey, for example, says in his note to this passage: "This is one of the most famous passages in Plato, and a source of the idea of the City of God . . ." (1970:414). The Platonists tend to take Socrates' words literally. But Aristotle, for one, is hesitant to do that. He says: "As a means to the end which he ascribes to the state, the scheme, taken literally, is impracticable, and how we are to interpret it is nowhere precisely stated. I am speaking of the premise from which the argument of Socrates proceeds, 'that the greater the unity of the state the better.' Is it not obvious that a state may at length attain to such a degree of unity as to be no longer a state?" (Aristotle 1972:1261a).

BIBLIOGRAPHY

Aristotle, 1908: Metaphysics. Translated by W.D. Ross, Oxford.

_____, 1951: Poetics. Translated by S.H. Butcher, New York.

_____, 1960: Metaphysics. Translated by Richard Hope, Ann Arbor.

_____, 1962: Nichomachean Ethics. Translated by Martin Ostwald, New York.

_____, 1972: Politics. Translated by H. Rackham, Cambridge.

Dodds, E.R., 1971: The Greeks and the Irrational, Berkeley.

Freeman, Kathleen, 1977: Ancilla to the Pre-Socratic Philosophers, Cambridge.

Fustel de Coulanges, Numa Denis, 1873: The Ancient City. Translated by Willard Small, Garden City.

Jones, W.T., 1952: A History of Western Philosophy: The Classical Mind, New York.

Hammond, Mason, 1972: The City in the Ancient World, Cambridge.

Isocrates, 1964: Panegyrics; cited by Horace M. Kallen in Aristotle: Politics and Poetics, New York.

Jaeger, Werner, 1944: Paideia: The Ideals of Greek Culture. Translated by Gilbert Highet, New York.

Nietzsche, Friedrich, 1956: Birth of Tragedy. Translated by Francis Golfing, Garden City.

Plato, 1967: Theaetetus. Translated by Harold North Fowler, Cambridge.

_____, 1970: Republic. Translated by Paul Shorey, Cambridge.

_____, 1971: Euthyphro. Translated by Harold North Fowler, Cambridge.

Strauss, Leo, 1964: The City and Man, Chicago.

Uemura, J.N., 1965: "Plato's Republic: An Antidote to Any Future Utopia." The Morningside Review, IV: 42-52.

Weber, Max, 1958: The City. Translated by Don Martindale and Gertrude Neuwirth, New York.

Windelband, Wilhelm, 1970: History of Ancient Philosophy. Translated by Herbert E. Cushman, New York.

Urban Problems in Ancient Rome

Edwin S. Ramage

Maps by Frank S. Ferry

Sources and Methods

When a sociologist turns to consider an aspect of life in one of our cities, he can expect to have a variety of source material at his disposal. Not only are there written records of all kinds, but contemporary institutions can be examined and human subjects interviewed. The situation is quite different for anyone attempting to deal with Rome, for not only is the human element missing but the institutions are also foreign to his experience. Moreover, the written record is far from complete, and the usefulness of what survives varies considerably from one source to another. The Romans wrote nothing on urban problems per se, so we must rely on the random comments of authors writing epigram, satire, history, technical treatises, and the like, where purposes and subjects only incidentally involve such things.

There are other sources, of course, and they present similar difficulties. The legal texts are helpful in reconstructing the problems that the law is expected to solve, but here too the record is incomplete, and without confirmation from elsewhere it is not always clear whether any real or anticipated problem has generated the legislation. Inscriptions, too, are important, but they are difficult to work with because they are frequently out of context and often fragmentary. At the same time they are usually terse and so offer a minimum amount of information. The archaeological record is far from complete for our purposes, since urban problems are often part of the mundane and ephemeral details of everyday existence that have long since disappeared.

Because of the incomplete and fragmentary nature of the evidence urban problems in Rome must be treated in fairly broad time periods. It is simply not possible to put together an account of the situation in a given year, not to mention a day in that year. But when they are approached in this way, the various sources have a substantial amount of information to offer on the subject. The period that is best documented and the one that will be dealt with here for the most part is the first century and a half of the Empire--the times of Augustus through those of Hadrian. But earlier and later material cannot be ignored, and it will be introduced for purposes of comparison and contrast.

In all of this the classical scholar does have one advantage over those investigating contemporary problems: he is involved with a terminal situation. The people and institutions with which he is dealing have run their course and their history is complete. This opens up the possibility of talking about long-term social, psychological, and economic developments and effects without having to rely completely on theory and prognosis.

The task of identifying the problems and estimating their effect is a large one, and what follows is not meant to be the last word on the subject. Research is not yet complete, and, besides, such a broad topic cannot be covered exhaustively in a few pages. Enough has been done, however, to make it possible to formulate a number of working definitions and to put together a tentative model consisting of the problems themselves, their psychological effect on the urbanite, and the search for solutions to them.

Factors Contributing to Urban Problems

Before considering the urban problems themselves, something must be said about location, population, and the lack of urban planning, all of which contributed to the situation in the city in the early Empire. As with most cities, Rome in all its periods was to a large extent the product of its location. The advantages of the site were clear to the ancients. They appreciated the breezy, healthful hills and a location that was separated from, but within easy reach of the sea via the Tiber River (Cicero, De Rep. 2.10; Livy 5.54.4). Cicero calls it a healthy place in an area that is generally unhealthy (De Rep. 2.11), while Livy has Camillus in 390 B.C. or shortly after observe that the site was "uniquely suited to the growth of the city."

Others like Strabo are a little more realistic. Rome was founded more out of need than by choice, and later expansion was subject to the exigencies of the site (5.3.2; 5.3.7). This is a fair appraisal of the situation. For, no matter how earnestly Cicero might insist that Romulus had chosen the site with a vision of Rome's future greatness before him, the early Iron Age people who established their villages on the Palatine and the other hills (Map 1) had only their own primitive concerns in mind. The hills were defensible sites; the marsh that later became the Roman Forum (Map 1: A) and the Tiber River offered defense in two different directions. At the same time, the river provided access to the sea, while the Tiber Island made contact with the people to the northwest easier as Rome's interests developed in that direction (Dudley, 1967, pp. 5-6). But, as Strabo suggests, these early assets became drawbacks for the developing city. The Romans themselves recognized the fact that the combination of hills and vallies limited urban communication and planning as the city grew. By the time of the late Republic they were ready to admit that Rome, which was "situated on mountains and in vallies," was topographically inferior to a city like Capua that was located in a plain (Cicero, De Leg. Agrar. 2.96). Cicero's mention here of apartment buildings, poor streets, and extremely narrow lanes suggests ways in which he feels the irregular topography has affected the city by his time. The situation did not improve much later; Martial, for example, describes the narrow street (semita) running from the Subura (Map 1: F) to the Esquiline (Map 1: No. 9) as having to be "overcome" (5.22.5-8). By comparing Maps 1 and 2 it is possible to see how closely the streets to the east and northeast follow the terrain.

The Tiber may have been an asset to the city, but as soon as Rome expanded from the hills to the lower levels it proved to be a liability

62

Map 1.   Topography and Walls of Rome

Hills
   1. Palatine
   2. Capitoline
   3. Quirinal
   4. Viminal
   5. Cispian
   6. Oppian
   7. Caelian
   8. Aventine
   9. Esquiline
  10. Janiculum

Areas
   A. Roman Forum
   B. Campus Martius
   C. Forum Holitorium
   D. Forum Boarium
   E. Velabrum
   F. Subura
   G. Docks and Warehouses
   H. Campus Vaticanus

SCALE
1 mile

as well. For it flooded regularly, as we shall see, inundating some of the busiest and most heavily populated parts of the city (Maps 1: A, B, C, D, E, G).

It is also possible that the unhealthiness of the city, especially in the summer and fall, that we hear about so frequently was at least in part due to the fact that Rome was located in "an unhealthy area" (Cicero, De Rep. 2.11). Although some Romans insisted that their city was a wholesome place in which to live (Cicero, De Rep. 2.11; Livy 5.54.4), such praise runs contrary to what other writers say about the common occurrence of fever in Rome at certain times of year (e.g., Horace, Ep. 1.7.5-9; Valerius Maximum 2.5.6). More will be said about this later.

Another factor conditioning the quality of life in any urban center is the size and mix of the population. In the case of any large ancient city this was even more crucial, since the lack of easy transportation made the population less mobile and reinforced a natural tendency to concentrate activities in a limited area in the center of the city.

The Romans of the Augustan period and later make frequent reference to overcrowding. Vitruvius, for example, speaks of an immense number of citizens needing countless places to live (2.8.17; cf. Seneca, Consol. ad Helv.6.2), and Tacitus keeps reminding his reader of the crowds of people that fill the streets (e.g., Hist. 1.8; 1.75). Various parts of the city are singled out for special mention. The Caelian and Aventine were heavily populated (Frontinus, De Aqu. 2.87); the Subura seethed with people (Juvenal 11.51) and was perhaps the most crowded part of the city (cf. Schol. ad Pers. 5.32). Getting through the streets was a struggle, especially if one was going against the tide of humanity (Horace, Sat. 2.6.28). People pushed, bumped, and trampled each other (Juvenal 3.243-48). The person who could find someone to go ahead and shoulder the opposition to one side was at a clear advantage (Horace, Sat. 2.5.94-95; Tibullus 1.5.63-64; Martial 3.46.5-6).

There is little agreement as to what the population of the city was at any given time. Estimates for the early Empire range all the way from 250,000 to 1,800,000 (Oates, 1934, pp. 101-102; Maier, 1953, pp. 321-22). Population figures have not survived and satisfactory methods of using the meager information that does exist have not been devised (Packer, 1971, pp. 78-79). A number of scholars have estimated the population of Rome at 1,000,000 people at the end of the Republic (Yavetz, 1958, p. 500; cf. Hammond, 1972, p. 284; Newbold, 1974, p. 858) and since this falls in the middle range of the estimates, it will suffice as a working figure here.

A city of a million people is hardly remarkable by modern standards, but the area into which they were squeezed is. In the fourth century after Christ Rome covered some 1783 hectares (4400 acres) or just under seven square miles (Homo, 1971, p. 113). There is no way of knowing how much the city had grown since the first century, though it seems safe to assume that some growth had taken place. But even if we take seven square miles as the space covered by the city at the beginning of the Empire, this is not a very large area for such an extensive population, for it leaves a per capita average of only eighteen square meters for all urban functions. But it must be remembered that much of the city was devoted to uninhabitable, low-activity areas such as gardens, public buildings, and the like (van Gerkan, 1943, pp. 217-27 (p. 219, fig. 1); Paoli, 1963, p. 4, fig. 3) which intensified the overcrowding in the other areas. The solution was the same for the Romans as it has been for us: they build upwards (Vitruvius 2.8.17). Some public buildings like basilicas, markets, and warehouses had a number of stories, but it was the insula or apartment/tenement house, at times reaching a height of seventy feet or more and containing as many as four or five stories (Meiggs, 1973, pp. 240-41; Werner, 1906, finds six or seven stories), that helped the Romans to pack so many people into so small a space. There is no way of knowing how many of these buildings existed in Rome in the first century. The Curiosum and Notitia, which were drawn up about 350 years after Christ, list 46,602 apartment buildings scattered throughout the city at that time. By contrast there were only 1790 homes. The figures are late and not without their problems, but combined with the frequent mention by authors like Vitruvius, Seneca, Martial, Tacitus, and Juvenal and the archaeological evidence of Ostia they enable us to conclude that the insula was important and well established in the early Empire (cf. Calza, 1914) and that we should project a large number of apartment buildings for Rome in the first century. We may also conclude that the overcrowding, unemployment, widespread poverty, debt, high rents, and the pressures of inflation meant that living conditions for the masses had not changed much since the late Republic when "most of the inhabitants of Rome lived in appalling slums" (Brunt, 1966, p. 13). It can be put even more pointedly: "The main population of the city . . . lived in cramped, noisy, airless, foul-smelling, infected quarters, paying extortionate rents to merciless landlords, undergoing daily indignities and terrors that coarsened and brutalized them, and in turn demanded compensatory outlets." (Mumford, 1961, p. 221; cf. Yavetz, 1958; 1969, p. 33; Bourne, 1969, p. 205; Hammond, 1972, p. 285; Frier, 1977, p. 34; Tacitus, Ann. 3.52; 4.6; 6.13; Hist. 1.89).

Another factor contributing to the problems of the city was a general lack of active urban planning (Homo, 1971, p. 55). The Romans were, of course, fine engineers and planners. New, well-planned and well-appointed cities were springing up continually throughout the Empire. Even the city of Pompeii shows careful urban planning in its later stages. But no general planning was attempted in Rome. This was not unusual; it is the fate of most large cities. Livy suggests one step in the process of unplanned growth when he describes the rebuilding of Rome after the Gallic sack of 390 B.C. (5.55.2-5; cf. Diodorus Siculus 14.116.8-9; Plutarch, Cam. 32.3). The city was rebuilt in a random manner (promiscue) without any attempt to lay out streets. This is the reason, Livy observes, that the city of his day looks more like one that has merely been taken over and filled up rather than one that has been carefully planned (occupatae magis quam divisae). What the historian says is important not only for the information it provides, but also because he is showing that he is fully aware of the reasons for the unplanned state of contemporary Rome and is tacitly admitting the desirability of some form of urban planning. The same conclusion may be drawn from Cicero's comparison between Rome and Capua that was mentioned earlier (De Leg. Agrar. 2.96).

A glance at the pattern of the streets of Rome (Map 2), confirms the general lack of planning mentioned by Livy and Cicero. Only a few of the major thoroughfares have been included on the map and hundreds of narrow, twisting streets and lanes must be added (cf. Vitruvius 6.6.6; Seneca, Controv. 2.1.11; Suetonius, Nero 38.1; Tacitus, Hist. 3.82). Actually, Rome must have been a maze of narrow, muddy (Martial 3.36.4; 7.61.6; 8.44.5-8; 10.10.8; 12.26.8), dusty (Horace, Ep. 1.17.6-7; Martial 12.2.2), slippery (Martial 4.18.2; Tacitus, Hist. 2.88; 3.82) streets that during the day were in constant shadow because of the high buildings lining them (Dionysius of Halicarnassus, Rom. Ant. 1.68.1) and at night were extremely dangerous because of a lack of any lighting (Tibullus 1.2.25-26; Juvenal 3.278-301).

There were three areas of Rome that testified to some awareness of long term planning on the part of the Romans: the Roman Forum (Map 1: A; Map 2), the Campus Martius (Map 1: B) and the gardens that eventually all but ringed the city. In the case of the Roman Forum it was largely fortune and the restricted use of the area that produced some regularity. In somewhat the same way the Campus Martius from an early time was designated a monumental area, and this identity seems to have been maintained through most periods in the history of the city. The very name of the Via Lata ("Broad Street": Map 2), which was a planned thoroughfare marking the eastern boundary of the Campus Martius, sets it off from the other crooked, narrow streets that predominated in the city.

The gardens are a special case. They had gradually come into the public domain since the time of the late Republic and were protected throughout the Empire from encroachment of any kind (Homo, 1971, pp. 68-69). The Romans recognized that the rest, relaxation, and pure, healthy air that these areas offered were important for urban living (Vitruvius 5.9.5-6). In fact, early in the time of Augustus, Maecenas cleared a large area of the Esquiline (Map 1: No. 9) of its cemeteries and established gardens there that he later willed to Augustus. He thus removed what the Romans felt to be a source of pollution and disease (cf. Varro, De Ling. Lat. 5.25) and replaced it with a healthful addition to the urban environment (Horace, Sat. 1.8.7, 14-16; Porphyrion, Ad Hor. Sat. 1.8.7, 14; cf. Lugli, 1952, vol. 4, pp. 24-26, Nos. 38-45). There is no indication that Maecenas viewed this as part of any overall plan for urban improvement, but he must have been aware that he was extending the ring of gardens that already existed to the north and northeast in the Campus Martius (Suetonius, Aug. 100.4) and on the Pincian, Viminal, and other parts of the Esquiline. In imperial times there was a conscious effort to establish garden areas in the Transtiber area. Julius Caesar, Augustus, the elder Agrippina, Nero, and Septimius Severus all promoted these (cf. Statius, Silv. 4.4.4-7; Lanciani, 1897, 544-60; Lugli, 1930, vol. 3, pp. 638-43, 680-88, 690-92).

There were other sporadic examples of planning, as we shall see. But there is no evidence to suggest that they were part of any master plan.

Map 2.   Some of the Main Streets of Rome.   The Roman Forum is the dark
         area; the Imperial Fora are hatched.

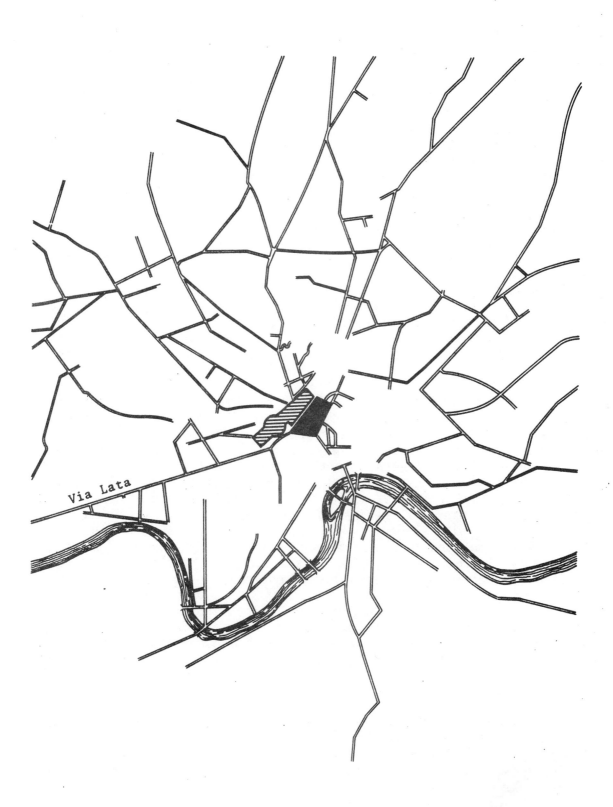

The Urban Problems

In the situation that has just been described, it was perhaps inevitable that urban problems should arise. Whether crime and violence were prevalent enough to be considered one of these is not yet clear. But we do hear of attacks by roving toughs, burglary, and crime in the streets (Juvenal 3.278-314; 10.19-22), and a person apparently had to be on guard in a crowd against possible knife attacks (Martial 7.61.7). Crime was certainly common enough to be included with fire and the other perils that Romans had to endure (Martial 5.42; cf. Catullus 23.8-11), and Augustus went out of his way to prevent it (Suetonius, Aug. 32.1) by ad hoc measures such as stationing guards throughout the city on holidays when citizens were away from home (Suetonius, Aug. 43.1). This was part of his use of the army, in particular the Praetorian Cohorts, as Rome's police force, a practice that continued under his successors (cf. Passerini, 1939, pp. 44-67).

There are strong indications that Rome had a serious traffic problem. While the majority of the traffic was made up of pedestrians, there were also a fair number of sedan chairs and wagons contributing to the congestion. As we have seen, the narrow, twisting streets and the hills added to the difficulties of getting around the city. The center of Rome must have been particularly congested with large numbers of wheeled vehicles, processions of all kinds, and milling crowds of people all coming together in the vicinity of the Forum (Horace, Sat. 1.6.42-44). The problem was aggravated by shops gradually pushing their displays out into the street (Martial 7.61).

The condition of the streets was another complicating factor. Though the Romans had begun paving the urban thoroughfares as early as 174 B.C. (Livy 41.27.5), there is no reason to believe that nearly all the streets were improved in this way. We have already noted complaints about muddy and dusty streets. Part of the reason was surely a lack of paving, but it is also possible that laws like Julius Caesar's so-called Lex Iulia Municipalis that provided for each citizen keeping the street in front of his place of residence swept and in good repair (C.I.L. 1.2².593; cf. Twelve Tables 7.7) were not observed and enforced. Apparently the mud and dirt accumulated even on roads as much traveled as the Sacra Via (Martial 12.2.2), in spite of the fact that these seem to have been flushed fairly regularly (Frontinus, De Aqu. 2.111).

Mention has also been made of the slipperiness of the streets. Martial shows how this would be an aggravation as he describes going from the Subura to the Esquiline (Map 1) over a paved thoroughfare that is never dry (5.22.6). The slipperiness combined with his having to go uphill to make progress difficult. It is entirely possible that flushing the streets added to the problem.

But it seems to have been wheeled vehicles that caused most of the difficulties (cf. Matthews, 1960; Mumford, 1961, pp. 218-19). To a large extent, the trouble that Martial had getting from the Subura to the Esquiline stemmed from the long lines of marble-filled wagons pulled by mules that were toiling up the hill (5.22.7-8). Not only did such vehicles block the road, but they were also a menace to pedestrian

traffic because they were often overloaded (Juvenal 3.254-61).
Actually, they could shake the buildings as they passed by (Pliny, _Pan._
51.1) or cause worry about the damage to the sewers and drains under the
streets (Pliny, _Nat. Hist._ 36.6). Apparently there were no load limits
in the city, but under the so-called _Lex Iulia Municipalis_ some attempt
was made to alleviate the noise, danger, and congestion. With a few
exceptions no wheeled traffic was allowed within the city limits or
outside the city where there was continuous housing during daylight
hours. If this kind of law was enforced, it meant, of course, that
there would be a great deal of wagon traffic at night. The unlit
streets would make these vehicles ll the more dangerous, and in places
the noise level would be so high that sleep would be impossible (Juvenal
3.232-38). Traffic may have been a problem in Rome, but, as happens so
often, attempts to remedy this one difficulty caused others.

In this climate accidents were inevitable, though we do not hear
about them often. A person might fall in the street and sprain an ankle
(Martial 8.75) or break a leg in an open sewer, as Crates of Mallos did
(Suetonius, _De Gramm._ 2). Apparently overloaded wagons that threatened
to lose their loads were a danger to the life and limb of pedestrians
making their way through the narrow streets (Juvenal 3.254-59). But
what seems to have bothered the Romans most was fighting the congestion
whenever they wanted to go anywhere in the city.

The crowds, the traffic, and the many activities concentrated in the
city produced a _noise pollution_ that must have reached levels at least
as high as those in some of our noisier cities today. The Romans called
it a "din" (_strepitus:_ Horace, _Ep._ 2.2.79; _Odes_ 3.29.12; Pliny, _Ep._
1.9.7) and a "roar" (_fremitus:_ Pliny, _Ep._ 3.5.14), and it must have
been greatest in the inner city areas such as the Subura (Map 1: F;
Martial 12.18.2; Juvenal 11.141).

The noise must have come to a large extent from the traffic that has
just been mentioned (e.g., Horace, _Ep._ 1.17.7-8; _Sat._ 1.6.42-44; Seneca,
_Ep._ 56.4), but there were many other sources: people plying their
trades, noisy professionals, the constant building, both public and
private, that was going on in the city, and the many indefinable noises
that a crowded situation produces to disturb the peace and quiet
(Seneca, _Ep._ 56.1-2, 4; Martial 12.57; _Spect._ 4; Statius, _Silv._
1.1.63-65).

Certainly much of the din that has come along with the industrial
age was missing from the streets of Rome. But this was compensated for
to a large extent by the fact that open doors and windows let more
sounds out and the narrow streets lined by high buildings tended to
concentrate the noise and thus exaggerate it. We should also not forget
that most of the apartment houses and other buildings in which the mass
of the population lived provided little insulation against noise,
whether it came from the outside or the inside. Seneca provides us with
a vivid picture of what must have been the situation in many apartments
in Rome. He lives over a bath and is beleaguered by the sounds of
people exercising, being massaged, playing ball, singing in their bath,
and swimming. From outside comes a whole array of noises that augment
these (Seneca, _Ep._ 56.1-4).

For many the noise of the city was so distracting that they could not follow their intellectual pursuits (e.g., Horace, Ep. 2.2.79-80, 84-86; Seneca, Ep. 56). Many urbanites, especially the poorer ones who could not afford country retreats or lodgings in the quieter parts of town, could not sleep amid the noise and hecticity that accompanied life in the big city (Martial 10.74; 12.57.3-4; 12.68). Evidently sleeplessness presented serious health problems for the city-dweller (Pliny, Nat. Hist. 26.111), and in some cases it was even fatal (Juvenal 3.232).

This was part of a general unhealthiness which threatened those living in Rome. More study is needed to determine whether this was a serious urban problem, but it does appear that late summer and autumn were particularly dangerous to many people's health (Horace, Ep. 1.7.5-9; Odes 2.14.15-16; Sat. 2.6.18-19). As has already been suggested, this unhealthiness was caused, at least in part, by the location of the city in an area that had a history of malaria. No doubt open sewers and sewage trenches contributed to the general unhealthiness, as did the fact that the Tiber, which was lower in the summer months, did not carry off the sewage emptied into it as quickly as it did at other times of year. This helps account for the frequent mention of fever in the Roman writers (e.g., Martial 2.40; 10.77; 12.90; Pliny, Nat. Hist. 26.115-17; Juvenal 4.56-59; 9.16-17) and for the existence of temples to Febris in the city (Cicero, De Leg. 2.28; Valerius Maximum 2.5.6). Plague must also have swept through Rome regularly (e.g., Livy 40.19.3; 40.36.14; 41.21.5; Suetonius, Nero 39.1; Titus 8.3, 4), and other communicable diseases must have spread quickly and easily in this overcrowded situation (Bourne, 1969, p. 206).

Also contributing to the Romans' ills was an air pollution made up of the dust from the streets and the smoke from the thousands of wood-burning fires throughout the city (cf. Horace, Odes 3.29.11-12). The general conflagrations that were constantly breaking out no doubt aggravated the situation. But there was another more serious kind of air pollution that came from the open sewers and open sewer trenches. Moreover, the Cloaca Maxima, great achievement though it was, emptied into the Tiber in the heart of the city just below the Aemilian Bridge, and there can be no doubt that the river was thoroughly polluted from this point for some distance downstream. It is perhaps significant that there is only one mention of the Romans drinking from their river (Frontinus, De Aqu. 1.4). This is balanced by Tacitus' account of the misfortunes of the Gallic and German contingents of Vitellius in A.D. 69 who, being unfamiliar with urban ways, not only encamped in the unhealthy parts of Transtiber, but also drank from the Tiber and so put themselves in double jeopardy (Hist. 2.93). Swimming in the Tiber and other similar activities that we hear about must have taken place further upstream away from the sewage, probably off the Campus Martius (Le Gall, 1953, pp. 270-71). This whole situation was aggravated by the periodic flooding of the Tibe. which backed up the sewers (Pliny, Nat. Hist. 36.105) and spread contamination over the lowlying areas of the city.

The result was what the Romans called a rather oppressive atmosphere and bad air (gravioris caeli, infamis aer: Frontinus, De Aqu. 2.88; cf.

Tacitus, _Hist._ 2.94: _intemperiem caeli_) which they attempted to combat in a number of ways. In the time of Nerva lapsed water was used to flush the streets and the sewers (Frontinus, _De Aqu._ 2.88, 111) with the result that Frontinus, at any rate, felt that an old problem had been solved and that the air was purer and the city cleaner.

Preserving and improving the ring of parks was a means of ensuring large amounts of fresh air within the city (Homo, 1971, pp. 68-69). Not only would this green belt bring about some dilution of the tainted atmosphere of the inner city, but it would provide a refuge from the pollution and noise as the parks in cities like Paris, London, Rome, and Madrid do today.

Flooding of the Tiber presented another threat to the well-being of a city-dweller. The inundations seem to have come with a certain frequency (Pliny, _Nat. Hist._ 3.55), so that at least some Romans viewed the city as being subject to floods (Suetonius, _Aug._ 28.3). Between 415 B.C. and A.D. 398 there were thirty years in which floods were recorded (conveniently listed in Le Gall, 1953, p. 29; cf. Lugli, 1952, vol. 2, pp. 62-66, Nos. 5-41). In 215 B.C. the Tiber flooded twice (Livy 24.9.6), while in 189 B.C. it seems to have overflowed its banks no fewer than twelve times (Livy 38.28.4). But if we simply take the total as thirty, this gives a frequency of one inundation every twenty-seven years or so. This is only part of the story, of course, since the record is far from complete. In modern times, between 1870 and 1930, the Tiber reached a flood level of thirteen meters or higher some 47 times (Le Gall, 1953, p. 15), which gives a frequency of one inundation every year and a quarter. The situation in ancient Rome may have been similar to this.

When the Tiber went over its banks a substantial part of the city was inundated, simply because so much of it was lowlying. The Campus Martius, the various fora along the river, and the Emporium were probably the first to be flooded (Map 1: B, C, D, G). But the water also made its way through the Velabrum into the Roman Forum and past the Circus Maximum to the southeast (Map 1; A, E; Map 4; No. 16). We should not forget that the Transtiber area on the right bank was also flooded, though no mention is made of this in the ancient sources (The references for this and for what follows are conveniently gathered together in Lugli, 1952, vol. 2, pp. 62-66, Nos. 5-41).

Since these are the areas of the city in which the population and everyday activities were concentrated, the effect must have been disastrous. We hear of bridges being swept away and of shops, tenements, and other buildings collapsing after being undermined by the water. Loss of life was extensive, especially when the flood came unexpectedly. We are told that some floods lasted as long as a week, so that we have to imagine urban life as being generally disrupted for this period of time. Pestilence from stagnating sewage must have been an ever present danger, while the displacement of the massive population combined with the disruption of dock facilities to produce a threat of famine.

Geography and climate together caused the flooding. The Tiber is a long river (403 km.) draining a basin of some 17,156 sq. km. made up of fairly mountainous country (Le Gall, 1953, pp. 4-6). By the time it reaches Rome it has collected its full supply of water. Three other characteristics combined with these to make the river a potential threat to the city: (1) it flowed in a fairly shallow bed some 3 m. deep (Lanciani, 1897, p. 9); (2) it wound (and still winds) through Rome in three sharp curves which makes a large part of the city a potential flood plain; (3) its level was always close to that of the parts of the city through which it passed. In this connection we should remember that the level of Augustan Rome was some 6 m. lower than that of modern Rome in the area of the Campus Martius.

The climatic factors could be expected to vary from year to year. A large part of the river's volume came from melting snows, and there is no reason to believe that the rate of melting was constant over any period of time. Again, rainstorms are reported to have caused flooding (Orosius, Adv. Pag. 4.11.6 (24) B.C.); Tacitus, Ann. 1.76.1 (A.D. 15); Ammianus Marcellinus 29.6.17 (A.D. 374), and this would be natural in this Mediterranean climate. The clustering of the floods in the ancient sources may be fortuitous, but it may also hint at unusual weather patterns. Floods are recorded, for example, for 193, 192, and 189 B.C., and the latter year is the one for which Livy reports twelve floods. It may be that a freak weather pattern is at work. There are similar clusterings in 203, 202 B.C.; 23, 22 B.C.; A.D. 12, 15; and perhaps in the undated floods under Nerva and Trajan.

The human factor may have played a part in the floods from time to time. The Romans seem to have been in the habit of dumping things in the Tiber. They regularly used it as a place to dispose of bodies that were denied burial (cf. Lugli, 1952, vol. 2, pp. 46-51, Nos. 254-96), and we hear of Nero throwing stale grain into the Tiber, presumably in quantity (Tacitus, Ann. 15.18). Whether such dumping was common enough to affect the flow of the river it is hard to say. Suetonius, at any rate, suggests that by Augustus' time both the debris thrown into the Tiber and buildings encroaching on it were contributing to the flooding (Aug. 30.1). Augustus cleaned out the riverbed and in A.D. 271 Aurelian seems to have "dug out the bed of the teeming river" again (Script. Hist. Aug., Aurel. 27.3). Aurelian's project may be an indication that such dumping did not stop and that periodic dredging of the Tiber was necessary because of it. In view of the lack of any provision for the disposal of garbage and other refuse, the Tiber must have presented an easy and perfectly natural way to the many people living near it of taking care of this need.

The fact that Augustus, Tiberius, Claudius, and Trajan all tried to remedy the flooding during the first century and a half of the Empire suggests that it was a serious problem. Actually, there are twelve inundations recorded for the years 27 B.C. to A.D. 138, of which six fell within forty years in the reign of Augustus (B.C. 27, 23, 22, 13; A.D. 5, 12, 15, 36, 69, Nerva (undated), Trajan (undated), Hadrian (undated)). Julius Caesar may have been the first to attack the problem. He seems to have promulgated a law in 45 B.C. to increase the size of the city (Cicero, Ad Att. 13.20.1; 13.33a.1; 13.35.1) by which the Tiber was to be diverted at the Mulvian Bridge and taken by the Vatican Hills (secundum montes Vaticanos). There is nothing about flood control in Cicero's description, and Caesar may indeed have been simply proposing a rerouting of the river to make the Campus Martius available for general building with the Campus Vaticanus replacing it as the city's monumental area. But there is also the possibility that he felt that by changing the course of the river in this way he would be removing the meanders that contributed to the flooding. He could also have been planning a deeper channel. Unfortunately, he did not live to carry out his project.

Augustus "widened the bed of the Tiber and cleaned it out, filled as it had been for some time with rubbish and narrowed by projecting buildings" (Suetonius, Aug. 30.1). He did this, Suetonius says, to control floods, but the fact that the flooding went on as before shows clearly that Augustus did not solve the problem. He may also have built an embankment (Hist. Pseudois. in Lugli, 1952, vol. 2, p. 67, No. 45; Pliny, Nat. Hist. 3.55), though this is unlikely (Le Gall, 1953, p. 119).

After the flood of A.D. 15 Tiberius appointed a planning commission of two to present proposals for solving the problem permanently (Tacitus, Ann. 1.76.1). They reported back to the Senate with a plan to divert tributaries upstream--in particular, the Clanis and the Nar (Tacitus, Ann. 1.79). But no action was taken either because of the opposition of the farmers and villagers who would be affected by the changes, because of the difficulties of carrying it through, or because of religious taboos.

An inscription of A.D. 46 (C.I.L. 14.85) describes Claudius as freeing the city from the danger of flooding through channels (fossis) running from the Tiber to the sea and dug in connection with the harbor works of Ostia. An undated inscription from Trajan's time, though in poor condition, seems to attribute a similar project with the same success to Trajan (C.I.L. 14.88). That neither was successful is clear from the fact that the floods continued. In fact, the younger Pliny specifically tells us that Trajan's fossa did not work (Ep. 8.17.2). This is not surprising, since it is difficult to see how channelling the river below the city would help reduce flooding higher up (Le Gall, 1953, p. 133). The only other work on the Tiber that is reported is Aurelian's dredging of the river bed and rebuilding of the river banks (Script. Hist. Aug., Aurel. 47.3).

Before leaving the Tiber and its flooding some mention must be made of the magistrates established by Augustus (Suetonius, Aug. 37) or by Tiberius (Cassius Dio 57.14.8) to look after the river--the "supervisors of the river bed and banks of the Tiber," as they were called (curatores alvei et riparum Tiberis). In Trajan's reign the sewers were added to their jurisdiction. They seem to have been concerned primarily with keeping the extensive river traffic moving and the harbor facilities functioning smoothly. They controlled both banks, and the area back from the river that was under their control was carefully delineated. One of their duties was no doubt to keep the riverbed free of debris and other obstructions. This would probably help prevent flooding in a minor way, but there is no indication that this was one of their major concerns (cf. Lugli, 1952, vol. 2, pp. 69-97, Nos. 1-169; Le Gall, 1953, pp. 175-83; Dudley, 1967, p. 46).

The most serious problem faced by the person living in Rome was that of fire. It was a "disaster only too frequent in the city" (Martial 3.52.2). Conflagrations were so common that they were taken for granted (Tacitus, Ann. 4.64: ultra solitum), and they were included at one time or another with money losses, runaway slaves, thieves, poisoning, falling buildings, crop failure, false mistresses, and sinking ships as a typical source of concern for everyone (Catullus 23.8-11; Horace, Ep. 2.1.121; Sat. 1.1.76-78; Propertius 2.27.5-13; Martial 5.42; Juvenal 3.7-9). They are the chief reason for the dramatic rise in the level of the ancient city (Frontinus, De Aqu. 1.18). And there are hundreds of references in the ancient sources to conflagrations of all kinds in all periods. All of this suggests that fire was simply part of the urban way of life.

Much has been written about fires in ancient Rome (e.g., Werner, 1906; Canter, 1932; van Ooteghem, 1960), although a modern, comprehensive study would be most welcome. Rather than begin a long historical narrative here, then, it will perhaps be better to limit ourselves to a few topics that show the effect that fires had on the city and the people living there: the kinds of fires, their distribution, the reasons for their being so common, attempts at combatting them, and their economic effect on the city.

When we think of fires in Rome, we usually think of the great conflagrations such as those of Nero in A.D. 64 or Titus in A.D. 80. But we have to remember that the urbanite was threatened by thousands of lesser fires each year as he went about his business. These might involve a single public building such as Pompey's theater, a gymnasium, the Pantheon, or the Colosseum (Tacitus, Ann. 3.72; 15.22; Orosius, Adv. Pag. 7.12.5; Script. Hist. Aug., Elag. 17.8). A garden might burn (Pliny, Nat. Hist. 35.51) or even ships in the Tiber (Tacitus, Ann. 15.18). Private houses burned down regularly also (Martial 3.52; 11.93), and so did the large apartment buildings or insulae that housed most of Rome's population. Juvenal shows what could happen to an apartment dweller living on the top floor of a burning insula (3.198-202). And these buildings could burn in great numbers (Script. Hist. Aug., Ant. Pius 9.1). Aulus Gellius provides a vivid description of an insula on fire as he and some friends approach the Cispian Hill (Map 1:5): "We catch sight of a certain apartment house, many stories in height, enveloped in flames and the whole neighborhood burning in a huge conflagration" (15.1.2). He does not tell us whether the inhabitants escaped.

If we plot the major conflagrations occurring between 31 B.C. and A.D. 412 on a map of Rome, we get a significant distribution (Map 3). The outlying regions seem not to have suffered a great deal, but as we move toward the center of the city destructive fires become more frequent. Region VIII, which included the Roman Forum and the densely populated inner city, burned no fewer than thirteen times. The only other region coming close to this is IX, and it covers a much greater area.

74

Map 3. The Fourteen Regions of Augustus. The regions are designated by
        Roman numberals.   The figures in parentheses represent the
        number of devastating fires that burned through each region
        between 31 B.C. and A.D. 412.

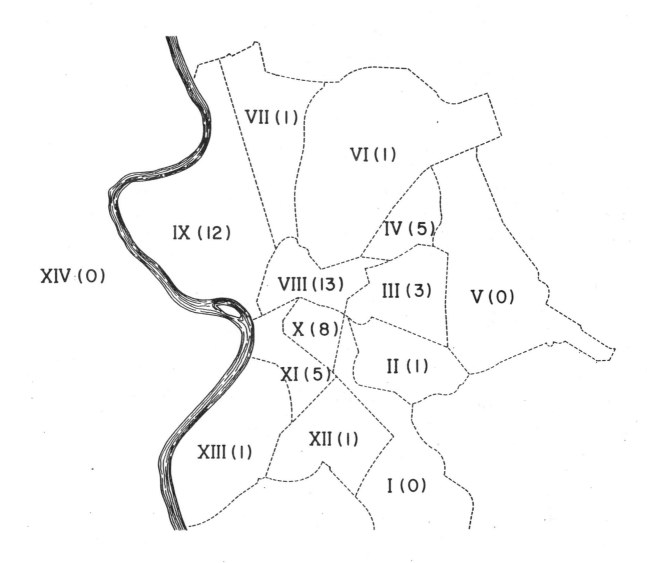

At least one of the reasons for the many fires is evident in the distribution. The conflagrations were most frequent and devastating where the crowding was densest. Vast numbers of people using open fires for cooking and heating made such disasters inevitable. Once a fire had started the narrow streets, high buildings, and party walls enabled it to spread quickly. Serious problems were caused by the combustibility of building materials used in shops, homes, and insulae. Large quantities of wood and perhaps even wattlework were used and some of the stone was subject to burning under the right circumstances. The seriousness of the problem is made apparent by the fact that a writer like Vitruvius chose to spend some time discussing the combustibility of various woods and stones (2.7.2; 2.9.6; 2.9.14; 2.9.16; cf. Pliny, Nat. Hist. 36.168, 169), and Nero put strict limitations on the use of wood as he rebuilt Rome after the fire of 64, stressing rather the use of hard, non-combustible stone like peperino (Tacitus, Ann. 15.43). Vitruvius becomes eloquent in rejecting wattlework, in spite of its providing added space quickly and easily: "I only wish wattlework walls had not been invented. . . . since they are like torches ready to go up in flames" (2.8.20). And just as the buildings themselves were tinder boxes, so many of the shops and warehouses scattered throughout the city were full of combustible goods just waiting to burn (cf. Tacitus, Ann. 15.38).

There were no doubt as many immediate causes of fire then as there are now. Simple negligence must have been a problem and was probably a factor in the "accidental" (fortuitus) fires which we hear about (Tacitus, Ann. 3.72; 15.18). The seriousness of the situation is underlined by the fact that the law provided a sound beating for a person convicted of causing a fire by negligence, if the magistrate so chose (Dig. 1.15.3.1).

Arson carried out by hired arsonists, freedmen, slaves, or other individuals or groups also seems to have been prevalent (Cassius Dio 50.10.3-6; Juvenal 9.97-99; 13.144-49; cf. Pliny, Nat. Hist. 36.115). This was the cause of the great fire of A.D. 64, whether at the instigation of Nero, Christians, or others (Tacitus, Ann. 15.38, 44). Arson went hand-in-hand with the rioting and civil war which regularly brought wide-spread devastation to the city. We hear of soldiers, civilians, and foreigners setting fires both in the Republic and the Empire (e.g., Plutarch, Brut. 20.4; Cassius Dio 58.12.2; 80.2.3; Tacitus Hist. 1.2.2; Script. Hist. Aug., Maxim. et Balb. 9.2; Maximin. 20.6).

Among the natural causes, lightning seems to have played its part (Pliny, Nat. Hist. 35.51; Tacitus, Ann. 15.22; Orosius, Adv. Pag. 7.12.5; 7.16.3). And we should imagine spontaneous combustion as a threat, especially where commodities such as grain were stored for any length of time.

Attempts to combat fires were made from an early time. As early as the Twelve Tables there were laws against cremating in the city (Twelve Tables 10.1), presumably because of the dangers involved (Cicero, De Leg. 2.58). The provision that a funeral pyre not be within 60 feet of another's building without the owner's permission (Twelve Tables 10.10; Cicero, De Leg. 2.61) reminds us of the Charter of Urso of 44 B.C. where it was forbidden that a crematorium be set up within a half mile of the city (Johnson, 1961, p. 99). There were also provisions against arson, as we have seen (Twelve Tables 8.10; Dig. 47.9.9).

In the early Empire Augustus seems to have attacked the problem from a number of different angles. Reference to at least one piece of his legislation has survived by which the height of buildings was limited to 70 feet (Strabo 5.3.7). This probably was aimed as much at preventing falling buildings as it was at increasing the effectiveness of the firefighters. Presumably, however, there would be fewer stories than in a taller building and this would mean fewer people to vacate. But a seventy foot building is still a tall structure, and it makes one wonder how tall buildings had become if this was set as a limit.

Augustus apparently was also interested in an informed public, for he drew their attention to Rutilius' speech On the Height of Buildings (Suetonius, Aug. 89.2). Again, by reading between the lines of Vitruvius' preface, we can imagine Augustus as encouraging the publication of the De Architectura which had as part of its purpose to promote safe building practices.

On a more practical level the Emperor sealed off his forum from the Subura behind with a high wall of peperino, a non-combustible stone. We may infer from a comment of Tacitus that such walls served as fire breaks (Tacitus, Ann. 15.38; cf. Werner, 1906, p. 49), and the usefulness of this wall may be inferred from the fact that Nerva and Trajan did the same thing in their fora.

Augustus also gave Rome its first fire brigade. There is not the time or space here to go into any detail on the subject, and, besides, others have provided full accounts of its organization and equipment (e.g., Werner, 1906, pp. 51-80; Baillie Reynolds, 1926; Homo, 1971, pp. 163-86). It is perhaps worth pointing out, however, that it was made up of night-watchmen and guards (Suetonius, Aug. 30.1: excubias nocturnas vigilesque), which suggests that both firefighting and fire prevention were part of the brigade's duties. How effective the system was we cannot tell, but the fires did not stop.

No other Emperor seems to have been as systematic about attacking the problem as Augustus was. It took the crisis of the fire in 64 to produce Nero's remedies, but he and his planners seem to have learned their lessons well. Just about every complicating factor was eliminated (Tacitus, Ann. 15.43). The narrow, winding streets were replaced by wide straight ones; the height of the buildings was limited; party walls were forbidden; wood was to be avoided as a building material for the most part with hard, non-combustible peperinos replacing it. In addition, porticuses were to be built along the front of insulae and houses, either to help with fighting fires (cf. Suetonius, Nero 16.1) or, as seems more likely, to help people escape from falling debris in the event of a fire (Hermansen, 1975, esp. pp. 170-71). People were also to keep firefighting equipment at hand.

Nero's limitations on the height of buildings and Trajan's setting a height of 60 feet (Aurelius Victor, Epit. de Caes. 13.13) are, of course, direct descendants of the Augustan legislation already mentioned. They suggest that the Romans were serious about limiting the height of their buildings, but also that legislation was not enforced and so had to be renewed (cf. Werner, 1906, pp. 47-51). Similarly, there is no indication that Nero's planning had any lasting effect, except perhaps in an improved pattern of streets. Fires continued to break out, and writers like Martial and Juvenal give us a picture of city that was pretty much the same as before (cf. Packer, 1971, p. 77). It may not be too farfetched to suggest that Nero's urban planning suffered the same fate as his Golden House and that a conscious effort was made to undo it. This becomes more likely when we remember that there was an element of the populace in Rome that did not approve of Nero's efforts at planning when he undertook them (Tacitus, Ann. 15.43). It is equally possible that the pressures produced by overcrowding simply led to the reuse of the space that had been left open and to the building of less substantial and so less expensive structures.

Our sources do not allow us to see clearly the economic effects of these fires on urban life, although it perhaps goes without saying that they must have been a constant drain on the economy. Nero's fire was an extreme case, but the ancient sources are more explicit about the financial burden caused by this fire than about any other (cf. Newbold, 1974). Expenses were incurred for the emergency measures taken at the time of the fire--mainly for the extra grain provided at less than market price and for temporary shelter of the homeless (Tacitus, Ann. 15.39). The facilities for distribution that were part of the extensive urban welfare system probably made this phase of the operation lest costly to administrate. At the same time, it may have been possible to charge at least some of the grain against the welfare budget. But there were other expenses for which new money had to be found: the removal of debris (Tacitus, Ann. 15.43) and the elaborate buiding program. Money had to be found to repair and rebuild the public buildings. Incentives had to be paid to individuals to ensure that houses and apartment buildings were completed by established deadlines (Tacitus, Ann. 15.43). And both Augustus and Tiberius had set precedents for such subsidies by assisting burned-out homeowners and landlords earlier (Velleius Paterculus 2.130.2; Suetonius, Tib. 48.1; Tacitus, Ann. 4.64; 6.45). Two complicating factors here must have been the less efficient use of expensive land under Nero's new plan and the use of more expensive building materials in the new structures. All of this evidently combined not only to strap Rome and Italy financially, but also to make inroads into the provincial treasuries (Suetonius, Nero 38.3; Tacitus, Ann. 15.45).

Nero's fire was one of a kind, but from its economic effects we can project the problems that accompanied the other conflagrations, especially the major ones. That the difficulties were there is hinted at in the attempts on the part of the various Emperors to enlist the help of private individuals in rebuilding operations (Suetonius, Vesp. 8.5; Tacitus, Ann. 3.72; cf. Suetonius, Aug. 29.4; Titus 8.4).

The fires combined with overcrowding to keep the housing and rental markets constantly inflated. Building and owning an apartment/tenement house in Rome was a high-risk venture, especially in the absence of any system of insurance. Thus the landlord had to keep his profits up (cf. Martial 4.37; Aulus Gellius 15.1.3). To do this he had to charge substantial rents (Yavetz, 1958, pp. 507, 514; 1969, p. 33; Frier, 1977, pp. 34, 36; cf. Newbold, 1974, pp. 859, 866, 868), and no doubt the constant demand for housing made this feasible. He also had to control overhead. This he did by building quickly and cheaply (Vitruvius 2.8.7; 2.8.20) and by limiting expenditures on upkeep (Juvenal 3.194-96).

Collapsing buildings may not have been as common as fires in Rome, but they constituted a serious problem for the city in all periods. In the late Republic Crassus had made his fortune by buying up buildings that had burned down or had simply fallen (Plutarch, Crass. 2.2-4). Juvenal suggests that such collapses were of common occurrence in his time when he includes them among the thousand perils of the city (3.7-8). They were so frequent that the word ruina ("ruin") was routinely used without qualification to refer to fallen buildings and to the idea of their collapsing (e.g., Catullus 23.9; Velleius Paterculus 2.35.4; Seneca, Contr. 2.1.11; Seneca, Oct. 831-32; De Clem. 1.26.5; De Tranqu. An. 11.6; Pliny, Nat. Hist. 36.106, 176; Juvenal 3.196; Suetonius, Aug. 43.5; Vesp. 8.5).

The causes are not difficult to find. Buildings fell because of fire and because of their own weight (Pliny, Nat. Hist. 36.103); flooding also played its part. Collapses are mentioned a number of times as a companion danger to fire (Catullus 23.8-11; Propertius 2.27.9; Velleius Paterculus 2.35.4; Seneca, Controv. 2.1.11; Seneca, De Clem. 1.26.5; De Tranqu. An. 11.6; cf. Yavetz, 1958, p. 510), and both Augustus and Vespasian are described by Suetonius as cleaning up the city cluttered with buildings that had burned down and collapsed (Aug. 30.2; Vesp. 8.5). We can easily imagine that the insulae, shops, and similar structures which were made largely of flammable material would collapse when wooden supports had been burned away.

Flooding must also have caused serious problems for all but the substantial public buildings (Livy 35.21.5; Script. Hist. Aug., Marc. Ant. 8.4-5). Structures like the insulae had their foundations undermined, and if they did not disintegrate at the initial onslaught of the water, they could be expected to collapse when the river subsided and the water around them went down (Tacitus, Hist. 1.86).

Buildings also just fell by themselves. Cicero, for example, tells us that two of the buildings he owns have collapsed and others are about to fall (Ad Att. 14.9.1). Martial describes a certain Regulus as just making it through a porticus at Tiber before it fell to the ground (1.82). Perhaps the worst tragedy of the times occurred in A.D. 27 at Fidenae about five miles from Rome when a jerry-built amphitheater collapsed killing some 20,000 people and leaving as many as 30,000 others injured (Suetonius, Tib. 40; Tacitus, Ann. 4.62-63). When such things happened during their lifetimes, it is no wonder that writers inveighed against undertakings like Curio's temporary wooden theatres with caveas that were moved with the people still in their seats (Pliny, Nat. Hist. 36.116-19). Nor is it surprising that spectators at the games in at least one instance needed assurance that the stands were not going to fall (Suetonius, Aug. 43.5).

The reason for permanent structures collapsing lay for the most part in improper building methods and materials and in poor upkeep. We have already noticed that financial considerations had to be uppermost in the minds of shop and apartment owners and that as a result they built cheaply and cut corners on upkeep. Vitruvius and Pliny suggest how this was done. The former, when talking about building materials in Book 2 spends some time describing how to avoid weak bricks (2.3.1-2), what sand not to use (2.4.2), and why some lime is inferior (2.5.2). All of these are factors contributing to structural weakness. Though he does not make an issue of it here, Vitruvius a little later shows the importance that he attaches to stability in structures by devoting a chapter to the subject (6.8). Pliny articulates the problem that lies behind Vitruvius' discussion and adds another element: "The main reason for the collapse of buildings in the city is the fact that stones (caementa) are laid without a suitable mortar (ferumine) because of the pilfering of lime (furto calcis)" (Nat. Hist. 36.176). Here is a hint that dishonest builders and contractors were at work then as now (cf. Yavetz, 1958, p. 509). Pliny goes on to say that he has found an old law to the effect that a contractor was not to use a slurry less than three years old and that this is the reason why older buildings do not show cracked plaster (Nat. Hist. 36.176). The implication here is that the law is no longer in effect; people build more quickly and so modern walls show cracks.

Indeed, cracking walls seem to have been a serious problem. Wattlework, which was quick, easy, and inexpensive to use, tended to cause plaster to crack and opus reticulatum routinely showed cracking (Vitruvius 2.8.1; 2.8.20). Thus it was that as a person went around Rome he could see insula walls that were "eaten away, covered with cracks, and out of plumb" (Seneca, De Ira 3.35.5: Parietes insulae exesos, rimosos, inaequales). Earlier Cicero had admitted that the tenements of his that had not fallen down were showing cracks (Ad Att. 14.9.1).

The philosophy of shortcutting seems to have extended to the upkeep of private buildings. In some cases there was no interest in a structure, since priorities lay elsewhere (Juvenal 11.12-13). This may have been the case with Cicero who does not seem worried that his buildings have fallen or are about to fall and that the tenants and even the mice have abandoned them. In fact, he plans to turn it all to a profit (Ad Att. 14.9.1). Juvenal's landlord, however, who "covers a gaping crack that has been there for a long time and bids (his tenants) sleep tight, though a collapse is ever threatening," (3.194-96) was one of a breed that was unwilling to have a proper job done, in spite of the danger to his tenants. And apparently the cost of such repairs was not exorbitant, since we hear that the job of propping up an insula which shows cracks in its lowest level could be done for a reasonable price (Seneca, De Ben. 6.15.7). Frier makes the point that "no source ever complains . . . about the landlords of Rome as a class" (1977, p. 36), but this does not mean that they did not deserve criticism. At least part of the explanation for the lack of complaints lies in the fact that the owners of the tenement/apartment houses came largely from the upper classes (Frier, 1977, p. 36), while most of their tenants were of lower station and so were not in a position to criticize. Eviction meant having to search for another place to live in a market where the demand was high and substandard accomodations predominated.

The Romans seem not to have found any lasting remedies for falling buildings. Rutilius' book on the height of buildings probably had little effect, and there is nothing to indicate that the legislation of Augustus, Nero, and Trajan limiting the height of buildings was successful in combatting collapses (cf. Dig. 32.1.11.4). Vitruvius' strictures on building stability may have had their influence on Nero, but there is no evidence that they had any lasting influence. Economic considerations overrode those of safety.

Psychological Effects

The Romans are quick to tell us about the negative effect that these less than ideal living conditions had on them. But as we turn to consider these complaints, we should accept what writers like Horace, Martial, Juvenal, and the younger Pliny say with some reservations. Not only were there others like Ovid who found city life very attractive and so had little negative to say about it (Ramage, 1973, pp. 87-100; cf. Tacitus, Dial. 9), but the writers who criticize and complain were throoughly committed to the city and the sophistication that it represented (Ramage, 1973, pp. 77-86, 132-43). The feelings of fear, frustration, disillusionment, and harassment that they give voice to were just a part of urban living. Moreover, it seems that in those days it was fashionable to complain about urban life just as it is now. In fact, in a writer like the younger Pliny who is so much a product of Roman urbanity, such complaints seem almost to have become commonplaces, so predictable are they within the rhetorical framework of his letters. But no matter how calculated such observations may be, they do stem from real pressures and real feelings.

It should also be kept in mind that most of the information that we have comes from writers who are spokesmen for the upper and upper middle classes, although some like Martial, Tacitus, and Juvenal provide some impression of the feelings of the educated poor. But the majority of the populace, those living in extreme poverty which left them completely dependent on the dole, have no spokesman. We can only imagine them as living a drab existence and as being subject to psychological problems of their own arising from trying to cope on their own level with various urban problems outlined above.

When we turn to consider what the urban dweller has to say about the effect of these urban problems we find that he is remarkably silent. From the few comments that do exist, however, it can be inferred that a constant apprehension nagged at some urbanites. They were naturally afraid of the unhealthy season and the threat of sickness and death that it presented for individuals and families (Horace, Ep. 1.7.2-9; Od. 2.14.15-16). Crime in the streets must have kept most city-dwellers at home after dark, while those who did venture out did so under heavy guard or else with some trepidation (Tibullus 1.2.25-26; Juvenal 3.278-314; 10.19-22). Flooding, when it occurred caused widespread panic, as might be expected (Tacitus, Hist. 1.86; cf. Livy 7.3.1-4).

But fires and falling buildings seem to have been the most frequent cause of anxiety for the urbanite (Catullus 23.8-11; Juvenal 3.6-9, 190, 197-98; Tacitus, *Ann*. 15.38), and given the frequency of these two disasters, the worry was probably constant. Vitruvius' emotional outburst against the use of wattlework walls may be taken as reflecting a genuine, continuing concern about fires and collapsing buildings (2.8.20). The elder Pliny's tirade against Curio's theater suggests almost a phobia about collapses (*Nat. Hist*. 36.118-19). That this feeling was widespread is clear from the story of the crowd in Augustus' time that was so concerned about the stability of the stands on which they were sitting that the Emperor had to go and sit with them to reassure them (Suetonius, *Aug*. 43.5). The same kind of apprehension seems to lie behind Seneca's observation that in Rome with its narrow streets and tall buildings "there is no defense (*praesidium*) against fire or any escape (*effugium*) in any direction from collapsing buildings" (*Controv*. 2.1.11).

But sickness, crime, flooding, fires, and collapses together represent just one aspect of the pressures felt by the educated Roman. They are only part of the general hecticity of life that took its toll on the person trying to follow his profession, keep his niche in society, or simply stay alive. This is not the place for a detailed account of a day in the life of a Roman (For this see, e.g., Friedlander, 1908; Carcopino, 1941; Paoli, 1963.). It is perhaps enough to say that what with appearing in court, making duty calls on people in various parts of the city, attending literary functions, and attempting to deal with frequent petitions of various kinds from friends and acquaintances, the Roman found his day very full (cf. Horace, *Ep*. 2.2.65-86; Martial 4.8; 10.70). These activities were often carried out under trying circumstances. The narrow, winding streets made it difficult to get from place to place in the city, as we have seen (Horace *Ep*. 2.2.72-75; Martial 5.22.5); there was always the crowd to fight (Horace, *Sat*. 2.6.28-31); one might be distracted by a change encounter with an undesirable character (Horace, *Sat*. 1.9; Martial 3.44); duties pressed in any kind of weather (Juvenal 5.76-69); and the constant din did not help matters (Horace, *Ep*. 2.2.79-80; Pliny, *Ep*. 3.5.14). It is no wonder that the Romans viewed these activities not only as duties (Horace, *Ep*. 1.7.8; *Sat*. 2.6.24; Pliny, *Nat. Hist*. 36.27; Martial 1.55.14) and business (*negotia*: Horace, *Ep*. 1.14.17; *Epod*. 2.1; *Sat*. 2.6.33; Pliny, *Ep*. 8.9.1), but also as work (*labores*: Horace, *Ep*. 2.2.66; Martial 4.8.3; 5.22.9; 10.58.8; 10.82.7; Pliny, *Ep*. 1.9.7; 3.5.14) and "city employments" (Martial 12 *praef*.; cf. Cicero, *De Or*. 1.21; Pliny, *Ep*. 2.8.3). Some people were so overwhelmed that they felt caught "amid the waves of affairs in the storms of the city" (Horace, *Ep*. 2.2.84-85) or "tossed on the high seas of the city" (Martial 10.58.7-8). We see such a person in Martial's Juvenal who rushes harassed (*inquietus*) through the noisy (*clamosa*) Subura and becomes dog-tired (*fatigant*) as he runs up and down the hills of Rome to wait on the wealthy (Martial 12.18.1-6).

Many Romans express a feeling that they are trapped and enslaved by this pressure-filled life. Rome imposes its burdens and keeps the city-dweller from doing what he really wants to do (Martial 10.12.6; 10.30.25-27; 10.51.5-6). He cannot escape the trap in any way at all;

the activities just keep piling up and the chains draw tighter every day (Pliny, Ep. 2.8.2-3). There are a hundred things to do, and even when the urbanite manages to escape to the country, they hound him and drag him back to Rome (Horace, Ep. 1.14.17; Pliny, Ep. 7.30.2). He asks a universal question that is really a plea: "When is a day here ever mine?" (Martial 10.58.7; cf. Cicero, Ad Qu. Fr. 3.1.7.) A frustration that is very modern comes through, and it must have been intensified by the conscientious Roman's feeling that he had to do all the things that were asked of him (Horace, Sat. 2.6.26; Pliny, Ep. 5.6.45; 8.9). It is this that makes Pliny's friend Verginius Rufus worry about being chosen for an important state committee (Pliny, Ep. 2.1.9). He has been ill and does not feel up to this kind of work, but if the appointment comes, he cannot refuse it.

Besides feeling frustrated, the Roman living in the city viewed much of his life as having little purpose: "On the day when you do these things they seem important and necessary, but these same things appear pointless (inania) when you realize that you've been doing them every day. (You feel this) even more when you've gone to the country" (Pliny, Ep. 1.9.3). Life is a meaningless rush (Pliny, Ep. 1.9.7: inanem discursum) consisting of useless tasks (Martial 10.82.7: vanos . . . labores; 3.4.6: vanae taedia . . . togae; 5.22.11: operis vani; Pliny, Ep. 1.9.7: ineptos labores) and insignificant, even mean worries (Pliny, Ep. 1.3.3). It is no wonder that many Romans found urban activities distasteful (Horace, Ep. 1.14.17; Pliny, Ep. 7.3.3) and thought that their lives were being wasted in these pursuits (Horace, Sat. 2.6.59; Martial 10.58.8; 10.70.4).

They felt, too, that this hecticity was debilitating and destructive. They were "ground down" by mighty Rome (Martial 4.8.1; 10.58.6; Pliny Ep. 7.3.3) and distracted from tasks like writing and study by the hecticity and noise (e.g., Horace, Ep. 2.2.65-66; Pliny, Nat. Hist. 36.27; Seneca, Ep. 56.1-5). It was a tiring life both physically and mentally (Martial 3.36.4-7; 5.22.9-10; 10.51.15; 10.70.13; 10.74.1-2; Juvenal 1.132) and one in which a person could not count on being able to find relief, especially if he were poor (Horace, Ep. 1.10.18; Pliny, Nat. Hist. 26.111; Martial 10.82.7; 12.57.3-4; Juvenal 3.232-38). For those who could afford it the answer was to escape from the city and its pressures, as we shall see. Those who did not have the means to do this simply stayed and suffered.

Solutions

As we have seen already, the Romans were constantly trying to find solutions to the various problems presented by urban living. But to find lasting answers was as difficult then as it is today--and for many of the same reasons. There was little possibility of organizing, controlling, or even compensating for the massive, unwieldy population crowded together in an unplanned environment. The great majority were poor and unemployed people who had neither the means of improving urban living conditions nor any real interest in doing so. History, too, was against any overall success, since centuries of growth without any planning made significant changes almost impossible. This is at least one of the reasons why Romans like Vitruvius speak of urban planning with reference to new cities and do not apply it to established centers (1.4-7).

Another factor with which reformers had to deal was that of public opinion. Caesar was not only laughed at by Cicero for his plans to enlarge the city, but he was also criticized for the way in which he went about clearing the area where he intended to build his theater (Cassius Dio 43.49.3). Again, as we have seen, lobbyists were probably a factor in defeating flood control legislation in A.D. 15. There were even people who felt that Nero's new, open plan of 64 let too much debilitating sunlight into Rome and that the old city with its narrow streets and tall buildings had been healthier (Tacitus, Ann. 15.43). Politics, tradition, personal interests, and jealousy motivated this opposition, just as they do today.

Religious superstition was another obstacle to reasonable solution. When an educated, thinking man like the elder Pliny calls the fires that plagued Rome a punishment for extravagance (Nat. Hist. 36.110), we can see how deeply such feelings went. Fires, floods, and sickness are frequently taken as acts of the gods (e.g., Cassius Dio 39.61.1-2; 41.14.2-3; 50.10.6; 53.20.1; cf. Pliny, Nat. Hist. 3.55). Procedures such as consulting the Sibylline Books in a time of flood (Tacitus, Ann. 1.76) and building temples to Febris to ward off sickness (Valerius Maximus 2.5.6; criticized by Cicero, De Leg. 2.11.28) surely came from an inability to cope with these situations in a rational way, but they also played their part in forestalling lasting solutions. Such attitudes were based in tradition and were for this reason difficult to combat.

It is significant that most of the institutions and structures that improved the urban environment were connected with individuals. One of the kings, whether he was named Tarquin or not, built the sewer system in Rome. The gardens which were so important to the health of the city had originally been in private hands and had gradually accrued to Rome. In the Empire urban improvements, as a rule, were initiated by the Emperor; the amount done depended on how interested he was in improving the situation. Augustus was the only ruler who attacked urban problems on a broad front, although most of his institutions and improvements, such as his administrative division of the city (Map 3), the curators of the Tiber, and the Vigiles became a permanent part of city life. It seems, however, that there had to be a disaster or at least a crisis before subsequent Emperors did anything significant about urban problems. Tiberius was spurred to action by the great flood in A.D. 15; Nero's improvements resulted from Rome's greatest fire; Vespasian had to clean up the city after a civil war; Titus and Domitian followed in the wake of another great fire.

Finally, we should not forget that many of the solutions produced further difficulties. Not the least of these was that of enforcement, a problem that plagues us today. As has already been pointed out, the fact that Augustus, Nero, and Trajan all instituted legislation limiting the height of buildings suggests that enforcement was not or could not be carried out. The difficulties of enforcing the law in Rome are reflected in Frontinus' discussion of Rome's aqueducts, where the author makes much of the abuses of the system and of the fact that he has successfully combatted these by insisting on strict observance of the rules and regulations (e.g., 2.67-115 *passim*; 2.130).

Specific projects produced specific problems. The law keeping wheeled traffic out of the city in the daylight hours, for example, resulted in a noise pollution at night. Nero's replanning of large parts of the city must have resulted in less intensive use of land with an accompanying displacement of large numbers of people and a rise in rents and in urban land prices (cf. Newbold, 1974). The welfare system, while solving the problem of mass poverty and unemployment at a minimum level, produced a large, lethargic, and dangerous element in the city.

But in spite of these drawbacks, the Romans persisted. Many of those who could afford it acted on their own and chose some form of retreat from the city as their solution. Some people abandoned Rome completely (Martial, 12.68; Juvenal 3.1-4, 315-22), though this seems not to have been common. It was more usual for Romans with money or willing patrons to look toward homes in the suburbs to escape the pressures of everyday urban life (e.g., Martial 8.61; 9.18.1-2; 9.97.7-8). The coinage of *secessus* ("retreat") without qualification to refer to this kind of life (Pliny, *Ep*. 1.3.3; 1.13.6; 2.13.5; 2.17.29; 3.5.14; 3.15.1; 4.23.4; 6.10.1; 6.31.2; 7.9.1; 8.1.3; 9.10.2) and the fact that by the younger Pliny's time land prices outside the city were very high (Pliny, *Ep*. 6.19.1) show clearly that it was common for urban dwellers to have such suburban retreats. This is also evident from the frequent comments the urbanites make about escaping to the country from the hectic, problem-filled life of Rome (e.g., Horace, *Ep*. 1.14; *Epod*. 2; *Sat*. 2.6; Pliny, *Ep*. 1.24; 8.1; Tacitus, *Dial*. 21). These suburbs are easily defined in a general way. They extended well beyond the city to include towns as many as twenty miles away (Homo, 1971, pp. 74-75, 120-23). Pliny's Laurentine estate, for example, was seventeen miles from the city (Pliny, *Ep*. 2.17.2) and Martial's farm at Nomentum lay some fourteen miles to the northeast (Martial 6.43; 12.57.1-2; cf. Catullus 44). The urbanite who was anticipating moving out to "the country," as he called it (Martial 3.58.51; 6.43.3; 8.61.6; 9.18.2), wanted something near the city with good connections. It had to have a limited amount of land and a modest house. In this way it was not a burden and distraction for its owner whose main interests and activities lay in Rome. It was there to provide rest, relaxation, peace, and quiet in a healthful atmosphere (Pliny, *Ep*. 1.24; cf. 2.17; 5.6; 7.3; 8.1). The fact that these establishments were notoriously unproductive (Martial 1.85; 3.47; 3.58.45-51; 7.31.8; Pliny, *Ep*. 4.6) and were even dependent on the city (Martial 3.58; 7.31; 10.94) reinforces the idea that they were simply meant to be extensions of urban living which solved some of its problems (cf. Varro, *Res Rust*. 3.2.6).

Many Romans did not go this far out, however, to escape the hectic city life, but chose to live in the outskirts (*continentia*; cf. Homo, 1971, pp. 75-77, 115-20), which are not as easy to identify as the suburbs. Augustine makes reference to a house just outside the old Porta Collina which was called *Quies* ("Peace and Quiet") for obvious reasons (*De Civ. Dei* 4.16). Martial twice mentions the "few acres" of

Julius Martialis on the Janiculum, where there is a pleasant country atmosphere conducive to study and where the proximity to the city enables one to see urban activities without experiencing the noise (Martial 4.64; 7.17). This estate seems to have a place in the long urban tradition already mentioned that saw private families establishing and living on the estates that were later to be preserved as the public gardens of the city. The remains of the apartment house built into the wall at the Porta Tiburtina (cf. Packer, 1971, p. 75) suggests that people had moved in numbers to the fringes of the city. Indeed, comments by Dionysius Halicarnassus (Rom. Ant. 4.13.4), the elder Pliny (Nat. Hist. 3.67), and Tacitus (Hist. 3.79) suggest that greater Rome included extensive outskirts where all kinds of buildings, winding streets, and gardens were to be found.

Another general solution that developed gradually over a long period of time was the decentralization of services and activities which then as now served to alleviate some of the problems caused by overcrowding. The process must have begun early, for it seems to have been nothing out of the ordinary for Julius Caesar to hold games in all the neighborhoods (vici) of Rome (Suetonius, Jul. Caes. 39.1). Augustus and Vitellius followed his example (Suetonius, Aug. 43.1; Tacitus, Hist. 2.95). It is likely that Caesar's proposed legislation for enlarging the city was meant to promote decentralization of the activities of business and government, though there is no way of knowing this for certain.

Augustus' careful division of the city into fourteen regions (Map 3) was a powerful impetus to decentralization. It made it possible to distribute facilities such as police and fire protection systematically throughout the city as well as to monitor and administrate all parts of Rome at the local level through the minor officials who were elected to run the wards into which the regions were divided. Augustus' partitioning of Rome was the beginning of thinking of the city in terms of a series of separate components each with its own needs.

If we turn to the major urban facilities and begin by plotting the large public paths on a map of Rome (Map 4: Nos. 1-10), a significant pattern emerges. These establishments are fairly evenly spaced throughout the city. It must be remembered that they were built over a span of 300 years, but the distribution is important as showing a continuing decentralization designed to bring facilities to the populace. It is tempting to imagine the Baths of Constantine and Caracalla as attempts to serve the population living in and near the outskirts of the city as well as those in their immediate vicinity. And they not only performed the obvious hygienic function, but also offered facilities for recreation, leisure pursuits, and social intercourse of all kinds, in some cases even providing pleasant shopping facilities.

Places of entertainment like the theaters and stadia tend to cluster closer to the center of the city (Map 4: Nos. 15-20). But even here there is clearly a movement in the Empire toward building the new stadia and naumachiae in the Campus Martius (Map 4: No. 14) and in the less congested parts of the Transtiber area (Map 4: Nos. 11-13).

Map 4. Baths and Other Places of Entertainment in Rome

Baths
1. of Agrippa
2. of Nero
3. of Constantine
4. of Diocletian
5. of Titus
6. of Trajan
7. of Helen
8. of Caracalla (Antonine Baths)
9. of Decius
10. of Sura

Stadia
12. Circus of Gaius and Neru
14. Stadium of Domitian
15. Circus Flaminius
16. Circus Maximus

Amphitheater
17. Colosseum

Theaters
18. of Pompey
19. of Balbus
20. of Marcellus

Naumachiae (buildings for mock sea battles)
11. Vaticana
13. of Augustus

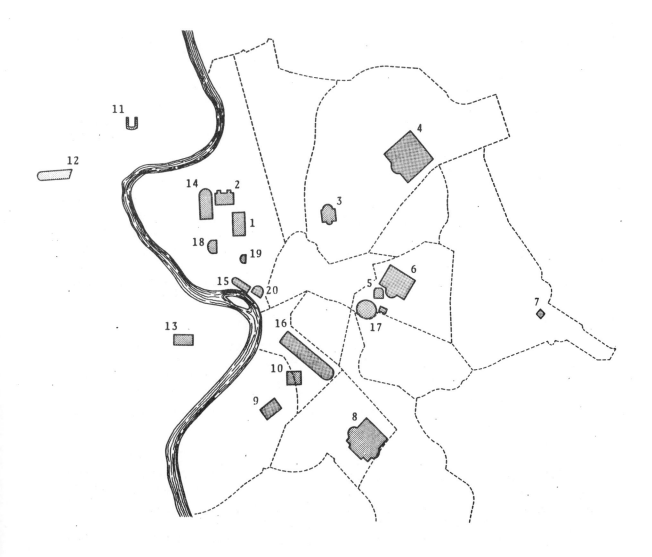

As far as facilities like markets and warehouses are concerned, much more work must be done by way of identifying and plotting these for which the fragmentary _Forma Urbis_ and archaeological remains will be indispensable. There can be little doubt, however, that these were scattered throughout the city (cf. Loane, 1938, 116-21, 127; _Script. Hist. Aug._, _Sev. Alex._ 39.3-5). The late itineraries, especially the _Curiosum_ and _Notitia_ of the fourth century after Christ, are of help here. We should remind ourselves that they are late and their figures may not be as reliable as we would like, but at the very least they can be taken to show an urban decentralization that had been growing over the centuries. If we take the figures for the number of warehouses, semi-private baths, and bakeries for each region we see a clear and fairly logical distribution:

Regions (map 3)	I	II	III	IV	V	VI	VII	VIII	IX	X	XI	XII	XIII	XIV
Warehouses	16	27	18	18	22	18	25	18	25	48	16	27	35	22
Baths	86	85	80	65	75	75	76	86	63	44	15	63	44	86
Bakeries	20	15	16	15	15	16	16	20	20	20	16	25	20	24

These three types of establishments served the everyday needs of the populace, and so the distribution we find here should not be surprising. It is confirmed to some extent by collateral evidence showing that Severus Alexander established public warehouses and baths in all the regions of the city (_Script. Hist. Aug._, _Sev. Alex._ 39.3-5). Moreover, when we add to this the fact that Septimius Severus built baths in the Transtiber area (_Script. Hist. Aug._, _Sev._ 19.5), we may at least tentatively posit a continuing decentralization of activities for the late second and third centuries.

While there was never any general urban planning in Rome, there were scattered attempts to replan parts of the city. Mention has already been made of Maecenas' work with the Esquiline and Nero's replanning and rebuilding after the fire of A.D. 64. It is also possible that Caesar's law for expanding Rome provided for replanning at least part of the inner city. The baths in a sense represent isolated attempts at urban renewal by which many acres of unplanned area were turned into large, carefully planned complexes.

But perhaps the most important attempts at urban planning and renewal are represented by the Imperial Fora and the Temple of Peace. These seem not to have been part of any published master plan, but were separate elements built over a century and a half between 46 B.C. and A.D. 113. Together, however, they constituted a gradually expanding, well-planned monumental center for Rome.

There were a number of reasons for their being built, but for the practical Romans need had to be the overriding consideration. Indeed, we are told that Augustus established his forum to take pressure off the Roman Forum and that of Julius Caesar (Suetonius, _Aug._ 29.1). Trajan's forum was probably motivated by the same need for space, and in its components it is strikingly similar to the Roman Forum: A plaza,

basilica, archives, a religious sanctuary, as well as monuments of
various kinds. This is just the combination that is found in the Roman
Forum, though there the separate elements are repeated (cf. Dudley,
1967, p. 135).

There can be no doubt that another important purpose of the various
forum builders was to provide a suitably elegant center for this
important city. Perhaps the most obvious evidence of this is the Forum
of Nerva which was in essence a monumentalizing of the Argiletum that
ran between the Subura and the Roman Forum.

It would also appear that there was another important consideration
in the building of the Imperial Fora. Both individually and
collectively they were designed as monumental oases of peace and quiet
in one of the noisiest and most hectic parts of the city. Each forum is
completely enclosed by its own walls with passageways and thoroughfares
running between and around them (Boethius, 1970, p. 189, fig. 84; Paoli,
1963, p. 9, fig. 5). The high back wall of the Forum of Augustus still
remains to suggest the care that this Emperor took to shut out the
sounds and smells of the Subura and to provide a fire break. The
absence of wheeled traffic from these fora (cf. Suetonius, Cal. 44.2)
prevented the noisy traffic jams that were experienced in other parts of
the city. This is not to say that they did not have their share of
noisy activities (cf. Lugli, 1952, vol. 6, pp. 13 (No. 74), 23 (No.
144), 33 (No. 191)), but even when there was a hubub in one of the fora,
the others would still offer relative peace and quiet to the person
desiring it. There are analogous situations in the Mediterranean
countries today where piazzas and plazas, even when they are crowded,
offer respite from the noisy, crowded, traffic-filled streets
surrounding them.

In this connection it is significant that Vespasian established his
Temple of Peace in close proximity to these fora. With its extensive
gardens and careful isolation from the surrounding city it served as a
natural complement to the Julian and Augustan fora that had been
preceded it. It is a matter of speculation, but there may be some
significance in the fact that the elder Pliny speaks of the need for
"great silence" if one is to appreciate art and in the next breath
mentions the Temple of Peace (Nat. Hist. 36.27).

Though the Imperial Fora are a prime example of successful urban
planning, we should not overlook the fact that then, as now, such
rebuilding, at least in the short run, must have caused almost as many
problems as it solved. There is little information on the subject, but
the fact that many acres of land in the heart of the city were swallowed
up for these projects must have complicated an already confused
situation. Large numbers of people were surely displaced, so that the
overcrowding became even worse. The over-intensive use of land in the
inner city had already inflated land values, and removing so many acres
from the market probably aggravated the situation (cf. Duncan-Jones,
1965, p. 225). Rents that were remarkably high to begin with must have
gone even higher and so must have other prices--at least those in the
immediate area.

There is just a hint from time to time in the sources that problems such as these are present. Augustus did not make his forum as large as he wished because he did not dare "to pry the nearby homes out of their owners" (Suetonius, Aug. 56.2), and indeed the back wall of his forum angles away to the southeast to show how the Emperor was forced to adapt his plans. The sensitivity of the situation helps to explain why Caesar and the Emperors were careful to buy the land for their projects and to use their own money for it. They took care to advertize this fact. It was no secret that Julius had paid 100,000,000 sesterces for the land on which his forum was built (Pliny, Nat. Hist. 36.103), while Augustus carefully pointed out to the world at large that his forum was built on his own property (in privato solo) and that financing came from booty (Res Gestae 21). The money for Trajan's forum came from his successful campaigns in Dacia (Boethius, 1970, p. 237), and the sculpture on his column and in other parts of the forum would be a constant reminder of this.

Such procedures seem to have been part of a general policy of an Emperor's providing fair compensation from funds at his disposal to cover the expenses of a project that he had instigated. The Theater of Marcellus, for example, was built "on land in large part purchased from individuals" (Res Gestae 21). The builders of the Baths of Diocletian are careful to point out that the buildings of the area had been bought in order to make way for that great structure (C.I.L. 6.1130). In the same vein are Ceasar's concern not to dispossess landowners while providing land for his veterans (Suetonius, Jul. Caes. 38.1) and the Roman policy of paying a fair price for the right of way for aqueducts (Frontinus 2.128).

Some form of expropriation must have been used, though there is no reference to such procedures in the sources. The Romans probably had many reasons for criticizing Nero and his building of the Golden House (cf. Newbold, 1974). But it is at least possible that when he was taken to task for stealing dwellings from the unfortunate populace (Martial, Spect. 2.8) and for plundering the citizens (Tacitus, Ann. 15.52) he was being criticized for not following accepted procedures such as those just outlined.

It is clear, then, from what we have seen that the Romans were attempting to find solutions to at least some of their urban problems in the early Empire. They had both successes and failures, though the latter seem to predominate. And this is not surprising, since then, as now, apathy, prejudice, self-interest, public opinion, politics, financial problems, and inadequate technology made progress difficult.

Bibliography

Boethius, A., and Ward-Perkins, I.B., 1970: *Etruscan and Roman Architecture*, Harmondsworth.

Bourne, F.C., 1969: "Reflections on Rome's Urban Problems" *Classical World* 62:205-209.

Brunt, 1966: "The Roman Mob," *Past and Present* No. 35:3-27 (repr. in M.I. Finley, ed., 1974: *Studies in Ancient Society*, London 74-102).

Calza, G., 1914: "La preminenza dell' 'insula' nella edilizia romana," *Monumenti Antichi* 23:541-608.

Canter, H.V., 1932: "Conflagrations in Ancient Rome," *Classical Journal* 27:270-88.

Carcopino, J., 1941: *Daily Life in Ancient Rome*, London.

Dudley, D.R., 1967: *Urbs Roma*, Aberdeen.

Duncan-Jones, R., 1965: "An Epigraphic Survey of Costs in Roman Italy," *Papers of the British School at Rome* 33:189-306.

Friedlander, L., 1908: *Roman Life and Manners under the Early Empire*, London.

Frier, B.W., 1977: "The Rental Market in Early Imperial Rome," *Journal of Roman Studies* 67:27-37.

Hammond, M., 1972: *The City in the Ancient World*, Cambridge.

Hermansen, G., 1975: "Nero's Porticus," *Grazer Beitrage* 3:159-76.

Homo, L., 1971: *Rome impériale et l'urbanisme dans l'antiquité*, Paris.

Johnson, A.C., 1961: *Ancient Roman Statutes*, Austin.

Lanciani, R.A., 1896: *The Ruins and Excavations of Ancient Rome*, Boston.

Le Gall, I., 1953: *Le Tibre, fleuve de Rome dans l'antiquité*, Paris.

Loane, H.J., 1938: *Industry and Commerce in the City of Rome (50 B.C.-200 A.D.)*, Baltimore.

Lugli, G., 1930: *I monumenti antichi di Roma e suburbio*, Rome.

_____, 1952: *Fontes ad topographiam veteris urbis Romae pertinentes*, Rome.

Maier, F.G., 1953: "Römische Bevölkerungsgeschichte und Inschriften-statistik," *Historia* 2:318-51.

91

Matthews, K.D., 1960: "The Embattled Driver in Ancient Rome," Expedition, Bulletin of the University Museum of the University of Pennsylvania, 2.3:22-27.

Meiggs, R., 1973: Roman Ostia^2, Oxford.

Mumford, L., 1961: The City in History, New York.

Newbold, R.F., 1974: "Some Social and Economic Consequences of the A.D. 64 Fire at Rome," Latomus 33:858-69.

Oates, W.J., 1934: "The Population of Rome," Classical Philology 29: 101-16.

van Gerkan, A., 1943: "Weiteres zur Einwohnerzahl Roms in der Kaiserzeit," Mitteilungen des Deutschen Archaologischen Instituts, Romische Abteilung 58:213-43.

van Ooteghem, J., 1960: "Les incendiés a Rome," Les Etudes Classiques 28:305-12.

Packer, J.E., 1971: The Insulae of Imperial Ostia, Rome.

Paoli, U.E., 1963: Rome: Its People Life and Customs, New York.

Passerini, A., 1939: Le coorti pretorie, Rome.

Ramage, E.S., 1973: Urbanitas: Ancient Sophistication and Refinement, Norman.

Reynolds, P.K., 1926: The Vigiles of Imperial Rome, Oxford.

Werner, P., 1906: De incendiis urbis Romae aetate imperatorum, Leipzig.

Yavetz, Z., 1958: "The Living Conditions of the Urban Plebs in Republican Rome," Latomus 17:500-17.

_____, 1969: Plebs and Princeps, Oxford.

The Roman City: A Philosophical and Cultural Summa

David G. Orr

"The greatest blessings that cities can enjoy are peace, prosperity, populousness, and concord" (Plutarch, Precepts of Statecraft xxxii)

Rome, by the middle of the first century A.D., had become the mother city of the western world. As Henry T. Rowell (1962:3) has stated Rome was ancient longer than any other period of time in her long history. She had established a Mediterranean hegemony by enforcing a Pax Romana of common law, government, and authority. Her authority (auctoritas) extended beyond the physical areas of influence and into the worlds of morality and even religion. With the settlement of the emperor Augustus, a century of bloody civil conflict was effectively terminated and a new pattern of government was born and with it severe constitutional adjustments. The Republic was shattered forever and in its stead a new Rome was created. New classes of people entered the political arena to serve the emperor's needs in a bureaucracy of gigantic influence and power. Rome was the axis of a vast realm of differing cultures, all of whom looked to her for sustenance and political leadership. Ironically, Rome sprawled around her seven hills; largely an unplanned town until the onslaught of imperial fora carving and building. Yet, the most regular orthaganal city plans went with her provincial organization and military aggrandisement. The city which centuriated and rectangularized so much of the Mediterranean world could hardly cope with the topographical challenges of her own situation.

Rome's urbanization schemes throughout her empire were rigidly self-conscious and carefully programmed. Municipal evolution in the Roman "constitution" was through a prescribed "cursus" not unlike the hierarchial patterns endemic in her culture. Grants of citizenship, the greatest gift of the empire, were given at one level while other advantages were contained in the lower rungs of the urban ladder. The desired end was always balance and stability. Just as her imperial fora (those of Augustus, Vespasian, and later Trajan) attempted to identify and control space and human movement in the capital, the Roman towns founded throughout western Europe attempted to reflect the imperial virtues of regularity, efficiency, and formal simplicity. Border towns like Carnuntum on the Danube, Eboracum in Britain, and Volubilis in Morocco, were not only microcosms of the mother city but also were individualized capsules of imperial purpose and identity.

Rome was an administrative and moral capital only. She exported authority and little else. Her ports unloaded the goods of her widespread holdings; little went back in return. Throughout her history as an imperial center this fact remained steadfast; her large population consumed, enjoyed, and ate the products of all her provinces. Her marketplaces were the largest Europe had ever witnessed; feeding her urban mobs became a main item of concern on the imperial agenda.

Not only were her urban political institutions aped by her provincial analogs. She became the exporter of city art, society, and amusements. Religious ideas, new fashions, novel technological advances, and philosophical concepts all appeared, however falsely, to eminate from her. The truth was that Rome was a triumph of cultural plagiarism. From Iberian short swords standardized as "the" Roman infantry weapon, to the popularity of Mithra among the soldiers, Roman urban culture transmitted much more than it created. Even her golden Augustan Age of literature and letters resulted more from an Italian migration to the capital than anything peculiarly "Roman." Roman greatness in the arts took place because the city was a magnet for talent; the towns of Italy effortlessly yielded their human resources to Rome.

But always Rome was the capital, the first great capital in western culture. She was the archetype for all subsequent European towns to mimic; Paris, London, Cordova, Vienna, Florence. She commanded the Imperium Romanum. As Aelius Aristides summed up:

> You have made the word Roman apply not to a city but to a
> universal people . . . . and, at that not just one of all the
> peoples there are, but equivalent to all the rest . . . ."
> (To Rome, LXIII–LXXI)

Perhaps that infelicitous word, Romanization, means just that. Roman urbanism was a collective identity; a striving toward an ideal which was mostly couched in political and material structure. We can argue the broad tenets of relative Romanization; that is, what areas were molded linguistically, philosophically, even spiritually. Unfortunately, what remains elusive is what the concept of urbs really meant to the far flung provincial capitals. It wasn't how long the ideas and values took to get to the provincial towns, it was what they meant when they got there.

This essay intends to select one model in which to examine the salient elements of Roman first century A.D. town culture. It further intends to heuristically denote this synthesis as a summa, i.e. a collective and combinative force which captures the summation of Roman town experience in the first century. Because of exigencies of space, arbitrary examples and expressions will be described. Throughout the narrative, reference will occasionally be made to towns not fully analyzed. Hopefully, the resultant mesh will not obscure the thesis. The truth is that any Roman town of this period would contain the basic ingredients, more or less appropriate for our argument. The same hierarchies of municipal evolution and stature within the empire would be discussed. Many of the same issues would be addressed. Rome may have been the capital of a world league of cities but it was simultaneously the arbiter of a multi-cultural association whose framework was delicately balanced between tyranny and chaos. Urban as the Roman world seemed, many of her subjects existed in tribal unities and scattered hamlets and villages. Surely the biting humor of Juvenal may not have played in most of Moesia, Dacia, and Pannonia. Our example, nevertheless, is a town where it would have played; Pompeii. Roughly seventy percent of this town has been unearthed to date. Since the eighteenth century Pompeii has fascinated the intelligentsia of Europe. Nineteen hundred years after her sudden destruction she has again emerged as an *exemplum virtutis* for the Roman town and its accompanying culture.

At the time of its destruction in 79 A.D., Pompeii had undergone only a century of full Romanization.[1] The well-planned Campanian town had acquired a Roman guise by a rather long process characterized by both organic development and a mutually worked out assimilation of Roman forms and values within its existing Italic framework.[2] As a Roman city it was at best atypical of those towns founded on the Roman *limes*. Certainly, it contrasted with the large ports, such as Ostia, which was expanding vigorously when Pompeii was destroyed. Yet, its significance lies in the simple truth that through the vagaries of fortuitous applications of volcanism it has been preserved as a marvelously intact town; cut off for all time by the events of August 24, 79 A.D. The power of Pompeii's unique record of Roman life rests in its candid intimacy, its unmatched preservation of the everyday trivialities of domestic and public performance.[3] Pompeii, (more formally *Colonia Veneria Cornelia Pompeianorum*), was never rebuilt after its destruction and the social changes and crises present in the town of A.D. 79 never saw a climax. The eruption of Vesuvius gave Pompeii a very fine archaeological *terminus post quem* but simultaneously gave the future much, much more. It represents our best evidence for the commercial, political, and social minutiae which interpreted holistically express for us the only complete portrait of Roman town society to survive.[4] An examination of her wall advertising, her household graffitti, her water supply system, and her religious shrines, for example, can shed light on aspects of Roman town life unknown even from the capitol of the vast empire itself.

Pompeii represents an extensive corpus for the analysis of the Roman town. Her urban institutions are, for the most part, materially preserved. Her evolution and change are faithfully recorded in the town plan and her public and private building. The Hellenic plan of the town was enclosed within a mural fortification system sometime before the end of the fifth century B.C. The early nucleus of the town was probably around the location of the forum (southwestern corner of the town) and the premural settlement expanded from there to the north and east (Eschebach 1970:45). The main north/south and east/west axes of the town corresponded to an existing road-system outside of the walls. Before the Roman advent in 80 B.C. Pompeii had already possessed a Forum dominated at one end by a large temple of Jupiter with a very impressive basilica located at the other end (Ward-Perkins and Claridge 1978:45-46). There were also Roman bath buildings, porticoes, a large theater, and large atrium houses. After the Roman installation of the colony, Pompeii underwent considerable change. The Capitoline triad of Jupiter, Juno, and Minerva now occupied the great temple at the Forum. Another Bath building located near the forum, the previously mentioned amphitheater, a covered lecture hall, and work on other Pompeian structures demonstrated the interests of the new inhabitants.[5]

After Augustus' settlement of the Roman world, Pompeii entered a new period of urbanism. Commerical establishments appeared in the forum and many of the smaller homes were revitalized for business interests. Pompeii never fully recovered from the disastrous earthquake of 62 A.D. and there is evidence that many of her city services, like water supply, were still in disrepair at the time of the eruption. Freedmen, accompanied by the nomenclature of the Hellenistic east and equipped with many orientalized trappings appeared to control the commercial life of the town. The town government responded with plutocratic fervor and Pompeii reflected the interests of different religions and nationalities with surprising ease (Tinh 1965 and 1971; Orr 1978; and Jashemski 1967 and 1977). Much land still remained within the walls of the town and it is mere speculation in wondering if the vineyards and vegetable gardens might one day have been replaced with commercial or industrial facilities (Jashemski 1979 and 1973). The Pompeii of 79 A.D. was a town still capable of a vigorous expansion yet at the same time valiantly attempting to rebuild from the earthquake which shattered it in 62 A.D. As Ward-Perkins and Claridge (1978:44) have noted, Pompeii's destruction came at a fortuitous time for the preservation of its material legacy. Several more decades might have found the town much less interesting from the standpoint of the built environment. Thus it was in 79 A.D. that Pompeii was arrested from further development while the town, and indeed the Roman world itself, was undergoing tremendous social and economic change.

Yet, a study of Pompeii's urban institutions reveals much about the summa mentioned in the introduction to this essay. Rome had effectively and powerfully fused the Hellenistic and western worlds into a rich culture which in turn was expressed best by the Roman town. In spite of its idiosyncratic urban mesh Pompeii brilliantly reflects this thesis. Urban life was constituted in Pompeii in a manner that demonstrates most of the prime elements present in Roman town society.

Urbanism in the Roman world begins and ends with literacy. No other quality is more needed in the social, economic, and political life of the town. It forms the basic division between the concepts of urbanitas and rusticitas (Marchese 1980:55-56). The urban "elite" in Pompeii responded to both wealth and family as the twin arbiters of status. Literacy was mandatory for the proper execution of most of the town's urban functions. Pompeii's inscriptions preserve this important aspect of its urban life with astonishing intimacy and diversity (Etienne 1966 and Onorato 1947). The town's plutocratic elections, whereby the ambitious members of the ordo could attain the municipal magistracies, are well documented (Castern 1975). The success of the Freedmen in the elections is also recorded by the electoral inscriptions (and public dedications) and shows the relationship of this group of "newcomers" to the imperial house which sponsored and encouraged them. Commercial accountbooks and tablets make up another group of epigraphical evidence (Andreau 1974). Here, the trade with Pompeii's neighboring hamlets and communities is described and the town's important mercantile role emphasized (Moeller 1976). The business records of the local auctioneer and banker, Lucius Caecelius Jucundus form a magnificent amalgam of daily transactions, inventories, and the very modus operandi of the no nonsense world of the Pompeian entrepeneur (Andreau 1974). Gladitorial edicta and programmata give us a glimpse of those families and individuals who were gaining status by lavish donations spent in the production of spectacular diversions. Private restorations[6] of buildings made possible by sporadic outbursts of civic munificence are preserved by beautifully cut inscriptions.

Yet it is the inscriptions which attest to the rather surprising fluid nature of Pompeian society which are most valuable for us. Freedmen, *liberti*, rose in the first century A.D. at Pompeii to positions of considerable importance. Children of persons manumitted by Roman citizens for meritorious service were legally at parity with other Romans. Since they generally adopted the names of those who had freed them it becomes difficult for scholars in our time to identify them (Lewis and Reinhold 1966:256-261; and Duff 1928). Yet, an analysis of the epigraphical evidence in Pompeii indicates that a great number of them lived in the town in 79 A.D. They were of prime importance in the mercantile life of the town and held large quantities of liquid capital. Many had eastern names, showing the commercial impact which the Hellenistic Mediterrannean had produced on western immigration in the Imperial age. More probably, many of the *liberti* maintained close contact with the eastern trade centers and profited from their ethnic and linguistic backgrounds. As our study of the electoral inscriptions proceeds, it will become possible for us to follow the careers of selected families and the rapid advancement of the freedmen into the elite circles of power which controlled the social patterns of the town. Certainly, the record of the inscriptions indicates a shift away from the old families that managed the affairs of the town and the manifestation of a new group made up of hitherto unenfranchised families and groups of freedmen. Wealth and the ability to raise it became increasingly more important for municipal political success. The post-Augustan landed aristocratic control of the town's political affairs rapidly declined after the reign of Nero. Throughout the Roman West Pompeii's governmental evolution was closely mirrored by similar developments in other Roman towns. Actually, what happened to Pompeii was simply a symptom of broad patterns of Romanization which can be seen by inscriptional analysis of the ruling classes of other Italian provincial communities. Several broad processes were at work by the second half of the first century A.D. Limes towns like Carnuntum on the Danube and ports like Ostia at the mouth of the Tiber were expanding to the detriment of Campania. Puteoli, on the Gulf of Naples, lost its once felicitous position as the port of Rome. Provincial imports competed strongly with those of Campania. Into this slowdown of economic expansion plunged the freedmen. Pushing the older families from power, their frenetic activity created crises of instability in Pompeii; crises which encouraged imperial intervention. Much of this fascinating account of social change in the first century A.D. can be found by close analysis of the epigraphical evidence.

If the epigraphical corpus of Pompeii proves the sophistication of its citizenry and its deep involvement in the urban problems of the first century it ambivalently records the intimacy of a wide spectrum of its inhabitants. Here, much of Pompeii's town culture and its literacy are preserved. The graffiti (literally scratched inscriptions) and their painted analogs suggest other urban themes. We read about a copper pot which is missing from a shop and the reward for its return. We sympathize with the latrine inscription which urges the user to

carefully refrain from eliminating in the wrong spot. We are touched by
the lovers' notes and their respective virtues. We read the list of
prices for bread and fish and a foul tasting local favorite called garum
(fish sauce). We are brought home by the prostitute's declaration, "I
am yours for two asses (copper coins)." And we are again reminded of
the broad base literacy when an inscriber reminds us that he wrote the
effort without any assistance. Pompeii's mural spontaneities form a
significant aggregate for Roman urbanism. Pompeian society was one
which was constantly bombarded with messages. Fronts of buildings
served the streetscapes as effective billboards offering the Pompeian up
to date neighborhood news items, political conflicts, commercial
comeons, coming attractions of cultural note, and most commonly, the
self-advertisements of much of the town's population. The wall writing
communicated much of the citizen's view of their civilization and their
desires and values. It reflects the dynamic at work in the freedmen's
struggle for power in the last decade of the town's existence and
underscores the literacy of the town's population.

One clear focus for our quick overview of the town life of Pompeii
is religion. Symbolically, the appearance of the freedmen dominated
local bodies known as ministri, who were involved in the local
administration of the districts into which Pompeii was subdivided.[7]
They performed religious activities, its true, but they were more
significant in other areas. They were involved in the financial
contributions which restored buildings and produced lavish spectacles in
the amphitheater. They formed a powerful co-fraternity of freedmen
(some slaves and free citizenry were included) which enabled them as a
group to "peddle" influence and vie with the other guilds and civic
groups in the town. The establishment of the imperial cult by Augustus
gave them more responsibilities. The Augustales (priests) which
venerated the Genius of the emperor gave them power beyond the
maintenance of a deceptively innocuous rite.[8] By worshipping the Genius
of the emperor the freedmen were not only making a pro forma
acknowledgement of the political power of the emperor and his capital
city but were also creating the tangible presence of the emperor's
prestige in the town. The material presence of the cult in Pompeii is
impressive indeed. The so-called Temple of Vespasian in Pompeii
contains a magnificent altar dedicated to the Genius of the emperor.
One would imagine that the Augustales were active in this structure.
However, the freedmen dominated imperial cult had its focii elsewhere in
Pompeii. In Pompeii the cult of the private and public Genius appeared
to mesh. The domestic Genius originally was a primitive force or numen
which was procreative in nature and embodied the alter-ego or spiritual
double of a man (Orr 1978:1469-1575). The imperial utilization was
conflated with other domestic deities and used an ancient festival, the
Compitalia (Fowler 1899:279-280), for its celebratory outlet. The cult
centered on the compitum, or crossroads, and shrines placed where two
streets intersected were accordingly dedicated to the imperial house and
managed by the Augustales. Using the visual iconography of the domestic
cult the shrines at the compita (street shrines) reminded the Pompeian
of his house shrine and of the continuation of his name and family.
Thus, the cult cleverly penetrated into the Pompeian home and blurred
the propitiatory ceremonies enacted daily in the house.[9] A glance at
the main east-west axis of Pompeii, the Via dell'Abbondanza, shows an

almost unbroken string of alters and shrines at nearly every intersection.[10] Perhaps the shrines reflected the districting which the ministri controlled. They do clearly demonstrate the permeation of the Augustales throughout the town at the time of its destruction. The archaeological evidence of the street shrines discovered at Pompeii clearly prove that the freedmen control of the compita rites was very widespread. The streetscape of Pompeii is typified by these shrines. What do they mean apart from their freedmen connections? One inescapable conclusion is that the formalization of the imperial cult appeared to conflate with the private religious rites which had already been practiced for centuries. The Lar (tutelary house spirit) of the emperor is very much like the Lar of the household. Both are depicted as mirthful, dancing youths whose hands hold brimming rhyta filled with overflowing wine, the great agricultural product of Campania (Orr 1978:Pl.IV No. 8). Venus, the patron deity of Caesar and his adopted heir Augustus, is the patroness of the town.[11] The Genius of the emperor parallels the Genius of the home, the "double" of the paterfamilias. Finally, the State Penates, the gods of the imperial household, appear with coincidental regularity in the house shrine paintings of Pompeii.[12] The religious rites of the Pompeian crossroads, dominated by the imperial rituals of the Augustales, nevertheless were conducted by elements of the town population which seemed sensitive to the traditional Roman domestic practices. Pompeii's energetic Freedmen seemed also to understand well the nuances of municipal politics; perhaps they were equally as successful in uniting the disparate elements which must have been present at their "block" parties.[13]

If the rites at the Pompeian intersections illustrate the urban crisis precipitated by the Freedmen and imperial intervention the rich spectrum of religions present in the town demonstrates the brilliance of the century in terms of Roman tolerance of foreign cults. Practically every known sect and/or cult was present in the town. Eastern religions such as Isis, a favorite with the freedmen mercantile community, were strongly intrenched. Isis even shared the humble niches of Pompeian houses with her Roman peers. Many eastern influences can be seen in the domestic shrines of the Pompeians (Boyce 1937:No. 372). In such religions one shared a great truth with other initiates and then in concert with others found a hope for immortality. Dionysiac cults, syncretized with eastern thought, were popular in the town together with the veneration of the Egyptian sects. Dionysus, an extremely complex diety, existed in the house shrines as a symbol of Campanian fertility but simultaneously was the nexus of an elaborate secret ceremony also practiced at Pompeii. Litholatry was even present in the rites of the Great Mother of Asia Minor. Pompeii had an active Jewish colony and no doubt welcomed a Christian or two.[14] All these had a wide appeal and Pompeii embraced them all, apparently without major difficulty. Other Campanian towns did as well; Herculaneum, for example, preserved an equal abundance of religious options (Orr 1978:1585-1587 and Maiuri 1958).

The town also gave symbolic veneration to the traditional Romano-Hellenic deities. Jupiter Capitolinus was honored in his magnificent Italic-type temple which dominated one end of the forum. Apollo's large shrine was comfortably situated nearby. Vesta appeared in many of the house shrines and was the patroness of the Bakers. Mercury was extremely popular in both the homes of Freedmen and the tabernae (taverns) which were liberally sprinkled throughout the town (Orr 1978:1581-1582 and Boyce 1937). This was probably due to the winged footed god being not only the god of commerce and financial transactions but also of thieves! Mercury is painted in the shrines and on the walls holding a bag of money in one hand. One remembers the slogan "Salve lucrum" (hail profit!) found on a Pompeian wall in connection with him. By far the most common image shown in the shrines of Pompeii is the goddess Fortuna (Boyce 1937:No. 372 & No. 13; and Tinh 1971). Originally an agricultural goddess, she evolved into a deity of luck and chance; more specifically, the luck of commerce and trade.[15] Sometimes syncretized as Isis-Fortuna, she is commonly shown holding fast to a rudder, a fine allusion to her mercantile responsibilities. Even the Sarnus, the river which connected the town of Pompeii with its neighbors to the west, had representation in the shrines of the town. One beautifully constructed aedicula (miniature temple) portrayed the river as a bearded river god who poured the Sarno's waters out of a jar.[16] Pompeii also fortuitously preserves several ancient pre-Roman Italic (Oscan?) shrines as exempla of the indigenous native deities found in the tribes which inhabited the nearby Latari and Appenine Mountains (Maiuri 1932:80; Maiuri 1933:98-106; and de Franciscis 1951:19).

The household shrines of Pompeii, the lararia, constitute our most important archaeological body of evidence for understanding how ancient Roman house cult ritual responded to the needs of the rapidly evolving first century A.D. town. Urbanism in Pompeii was reflected in the construction and location of these humble niches and tempetti. Moreover, these shrines act as typological reference points for the entire Roman world, for no other Roman town equalled their number, diversity, and quality. Large numbers of them have been excavated in shops and small industries and many of these establishments are provided with multiple shrines.[17] Most of the shrines have been found, quite naturally enough, in gardens and kitchens where they respond to their respective roles as agricultural deities and guardians of the hearth fire. Besides the deities mentioned above, some shrines have been associated with more bizarre spirits, such as eastern moon gods, Phrygian seeresses, and even sacred trees, planted conveniently adjacent to the shrines. Inscriptions on the lararia attest to the activity of Freedmen and their desire to fulfill various votive. Decorative schemes include the cementing of conch shells and scallops around the shrines, a sure commentary on the maritime life of the Naples area.

Pompeii's municipal government provided sumptuously for the entertainment of all aspects of its urban population. The amphitheater was built at the same time the Roman colony was founded (80 B.C.) and decades before a similar structure was erected in Rome itself (Boethius and Ward-Perkins 1970:292-293 and 297). Its arcade is a feature which was novel at the time of its construction. Architecturally speaking, Pompeii presents a material cultural analog for the summa we have been arguing in other topics. Italic forms are there in the so-called Samnite atrium house with its first style (rectangular blocks of color) decoration. Hellenic forms are omnipresent; witness the old Doric temple in the triangular forum, the Hellenistic porticoes, and the Greek planning used in the design of the earlier town. After the beginning of the reign of Augustus the town acquired more Roman forms like a gravity fed water supply system with _aquae castellae_ (water towers) built throughout the city at key points. Bath buildings, a large open air theater, a lecture hall (_odeon_), a large _palestra_ for athletics, a voting precinct, and a substantial _macellum_ (market building) complete with painted shrine provided the range of services necessary for a Roman town. Beyond this, other amusements were in evidence in the town. The _Lupanar_ is no doubt the finest one to survive from the Roman world. Each prostitute was provided with a dimly lit room. The walls of these were covered with the graffitti one would associate with these occupations.

The great luxuriously fitted atrium and peristyle houses of Pompeii; probably the most memorable edifices on any visit to the site fell upon hard times in the last years of the town. There is much evidence to support the thesis that many of the wealthier aristocratic Pompeians abandoned the town and some of the fine dwellings were jury-rigged to serve as hostels and small hotels. Others were pinched by the rise in land values and added new facades, galleries, and shop niches. Yet, much of the land in the town was still open; vineyards, vegetable gardens, and large ornamental _horti_ (gardens) sometimes filled whole city blocks. Humbler abodes were also in evidence and much of Pompeii's population were provided with only small poorly ventilated apartments (Parker 1975). Industry and agricultural activity continued also in the town up until its last days. Potters, bakers, fullers, vintners, and metal workers survived the economic decline felt in Campania during the Flavian period.

Finally, a word of caution about gladiatorial contests. Much of our popular culture has dwelt upon the bloody business of the arena. Epigraphical studies on the subject at Pompeii, based on the graffitti and _programatta_ indicates that death was not inescapable (Kummerow 1975). Names of the gladiators have been found with their victories recorded and the results of other contests trumpeted. Although grim by our standards, the contestants apparently fought according to a closely followed regimen. There may have even been a referee to indicate "fouls" and separate contestants. The gladiators led a fairly good life, if not occasionally and suddenly abbreviated. One particular fellow, Paris, was mentioned in the graffitti as a person who won the hearts of all the young ladies in the town.

Pompeii obviously has encapsulated a great deal of its material memory. From the Street of the Tombs we learn the names of its wealthy citizenry and how the dead were venerated in the Roman town. From her great Hellenistic fortifications we can study the fourth century B.C. wall and its construction and strategy in detail down to its Samnite mason's marks. Pompeii's marvelous drainage system efficiently swept away the sudden winter rain storms. Her great basilica dealt Roman justice to its people. Her porticoed _palestrae_ sheltered theater goers when their plays were halted by inclimate weather. Her _thermopolia_ (fast food snack bars) ladled out warm stew to customers who consumed it standing on the sidewalk. The intimacy generated by the circumstances of excavation is hard to duplicate in any other Roman site. The carbonized basket of eggs consumed by workers who were decorating a large peristyle at the time of the eruption; the furniture pushed to one side and the scaffolding miraculously preserved. The silver statue of Mercury, found outside the _fauces_ (entryway) of a Roman house, and a small gold _bulla_ (a symbol of childhood worn by young boys and girls before they came of age and then dedicated in their house shrine during the ceremony commemorating their adulthood) tied around its neck. Was it rescued from its familiar niche by its proud owner and then tragically lost during the mad rush to escape? More direct are the confrontations we make at Pompeii with the plaster casts of vine roots, tree trunks, dogs, bread, and even the Pompeians themselves. All of this part and parcel of the massive _summa_ which the town has provided.

This essay is meant as Prologomena only. The Roman town of the first century A.D. has only begun to receive the scholarly attention it richly deserves. Pompeii has not had a major holistic analysis since Mau's volume appeared at the turn of the century. Comparisons between the _limes_ town of the frontier and their contemporary eastern and western urban centers need to be considered. For too long we have judged the Roman world from its great literature and its great architecture. We need to approach its civilization from the vernacular level in order to ascertain exactly how brilliant it really was. In reality, as Pompeii has so clearly shown, it was the lower order of society, the anonymous populace of the town which encouraged the social dynamism which in turn led to social and cultural change. Pompeii was desperately trying to diversify its economy in order to cope with imperial competition at the time of its destruction. It realized that it could not survive simply on the agricultural and commercial surplus generated by the small towns of Campania which fostered it. Its institutions responded in a surprisingly fluid manner to the crisis.

Pompeii was called _Colonia Cornelia Veneria Pompeianorum_. The four elements of the name respond to the status it enjoyed in the empire, the family of the general who conquered it, the goddess who protected it, and the continuation of the ancient name it called itself. It possessed territory (its _pagi_ and _vici_) and it benefitted from self-government and considerable autonomy. Its _ordo Pompeianorum_ deliberated important issues and its elected magistracies decided executive matters. Its _fiscus_ (treasury) was well run and its city services seemed to be effectively managed. But above all else, it prospered under a sense of both indigenous legacy and contemporary acceptance. It was home to a varied population. Other towns, like veteran colonies containing mostly ex-soldiers, possessed more homogeneous populations. Each Roman town's nuances and values were different. What typified them were their institutions. In many ways, they were the same institutions which served as archetypes for much of subsequent European urban life.

Notes

1. Pompeii had been a Roman colony since 80 B.C. but had been Romanized only since the reign of Augustus. At the time of her destruction, she was still an Hellenized Italic town. (For recent accounts of her history see Ward-Perkins and Claridge 1978; Andreae 1975; Andreae and Kyriekis 1975; and Jashemski 1979. For good bibliographies consult all of the above works.)

2. The material culture of the town dramatically underscores this assimilation as the Roman forum in Pompeii was built and as the Italic houses were cut up to serve the needs in the first century A.D. Bath buildings, temples, shrines, and public squares were developed under Roman hegemony. For example, the amphitheater (oldest in the Roman world), took advantage of a large vacant area located on the eastern fringe of the town.

3. Much of this insight revolves around the Pompeii streetscape. Electoral notices, lover's messages, political insults, religious pleas, shop advertisements; all cover the walls of the town. Even the erotic life of the town survives to be studied (see Grant, De Simone, and Merella 1975; Ciprotti 1959; and della Corte 1965).

4. Minutiae examples: commercial - a painted shopsign showing feltmakers at their trade (see Moeller 1976). For political examples reference is made to the numerous inscriptions urging the passerby to vote for candidates for Pompeian public office. The feltmakers, fruit sellers, fish sauce makers', even the late drinkers, all have candidates! Social minutiae of interest include ABC's written on the walls, the first lines of Vergil's Aeneid, warnings to passersby not to defile the walls, and even lover's quarrels.

5. Pompeii's architecture has never been treated in a single coherent monograph. A quick introduction to its buildings can be found Mau (1902). Unfortunately this is quite out of date in its interpretations of the forum of the town.

6. A good example is the inscription recording the rebuilding of the Temple of Isis (see Ward-Perkins and Claridge 1978:120).

7. The subdistricts were termed pagi and vici. Some of the ministri were slaves.

8. Many of the formal priesthoods at Pompeii were elected magistracies and were held by members of the senatorial class, the ordo. But the Augustales were held mostly by freedmen (see Duthoy 1978; Taylor 1914:231-253 and 1931; Niebling 1950:147-150 and 1956:303-331; Boak 1916:25-45; and Eisenhut 1964:739-740).

9. Some of the shrines seem to actually depict large street sacrifices.

10. Some of these shrines are simply altars while others are provided with large mural decorations and painted inscriptions.

11. *Venus Pompaiana, the patron deity of the town, was probably borrowed from Sulla whose family's geneology traced themselves back to several ancestors who benefitted from the goddess in one way or another.*

12. *The <u>Lares</u> <u>Praestites</u>, the guardians of the state of Rome, were especially concerned with the maintenance of the Imperial cult.*

13. *The "blockparties" got out of hand as far back as Augustus' time. The festivals of the Comitalia had to be controlled.*

14. *A possible Christian shrine has been found at nearby Herculaneum (see Kahn n.d.).*

15. *Fortuna also was popular in small shops and taverns. Perhaps her presence in the taverns reflects her favors in games of chance!*

16. *This same shrine shows a commercial scene on the river in some detail (see Orr 1978: VII, no. 4).*

17. *The Study of household religion has not produced a major monograph which contains both archaeological and documentary analysis. The bibliography is dated and parochial (see Marchi 1896; Samter 1901; Latte 1960; and Mau 1886).*

Map 1. Italy and its Environs (After Axel Boethius and J.B. Ward-
         Perkins. Etruscan and Roman Architecture. Middlesex Penguin
         Press: 1970, p. xxx)

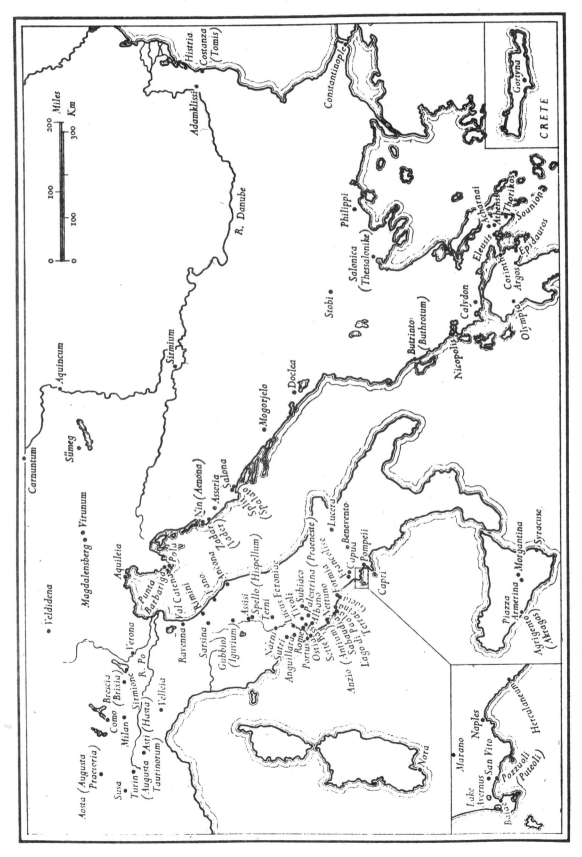

Map 2. *Pompeii (After Wilhelmina Jashemski. <u>The Gardens of Pompeii</u> Caratzas Brothers, New Rochelle: 1979; p. 4).*

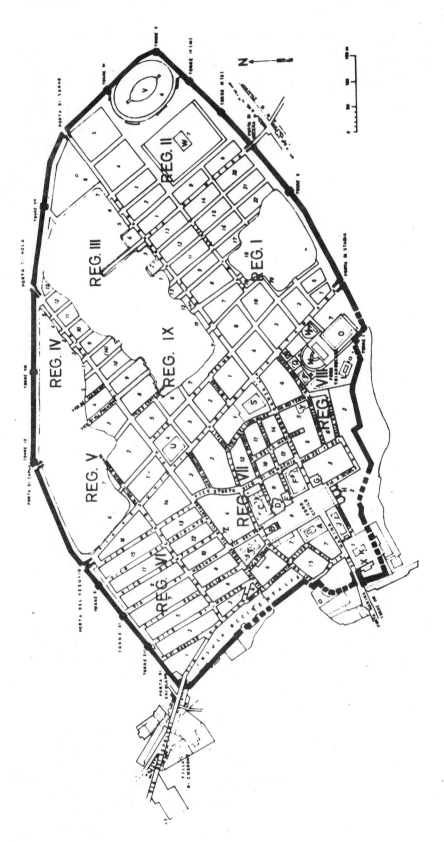

Bibliography

Andreae, Bernard, 1975: _Pompeji: Leben und Kunst in den Vesuustädten_, Recklinghausen.

Andreae, Bernard and Kyriekis, H. (eds.), 1975: _Neue Forschungen in Pompeji_, Recklinghausen.

Andreau, Jean, 1974: _Les Affaires de Monsieur Jucundus_, Rome.

Boak, A.E.R., 1916: "The Magistri of Campania and Rolos." _Classical Philosophy_ II:25-45.

Boethius, Axel, and Ward-perkins, J.B., 1970: _Etruscan and Roman Architecture_, London.

Boyce, George K., 1937: _Corpus of the Lararia of Pompeii, Memoirs of the American Academy in Rome_ 14, Rome.

Castren, Paavo, 1975: _Ordo Populusque Pompeianus: Polity and Society in Roman Pompei_, Rome.

Ciprotti, Pio, 1959: _Conoscere Pompei_, Rome.

de Franciscis, Alfonso, 1951: _Il Ritratto Romano, a Pompei_, Naples.

della Corte, Matteo, 1965: _Case ed Abitante di Pompei_, Naples.

Duff, A.M., 1928: _Freedmen in the Early Roman Empire_, Oxford.

Duthoy, Robert, 1928: "Les Augustales" _ANRW_, Berlin.

Eisenhut, W., 1964: _Augustales, Kleine Pauly_ I.

Eschebach, Hans, 1970: _Die Slädtbauliche Entwicklung des Antiken Pompeji_, Heidelberg.

Etienne, R., 1966: _La vie Quotidienne a Pompei_, Monaco.

Fowler, W. Warde, 1899: _The Roman Festivals of the Period of the Republic_, London.

Giordano, C. and Kahn, I. n.d.: _Gli Ebrei in Pompei e in Ercolano e nelle citta della Campania Felix_, Pompei.

Grant, Michael, De Simone, A., and Merella, M.T., 1975: _Erotic Art in Pompeii_, London.

Jashemski, Wilkelmina F., 1979: _The Gardens of Pompeii_ I, New Rochelle.

_____, 1977: "The Excavation of a Shop-House Garden at Pompeii", _American Journal of Archaeology_ 81:217-227.

_____, 1970:   "The Discovery of a Large Vineyard at Pompeii, The University of Maryland Excavations, 1970", _American Journal of Archaeology_, 77.

_____, 1967:   "The Caupona of Euxinus", _Archaeology_ 20:44ff.

Kummerow, Burton, 1975:   _Gladiators of Pompeii: An Epigraphical Study_, Unpublished M.A. thesis, The University of Maryland.

Latte, Kurt, 1960:   _Römische Religionsgeschichte_ 4, Munich.

Lewis, Naphtali and Reinhold, Meyer, 1966:   _Roman Civilization Sourcebook_ II, New York.

Maiuri, Amendeo, 1970:   _Pompeii_, Rome.

_____, 1958:   _Ercolano: I Nuovi Scavi (1927-1958)_ I, Rome.

_____, 1933:   _La Casa del Menandro e il suo tesoro di Argenteria_, Rome.

_____, 1932:   _La Villa dei Misteri_, Rome.

Marchese, Ronald, T., 1980:   "Urbanism in the Classical World: Some General Considerations".   In F.E.H. Schroeder, _5000 Years of Popular Culture_, Bowling Green.

Marquardt, Joachim and Mau, A., 1886 (1965): _Das Privatleben der Römer_, Leupzig.

Mau, August, 1902:   _Pompei_, New York.

Moeller, Walter, 1976:   _The Wool Trade of Ancient Pompeii_, Leiden.

Niebling, G., 1956:   "Laribus Augustis Magistri Primi," _Historia_ 5: 303-331.

_____, 1950:   "Zum Kult des Genius und der Laren." _F & F_ 26: 147-150.

Onorato, G., 1957:   _Iscrizioni Pompeiane La Vita Publica_, Florence.

Orr, David G., 1978:   _Roman Domestic Religion: The Evidence of Household Shrines_, Berlin.

Packer, James, 1975:   "Middle and Lower Class Housing in Pompeii and Herculaneum: A Preliminary Survey." In Andreae, Bernard, and Kyriekis, H. (eds.), _Neue Forschungen in Pompeji_, Recklinghausen.

Rowell, A., 1962:   _Rome in the Augustan Age_, Norman.

Samter, Ernst, 1901:   _Familienfeste der Griechen und Römer_, Berlin.

Taylor, Lily Ross, 1931:   _The Divinity of the Roman Emperor_, Middletown.

_____, 1914: "Augustales, Seviri Augustales and Seviri", _Transactions of the American Philological Association_ 45:231-253.

Tinh, V. Tran Tam, 1971: _Le culte des divinités Orientales à Herculanum_, Leiden.

_____, 1971: _Le culte des divinités Orientales en Campanie_. Leiden.

_____, 1964: _Essai sur le culte d'Isis à Pompéi_, Paris.

Ward-Perkins, John and Claridge, Amanda, 1978: _Pompeii_ A.D. 79., New York.

Bostra in Arabia

Nabatean and Roman City of the Near East

Doris S. Miller

Introduction

The ruins of ancient Bostra, onetime caravan city of the Nabatean Arabs and capital of the Roman province of Arabia, lie southeast of Damascus just north of the present day Syrian-Jordanian Border. The site today is Bosra eski Sham, a small town remote from the political and economic mainstream of contemporary Syrian life. Interspersed among the streets and buildings of the modern town are magnificent standing monuments from the Nabatean and Roman periods. They evoke comparison with the famed ruins of Palmyra and Petra, but, unlike these other caravan cities of the Near East, Bostra's role in the history of ancient urbanism has been relatively unexplored.

Bostra is a remarkable subject for urban study, offering for investigation a unique combination of archeological, environmental and historical factors. Bostra's archeological remains--streets, gates, walls, reservoirs and buildings--are diffused throughout a living settlement whose size, internal organization and economic relationships with the surrounding hinterland notably correspond to those of the ancient city. The evidence of Bostra's monuments, many of which are in an almost perfect state of preservation, and of the epigraphical and numismatic material, has made it possible to recover the main outlines of the city plan and to resurrect the life of the Roman city.

The environment of the site today is rich in ancient parallels and the interaction between settlement and hinterland is highly visible. The modern town occupies approximately the same area as that of the ancient city and many of its activities demonstrate a relentless continuity with the past. Bostra's location on the edge of a vast agricultural heartland adjacent to the Syrian steppe has timelessly involved the community with the economies of grazing and farming. Bedouin tents and grazing herds of sheep and goats still mark fallow fields near Bostra, and numerous farming villages in the area, many of which began their existence in Roman times, still market their cereal crops at Bostra.

The development of the city in the Hellenistic period was carried out, not by the city-building successors of Alexander, but by the Nabatean Arabs. The planning and design of pre-Roman Bostra were not, therefore, necessarily based on the ideals of urban life inherited from Greek tradition which found expression in the layouts of Ptolemaic and Seleucid foundations. Bostra offers us another model of the Near Eastern Hellenistic and Roman city. Like other sites, its archeological endowment, environmental contexts and particular history inform about the organization and functions of the ancient city. Distinctive to Bostra, however, during its evolution from Aramean settlement to Roman city, is an important stage of growth that was, not Greek, but Arab.

110

The Geographical Setting

Bostra's immediate environs form the southeastern quarter of the lava lands of southern Syria, a large rectangle of connecting basalt plateaus stretching south of Damascus from the upper Jordan valley and the Sea of Galilee eastward to the Syrian steppe. The central area of the lava lands is the wide fertile plain of ancient Bashan or Batanea, known today as the Nuqra ("Hollow"). It is bound on the east by the rising western slopes of the Jebel Hawran (or Jebel Druze), and on the west by the highland and lowland terrains of the Golan. Several lava fields, including the Leja ("Refuge") border the region on the northeast (Peters 1980:111; and Wirth 1971:408-421).

Bostra stands slightly above its surroundings at an elevation of 850 m. To the north and northwest the site overlooks the Nuqra plain. Some 40 kms. to the west lies the city of Der^{c}a (ancient Adraa). Beyond Der^{c}a the Yarmuk river system feeds westward to the Jordan tracing the southwestern boundary of the lava lands. To the east Bostra is sheltered from the Syrian steppe by the massif of the Jebel Hawran. Its slopes rise from the Nuqra plain to a summit plateau at 1500 m. crowned by several volcanic peaks reaching heights of 1800 m. South of Bostra the wide seamless expanses of the Nuqra give way to a rougher and rockier terrain, the plain of the southern Hawran. This landscape extends southwest to Umm al-Jimal in Jordan and southeast to the oasis of Azraq and the open steppe.

Azraq is the northern terminus of the Wadi Sirhan, a long depression east of the Jordanian watershed which runs for over 300 kms. southeast to the oasis of al-Jawf in northern Arabia. This watered and traversable track has been for millennia a natural passageway for human traffic from Arabia into southern Syria (Glueck 1940:40-41; and Winnett and Reed 1970:56).

The climate of Bostra is essentially a bi-seasonal one of warm dry summers and cool wet winters. The area receives annual averages of 200-300 mm. of precipitation and is superb dry farming country. The slopes of the Jebel receive more rainfall than the plain and there summer crops have been harvested over millennia. In this minimally watered region the site of Bostra is notable for its permanent water supply, one provided by several perennial springs supplemented by seasonal runoff from the nearby Wadi Zaydi (Wirth 1971 Map 3; and Dufourg 1955:311).

Bostra's physical characteristics of location, topography and climate have timelessly welcomed the economies of agriculture, nomadism and commerce. To the north and west, the site fronts immensely fertile land capable of supporting intensive sedentary settlement. To the south and southeast, Bostra is exposed to a different domain, however, that of the camel nomad whose cyclical patterns bring him off the steppe in summer into the milder environs of the site in search of pasturage and water (Raswan 1930:498-499). In antiquity goods from the Persian Gulf and southern Arabia collected at al-Jawf and were channeled northward along the Wadi Sirhan. Bostra's location between Damascus and Azraq, together with the site's water resources for the caravaneer, fixed it as a natural transit point along the Jawf-Damascus axis.

Nabatean and Roman Bostra: 163 B.C.-305 A.D.

The Semitic name, Bostra, means "fort," and suggests that Bostra may have been a fortified settlement from its beginnings (Waddington 1870: no. 1907). Second millennium documentation in Egyptian texts such as the Tell el-Amarna tablets' place name, Busruna, cannot be ascribed to Bostra with absolute certainty (Jones 1971:232, 447, and n.6). The account in Deuteronomy which specifies Der^Ca and Salkhad, Bostra's immediate neighbors to the west and east, among the sixty fortified towns of the kingdom of Bashan does not mention Bostra (Deut. 3:4-11). The earliest most certain reference in the literature appears much later in the description of the campaigns of Judah Maccabeus in the Books of Maccabees. In 163 B.C. Judah encountered east of the Jordan some Nabateans who gave him information about the area after which he went "by the desert road to Bostra" where he first sacked, then set fire to the town (1 Macc. 5:28; and Peters 1977:264).

Emerging out of an almost total historical obscurity, the site is thus linked with the mention of Nabateans in the lava lands, Arabs still living in tents as nomads, traders and mercenaries (1 Macc. 5:39). Following their establishment at Petra in the fourth century B.C., the Nabateans during the course of the next two centuries built a kingdom whose prosperity depended on a network of fortified, policed and watered caravan routes between northern Arabia and the Mediterranean. As Seleucid power in southern Syria declined, they moved almost effortlessly northwards taking control of key routes, notably the desert al-Jawf, Wadi Sirhan and Azraq passage towards Damascus (Peters 1977:264-265). The earliest Nabatean inscription found at Bostra dates to the end of the second century B.C. (Starcky 1964:930). It is perhaps to this period of Bostra's history that a text of Damascius refers: "Bostra in Arabia was not an ancient polis; it received its polis status under the emperor Severus. In ancient times it was a fortress (phrourion) and its walls were built by Arab kings as protection against the people of Dioynsias (Peters 1977:266). Nabatean troops were in the area in 93 B.C. when they skirmished with the forces of Alexander Jannaeus in the Jawlan (Josephus, Ant. XIII, 13, 5; and Schürer 1973:577). Down through the first century B.C. we can place the Nabateans not only at Bostra but on the southern and western slopes of the Jebel Hawran as well, at Salkhad, Suwayda, Qanawat and, particularly, Si^Ca where construction of a great temple to Ba^Cal Shamin began in 33/32 B.C. (Butler 1919:374-385).

The brief regime of the Nabatean king Arethas III at Damascus (ca. 85-72 B.C.) marked the fullest territorial extent of Nabatean influence in the lava lands. The annexation of Syria by Pompey in 63 B.C. and a succession of land grants made to the Herodians beginning in 23 B.C. restricted Nabatean control to the southern Hawran from the line Der^Ca, Bostra and Salkhad southward. The Nabateans' primary objective in the lava lands was commerce, and their continued control over the Wadi Sirhan route and their defensive strategies towards nomadic groups to the south must have been more critical than playing politics in the lava lands. In fact, Herod's presence in Batanea and Trachonitis insuring the safety of caravans passing between Bostra and Damascus probably suited the Nabatean interests very well (Peters 1977:266-271).

We can piece together an outline of Bostra's development during the first century A.D. from a number of external and local factors. These include changes in the pattern of trade in the southern Nabatean kingdom, the possibility that Rabbel II (70-106 A.D.), the last Nabatean king, ruled from Bostra rather than Petra, the existence of a network of agricultural villages in the Bostra area and, finally, the presence in the city of certain monuments, undated but in the unmistakable Nabatean style, whose execution, function and relationship to one another suggest an urban center of some significance and complexity.

As Strabo noted, the Romans early in the century began transferring goods directly from the Arabian coast across the Red Sea to Egyptian ports (Strabo, Geography VI, 4.23-24). The volume of Mediterranean-bound trade through Petra declined, but trade along the interior routes flourished as the growth of caravan cities like Jerash (Gerasa), a city of the Decapolis southwest of Bostra, and Palmyra, out on the steppe to the northeast, confirms (Bowersock 1973:136-139). This prosperity inland and to the north was not lost on the Nabateans. A series of coins and inscriptions describing a special cult of Dushara linked both to the person of Rabbel II, "he who has given his people life and freedom" and to the city of Bostra is grounds for conjecture that Rabbel II made this caravan city the northern capital of the kingdom (Peters 1977:272-274). Moreover, between Bostra and Umm al-Jimal to the south, in the dry farming region of the southern plain, there are many villages where Nabatean temples, tombs and inscriptions have been found (Butler 1919:63-213). These villages present three points of interest: one, their existence required a local regime capable of providing protection and water; two, their agricultural surpluses were likely to have been marketed at Bostra; and three, certain of their inscriptions date to the years of Rabbel II (Negev 1977:637-640). The Nabatean monuments at Bostra will be described later. It should be noted now, however, in connection with Rabbel's possible rule from Bostra that an impressive palace residence that housed the Roman governor may predate the Roman period. This conjecture is based on certain decorative elements applied to the palace itself, its lack of orientation to what is known of the Roman street layout and its location near the remains of a Nabatean temple complex (Butler 1919:255-260; and Peters 1977:273-274). Thus the panoply of functions that we may see in the administrative, economic, religious and cultural life of the Roman city finds precedent in similar activities however dimly perceived and undeveloped carried out by the Nabatean city during its last pre-Roman century.

During the reign of Trajan in 106 A.D., presumably on the death of Rabbel II, A. Cornelius Palma, consular legate of Syria, incorporated the Nabatean kingdom into the eastern Roman system as the province of Arabia. The boundaries of the new province were essentially those of the former Nabatean territories plus the Nuqra plain and parts of Transjordan including the city of Jerash. These boundaries were later readjusted, once under Septimius Severus in 195 A.D. when the northern

Hawran was joined to Arabia, and again during the reign of Diocletian when much of the southern portion went to Palestine (Brünnow and von Domaszewski 1909:261-270; and Bowersock 1971:228-231).

The city, renamed Nea Traiana Bostra, became the capital of the new province, the seat of the governor and the headquarters of a legion (Jones 1971:291, 468, n. 90; and Bowersock 1971:231). The legion permanently stationed at Bostra was the III Cyrenaica whose career was associated with the city down through succeeding centuries (Speidel 1977:689-698; MacAdam 1979:136-145). Bostra was subsequently elevated to colonial status, either under Elagabalus (218-222 A.D.) or Alexander Severus (222-235 A.D.). During the middle of the third century it was given the title of metropolis by Philip the Arab (244-249 A.D.) (Butler 1919:Part 4, xxxii, xxxiii; Bowersock 1971:234).

The Romans released formidable new energies into the region. Vital objectives were security, communications and water supply. Immense construction projects were initiated that stimulated development for the province and for its capital city which was graced with the features and amenities characteristic of Roman city planning at its best. Military detachments were deployed throughout the province and eventually east of the Jebel Hawran in response to inherited concerns of security of trade routes and control of the steppe (Peters 1978:315-326). Roman roads converged on Bostra from almost every direction. The most ambitious road building project was the Via Nova Traiana, accomplished over the years 111-115 A.D. It connected Bostra as the caput viae in the north through Amman (Philadelphia) to Aqaba (Aila) on the Red Sea (Bowersock 1971:282; and Thomsen 1917). Cornelius Palma oversaw the construction of an aqueduct that channeled water from springs on the Jebel Hawran down into the Nuqra plain to Karak (Kanata), a village that lay within Bostra's own territory (Dunand 1930:272-279; and Alt 1951:235-245). Reservoirs and cisterns began to dot the region, particularly out across the Nuqra which experienced systematic agricultural development for the first time (Peters 1980:118). Bostra itself was transformed. Climaxing the building of temples, colonnaded streets, arches, fountains, baths, warehouses and shops was the achievement of a great freestanding theater completed sometime in the first half or middle of the second century. Like the construction of roads, bridges, aqueducts and reservoirs, the theater project must have engaged, the engineering skills and labor of the legion (Sartre 1976:44; and Frézouls 1959:222).

Documentation from Bostra and other sites in the lava lands during the third century reflects a preoccupation with political and cultural changes affecting the entire eastern empire: the decline of the Parthians and ascendency of the Sasanians in Iran which created new tensions on the frontiers, the challenge to security and trade by newly-arrived nomadic groups out on the steppe and the impact of the spread of Christianity. The Sasanians invaded deep into Syria in the middle of the century. They were followed by the Palmyrenes who overran Arabia in 270. At Bostra they destroyed the temple of Zeus Ammon, tutelary god of the III Cyrenaica (Seyrig 1941:44-48). Inscriptions from Bostra, Der[c]a and elsewhere record a succession of building activities down through this century, many clearly for purposes of fortification and defense. They include the construction (or reconstruction) of a fortress at

Dayr-al-Kahf on the southern slopes of the Jebel Hawran in 306 A.D. (Butler 1919:70-74, 145-148; and Pflaum 1952:307-330).

We do not know the date or circumstances of Bostra's earliest exposure to Christianity, but by 245 A.D. the city's importance as a Christian center can be measured by the tradition that Origen journeyed there to challenge the views of its bishop Beryllus. By the middle of the fourth century half of the population of Bostra was accounted to be Christian (Waddington 1870:no. 1907; Sartre 1976:48). On the strength of the archeological and literary evidence, the city thrived throughout the Byzantine period as it continued to do as a major caravan and pilgrimage center under Islam.

Out of a dearth of reporting from the classical historians and geographers come two fleeting contemporary references to the Roman city. One is a brief notice in a fourth century travel guide which stresses Bostra's proximity to both the Persians and the Arabs and the importance of her commercial activity. It also speaks of the tetrapylon, one of her public monuments, as a marvel (Expositio:176-177). The other commentary comes from Ammianus Marcellinus. He describes (14.8, 13) Arabia as a province rich from a variety of products, well fortified against the depradations of nomads and possessing great cities, one of which is Bostra.

The Appearance of the Ancient City

Bostra presents a striking visual unity of site and setting. This unity can be attributed to the almost exclusive use of basalt for the construction of walls, streets and buildings and of outlying pasture and threshing enclosures. The sight of nearby cultivated fields, of threshing floors lining the perimeters of the site and of the daily passages of sheep and goats between town and pasture enhances the visual association. The area of the modern town is essentially the same as that of the ancient city. Daily activities of marketing and water collection echo those of the ancient settlement and they are carried out in precisely the same places.

The streets and monuments of Nabatean and Roman Bostra, as well as those of the Byzantine and early Islamic periods, lie in a tangle of modern lanes and buildings many of which are built out of reused stone or are subdivisions of ancient structures (See Plan 1). Three prominent features provide a sense of orientation to the site. One is the perennial spring surrounded by a grove of trees in the northwest section of the town which has been a major water source for the settlement throughout its history. Another is the massive form of the Ayyubid citadel which encloses the Roman theater on the southern edge of the site. The third is the horizontal line of the main east-west street that was in antiquity as it still is today the principal avenue of the city. It runs from the ancient West Gate eastward for over 800 m. and terminates on slightly higher ground at an arch about three-quarters of the way through the site. This street provides Bostra with its longest axis and its major orientation of east-southeast, west-northwest.

115

Bostra has been only partially excavated. The many accounts of nineteenth century travellers have been collected in the monumental work of Brünnow and von Domaszewski on the province of Arabia (1909:1-84). The most comprehensive study of the city is that of the Princeton University expeditions early in this century which recorded, photographed and surveyed the site and published its inscriptions.[2] A series of excavations in recent decades sponsored by the Department of Antiquities of the Syrian-Arab Republic has cleared the Roman theater and recovered such features of the Roman city as the tetrapylon and cryptoportico. Ongoing excavation has been facilitated by the clearing of modern buildings, an undertaking made possible by the gradual resettlement of residents from the old town to new suburbs nearby.[3]

The location of the pre-Nabatean Aramean settlement was in the western section near the principal spring. Remains of a semi-circular wall constructed of rough boulders in the southwest corner resemble walls of unhewn stone found at other very early sites in the southern Hawran (Butler 1919:218 and 225). Most of the monuments of the Nabatean period, however, are located on the higher ground at the eastern end of the site. These include the monumental East Arch, an engaged Nabatean half-column just east of the arch and other smaller half-columns which were all part of a large temple complex. In the same area a piece of Nabatean relief sculpture built into a modern house and fragments of Nabatean ceramics have been found (Butler 1919:236-243 and 249-251; and Gualandi 1978:43-44). To these few, albeit impressive, remains one must also consider the two great reservoirs, the palace and the West Gate as possible constructions of the Nabatean period (Moughdad 1978:29-32; and Butler 1919:229-230).

The Roman city circuit can be traced by moving clockwise from the southwest corner where the Romans set a tower into the pre-existing walls, north past the West Gate, then east to the site of the North Gate and to the remains of Roman walls incorporated into the Mabrak Mosque. The northern portion of the circuit features a large enclosed area of ca. 350 x 400 m. where foundations for towers and a gate have been found. This is probably the site of the legionary camp (Moughdad 1976:71-73; and Peters 1983). From the Mabrak Mosque the line of the Roman city continues south to the Southeast Reservoir, then turns westward to the theater to complete the circuit. The Roman walls no longer stand, having been dismantled and used in the construction of the Ayyubid citadel, but masses of stone from the inner core can be seen along the western and northwestern sides (Butler 1919:225-226). The West Gate gave directly onto the road to Derᶜa and the North Gate to Suwayda via Jamarrin where a Roman bridge still spans the Wadi Zaydi. The exits east and south of the city as well as the line of the southern wall continue to be a matter of speculation, but a Roman road ran due east to Salkhad.

A network of principal and secondary streets establishes the interior layout of the Roman city (See Plan 2). The principal avenue, three secondary transverse streets, and two streets north of and parallel to the main street are indicated on the Princeton survey plan. Information about additional streets and extensions of streets is coming to light as new excavation proceeds (Cerulli 1978:81-93). The main street does not bisect the city from gate to gate, but stops at the East Arch partway through the city, a layout that is similar to the main street layout at Petra (Starcky 1964:948; Peters 1977:n. 8, 273; and Peters 1983). Three important transverse streets oriented approximately north-south lead to the spring, theater and North Gate. The meeting of the theater street with the main street is marked by an imposing triple arch (Butler 1919:243-247).

The visual splendor of the sites of ancient Gerasa (Jerash) and Palmyra is enhanced by the array of colonnades that still line their principal intersecting streets. Bostra's colonnades unfortunately have disappeared, but the remaining columns and column bases indicate that not only were the main street and the North Gate street colonnaded, but all of the others noted above as well (Butler 1919:230-235). The main street has other features also found at Jerash and Palmyra. An oval forum lies inside the West Gate, the outline of which is visible on the north side of the street. Its location coincides with the point where the street shifts direction slightly to the south (Cerulli 1978:93, figs. 1 and 8). Further east the bases of a tetrapylon have been recently excavated at the intersection with the street that leads to the spring (Cerulli 1978:figs. 1, 6, and 7 and 91-93). The Roman main street was paved, the patterns of the paving stones varying from one section of the avenue to another.

Many of the individual monuments of Roman Bostra, some of which are described below, can be dated either on epigraphical or stylistic grounds, and in many cases their functions -- commercial, religious and cultural, etc. -- can be identified. A compact commercial unit of some architectural complexity is located on the north side of the main street just east of the tetrapylon. An underground warehouse called a cryptoportico is surmounted by a row of shops facing the main street. The handsomely detailed shop entrances are approached by several steps above the colonnaded sidewalk. More shops line the north and rear side of the cryptoportico whose doorways opened onto a wide paved area. The cryptoportico, built during the second century A.D., extends over 100 m. in length along the main street. A long row of narrow skylight vents just above the sidewalk level admit light and air into the interior (Moughdad 1978:15-16; and Voûte 1971-1972:128). Another commercial complex, a massive market or khan, stands on the western side of the street leading to the North Gate. Its two doorways from the sidewalk gave entrance into a vast unroofed oblong court lined with many recesses and doorways. They in turn opened into three great vaulted roofed halls. Although the date of construction is unknown, epigraphic evidence indicates that the market building could not have been built before the third century A.D. (Butler 1919:270-273).

The inscriptions and coins of ancient Bostra, with their representations of shrines and temples, are testimony for the presence of a variety of religious buildings (Zouhdi 1977-1978). The remains of a fountain shrine or Nymphaeum stand at the intersection of the main street and the street leading to the North Gate. This was an apsidal building set on a diagonal to the intersection behind four surviving columns noted for their exceptional beauty of proportion and design. The Nymphaeum is directly across the street from the ruins of a building of a later date called a "Kalybe" after a type of open-air shrine found elsewhere in the Hawran (Butler 1919:251-255).

Bostra has two bath complexes, one located in the north enclosure area and a more imposing and elaborate structure in the center of the city south of the main street. This South Bath has a large main hall with an eight-sided dome behind which lie the various chambers typical of the Roman bath establishment (Butler 1919:260-265). Beyond the South Bath is the great Roman theater, sited along the same axis as that of the main street. Because most of its components, scene, orchestra, dressing rooms, loges, cavea, and exits, etc., are virtually intact, it is one of the most perfectly preserved Roman theaters in existence (Brünnow and von Domaszewski 1909:47-84; and Butler 1919:273-277). A hippodrome lay south of the theater, the outlines of which the Princeton survey was able to trace (Butler 1919:275-276).

A magnificent basilica with a large elliptical entrance and apse stands north of the East Arch area. This great unadorned hall, lit by plainly designed windows placed high on the walls, had external colonnades on both sides. Near it are the ruins of smaller apsidal structures. Together they form a complex that may have been the setting for some of the administrative activities of the city (Butler 1919:265-270). Butler, in the Princeton survey, concluded that the basilica was pre-Christian, indeed, possibly even of second century construction, because of certain design and construction elements. In any case, the construction of the basilica and neighboring apsidal structures represents the expansion of the city plan under Roman administration.

Life in the Roman city

Bostra's political, cultural and economic functions informed the physical layout, organization and character of the ancient city. In the course of their description we may read the interdependence of the city and the larger geographic and economic landscape that composed its hinterland.

Bostra's administration operated at two levels, the gubernatorial supervision of the affairs of the province and the internal municipal organization of the colony itself. In Arabia the governor was both legionary and civil commander. He drew his general staff from the legion and had assigned to his person a guard of footsoldiers and cavalry that included a detachment from the camel corps (Speidel 1977:696). On occasion, military and judicial duties such as the holding of assizes elsewhere in the province took him away from the city (Bowersock 1971:224 and 231-232). When at Bostra, his headquarters was the palace, as it may have been Rabbel II's before him. Its storied apartments, colonnaded porticos, towers and walled central courtyard provided the public and private spaces suited to an official residence with rooms for conducting audiences and for housing archives, stores and weapons.

Bostra was a colony, then a metropolis, with the right to mint coins. The organization of municipal life with a citizen body, council and magistrates responsible for food and water supplies, public safety, market affairs and amenities like the public baths must have occurred soon after the Roman takeover (Jones 1971:291; and Sartre 1973:228). The Greek and Latin inscriptions detail the activity and influence of the military presence on the day-to-day affairs of the city. A legionary centurion was in charge of the public prison (Speidel 1977:696). Veterans of the army settled in retirement at Bostra or in nearby villages, where they became members of the local aristocracy as councillors and magistrates (Rey-Coquais 1965:70; and Speidel 1977:721). A coin issue during the reign of Decius (249-251 A.D.) cites the harmony of the "Bostreni" and shows the legionary god, Zeus Ammon, holding hands with the Tyche of Bostra (Butler 1919: Part 4, xxxiv, xxxv; Sourdel 1952:89-92).

The composition of the permanent and transient populations of Bostra was a mix of Greeks, Romans, Syrians and Arabs; of pagans and Christians; of functionaries of the governor's staff, soldiers and veterans of the legion some of whom came from the western provinces of the empire, councillors, magistrates, landowners, priests, merchants, caravaneers, shopkeepers, craftsmen and slaves. The representations of Nabatean and Roman deities and temples on coins, the theater which was the setting for the Actia Dusaria, the reconstructions of the handsome colonnades, the baths, even the dedication of a torch bracket on a column on the main street by a citizen denote some of the cultic and social facets of life in the city (Price and Trell 1977: fig. 277; Waddington 1980: no. 2023; Butler 1919:254; MacAdam 1979:171-180.

Bostra was a market and transhipment point for long distance and local trade. The elaborate road system (including a road cut by the Romans through the formidable lava landscape of the Leja) tied the city into the circuit of coastal and inland routes that linked the sources of origin of goods and their ultimate markets from China to Europe. Syrian and Arabian land routes connected the Tigris and Euphrates and the Persian Gulf to the Red Sea and the Mediterranean. The chief cargoes of the Persian Gulf and Yemenese trade borne northwards along the roads to Bostra were the low bulk, high value goods of incense, spices, aromatics, precious metals and textiles (Rostovtzeff 1932:1-35). Detachments of the legion protected the roads as had the Nabateans at posts as far south as al-Jawf and Mada^C in Salih (Speidel 1977:694). In Roman times merchants came to Bostra from cities on the coast to buy gold, semi-precious stones and incense (Levine 1975:55). Among local goods exported were wine from the vineyards of the Jebel Hawran, grain from Auranitis and Batanea, figs, salt from Azraq, and in all likelihood, nomadic products of hides and wool (Bowersock 1971:241). Roman Bostra provided the caravaneer with facilities for watering, revictualling, marketing, storage and distribution, services that had their counterparts in Nabatean times.

Given the variety and volume of commercial activity that filled Bostra's streets, her colonnaded sidewalks were not so much an amenity as a practical necessity for the separation and free passage of pedestrian and street traffic. The cryptoportico and great market building may have been used for storing different types of goods. The cryptoportico's smaller area, underground situation and limited access seem particularly suitable for high value commodities. The market had an immense storage capacity and its outer court was so designed that a variety of retail operations could have been conducted there.

The terms "capital city" and "caravan city" signal political prestige and commercial prosperity, and Bostra's transition from fortified trading settlement to foremost city of Arabia was undeniably stimulated and fostered by its administrative and mercantile activities. The principal impetus to growth, however, came from the economic support provided by a stable, productive and prosperous agricultural hinterland. The Nuqra plain, which in Herod's time had been predominantly grazing country, was intensively settled under the Romans with farming villages (Peters 1980:115). Parallel to the development of the hinterland's capability for surplus grain production was the growth of the city as a major consumption and distribution center.

Agricultural production then as now was the function of the peasant village. The survival and productivity of the village depended on sufficient water for the drinking needs of inhabitants and livestock and on security against raiding and brigandage (Peters 1980:116-118). The Romans introduced these two factors critical to stable village settlement, their technology securing water supplies by the construction of cisterns, reservoirs and aqueducts and their arms guaranteeing the control of intrusive nomadic movements in and out of the area (Peters 1980:118; and Peters 1978). Intensive and widespread settlement became possible where formerly villages had existed only at easily defensible and naturally watered sites. We can look back to the Nabatean village settlement in the southern plain as a small-scale prototype for the form and process of later Roman development.

Conclusion

The successors of Alexander in the Near East founded cities on a model which earlier and successfully had been applied to sites in Asia Minor. The plans of Seleucid foundations in Syria and Mesopotamia uniformly and repetitively display the orthogonal grid layout attributed to Hippodamus of Miletus (Wycherley 1962:15-27; and Ward-Perkins 1974:18-21). The main feature of this plan was the even distribution over the site of several or many avenues intersected by transverse streets at right angles to create rectangular blocks or insulae of uniform size. Open areas or groups of insulae were reserved for large public spaces and buildings such as the agora or a major temple complex (Sauvaget 1941:Pl 211).

Whether the Romans build anew or altered the classical Hippodamian layout, the pragmatic and esthetic values of their planning resulted in the predominance of a single main street and its axial relationship to one or a few secondary arterial streets. Where the Romans worked afresh, or in a relatively undeveloped settlement environment, as at Shahba (Philippopolis) and Jerash (Gerasa), they laid out one long principal avenue which was intersected precisely at right angles by

120

transverse streets (Butler 1904:376-396; Brünnow and von Domaszewski 1909:145-179; and Kraeling 1938). Elsewhere, at Aleppo, Damascus and Dura Europus, for example, they widened, paved and colonnaded the earlier Hellenistic arterial streets. Characteristic accents of the eastern Roman main street such as arches, oval forums and circles with tetrapylons fulfilled practical and visual aims, organizing internal communication, allowing for the flow of wheeled and foot traffic, providing for shelter from the sun and in some instances disguising deviations and irregularities in the plan (Ward-Perkins 1974:27-36).

It is possible to trace the Greek orthogonal and Roman axial stages in the layouts of many ancient cities of the Near East. At Bostra many of the elements of the Roman plan are obvious, but the definition and progression of the pre-Roman layout are not. At the time Seleucus Nicator was laying down his new foundations (ca. 300 B.C.), Bostra was still only a fortified settlement whose hinterland was predominantly nomadic and where grazing rather than agriculture persisted as the major form of land use. The development of the city followed upon the arrival of the Nabatean Arabs during the second and first centuries B.C. It was they, not the Greek successors of Alexander, who initiated the new planning and construction seen in the monuments attributed to Rabbel II in the first century A.D.

The present state of our knowledge does not permit definitive conclusions about the Nabatean plan. We can pinpoint, nonetheless, certain specific problems for study that further excavation may help to resolve. Among them are the linkage between the original Aramean settlement at the western end of the city and the major Nabatean construction in the eastern section; the termination of the main street in an arch behind which lay a temple complex, resembling the via sacra, arch, temenos arrangement at Nabatean Petra (Peters 1983); and the layout of two transverse streets (to the spring and to the North Gate) which join the main street at oblique angles, junctures that adhere neither to the Greek orthogonal nor the Roman axial ideal. The Roman contributions to the street design are evident. They include the colonnades, paving and the right-angled alignment of the theater's transverse street to the main street. Moreover, the settings of the oval forum, tetrapylon and Nymphaeum as they disguise deviations in the main and transverse streets accord with preferred Roman visual traditions.

Bostra's experience illuminates two important considerations for the history of ancient Near Eastern urbanism. One is the specific problem of a Nabatean phase of development, the other, the more comprehensive subject of settlement transformation. Roman Bostra owed its character to a setting between sedentary lands and a steppe frontier and to an evolution stimulated by Arabs rather than the Greek heirs of Alexander. Essential to the development of Bostra during the late Hellenistic and Roman periods was the conversion of land use in the area from grazing to agriculture which eventually established a flourishing hinterland capable of supporting a great city and its varied non-agricultural functions. This conversion required two fundamental elements, security and a dependable water supply for farming villages. The Nabateans and Romans provided both although on very different scales. The transformation of Bostra, unique in itself, rests within a larger phenomenon of regional change that led eventually from nomadism to sedentarization and from tribalism to Roman urbanism across the lava lands.

Notes

1. The writer gratefully acknowledges the courtesy and cooperation of the Department of Antiquities and Museums of the Syrian Arab Republic, in particular, of the late Mr. Sulayman Moughdad, Curator at Bostra, during field researches in Syria.

2. The Princeton publications are cited in full in the "Bibliography" of this paper. Since this paper was written, a complete corpus of inscriptions from Bostra, edited by Maurice Sartre, has appeared as Volume XIII. fasc. 1 of the _Inscriptions Grecques et Latines de la Syrie_ Series (Paul Geuthner:Paris, 1982).

3. Publications of recent work include S. Moughdad, "Bosra," _Felix Ravenna_ CIX-CX (1975), pp. 7-12; S. Cerulli, "Bosra note sul sistema viario urbano e nuovi apporti alla comprensione delle fasi edilizie nel sanctuario dei Ss. Sergio, Bacco e Leonzio," extract from _Felix Ravenna_, CXV, fasc. 1 (1978), pp. 79-120. For the location of new suburbs see the plan in S. Moughdad, _Bosra_, tr. H. MacAdam (Damascus, 1978), p. 57.

Bibliography

Alt, A., 1951: "Das Territorium von Bostra." Zeitschrift des Deutschen Palästina-Vereins 68:235-245.

Ammianus Marcellinus, 1935: Tr. by J. Rolfe. Vol. I. Cambridge, Mass.: Loeb Classical Library.

Bowersock, G.W., 1971: "A Report on Arabia Provincia." Journal of Roman Studies 61:219-242.

_____, 1973: "Syria under Vespasian." Journal of Roman Studies 63:133-140.

_____, 1975: "Old and New in the History of Judaea." Journal of Roman Studies 64:180-185.

Brünnow, R.E. and von Domaszewski, A., 1909: Die Provincia Arabia III. Strassburg.

Butler, H.C., 1904: The Publications of an American Archaeological Expedition to Syria in 1899-1900 II, Architecture and Other Arts. New York: The Century Co.

_____, et al., 1919: Syria. Publications of the Princeton University Archaeological Expeditions to Syria in 1904-05 and 1909. Division II. Architecture. Section A. Southern Syria. Leiden.

Cerulli, S., 1978: "Bosra note sul sistema viario urbano e nuovi apporti alla comprensione delle fasi edilizie nel sanctuario dei Ss. Sergio, Bacco e Leonzio." Felix Ravenna CXV, fasc. 1, (Universita degli studi di Bologna Istituto di Antichita Ravennati e Bizantine), 79-120.

Dufourg, J.P., 1955: "Premieres notes sur les problemes de l'eau au Djebel ed Druz." Revue de geographie de Lyon 30:309-328.

Dunand, M., 1930: "Kanata et Kanatha." Syria 11:272-279.

Eusebius, 1932: Ecclesiastical History. Tr. by K. Lake and J. Oulton. Vol. 2. New York (Loeb Classical Library).

Expositio totius mundi et gentium. 1966: Ed. and tr. by J. Rougé. Paris: Les Editions du Cerf.

Frézouls, E., 1959: "Recherches sur les theatres de l'orient syrien." Syria 36:202-227.

_____, 1961: "Recherches sur les theatres de l'orient syrien." Syria 38:54-86.

Glueck, Nelson, 1940: The Other Side of the Jordan. New Haven: American Schools of Oriental Research.

Gualandi, G., 1978: "Bosra: la seconda campagna di scavi nella chiesa dei Ss. Sergio, Bacco et Leonzio." _Felix Ravenna CXV_, fasc. 1, (Universita degli studi di Bologna Istituto di Antichita Ravennati e Bizantine), 9-69.

Jones, A.H.M., 1971: _The Cities of the Eastern Roman Provinces_. 2nd ed. Oxford: The Clarendon Press.

Josephus, 1926-65: _Opera_. Tr. by H. St. J. Thackeray, R. Marcus and L.H. Feldman. 9 vols. Cambridge, Mass.: Loeb Classical Library.

Kraeling, C.H., 1938: _Gerasa, City of the Decapolis_. New Haven.

Levine, Lee I., 1975: _Caesarea under Roman Rule_. Leiden.

MacAdam, H.I., 1979: "Studies in the History of the Roman Province of Arabia." Ph.D. dissertation, University of Manchester.

Moughdad, Sulayman, 1975: "Bosra." _Felix Ravenna CIX-CX_, (Universita degli studi di Bologna Istituto di Antichita Ravennati e Bizantine), 7-12.

_____, 1976: Busra. _Dalil athari wa tarikhi_. Damascus.

_____, 1978: Bosra. _Historical and Archaeological Guide_. Tr. by H. MacAdam. Damascus.

Negev. A., 1977: "The Nabateans and the Provincia Arabia." In _Aufstieg und Niedergang der römischen Welt_ II, 8, edited by H. Temporini and W. Haase, Berlin: De Gruyter, 520-685.

"Note préliminaire sur le cryptoportique de Bosra (Syrie)," 1973: in _Les cryptoportiques dans l'architecture romaine. Ecole française de Rome, 12-23 Avril, 1972_. Coll. de l'école francaise de Rome. Rome, 411-412.

Paret, Roger, 1960: "Les villes de Syrie du Sud et les routes commerciales d'Arabie à la fin du vi^e siècle." _Akten des XI internationalen Byzantinisten-Kongresses_, Munchen, 1958. Munich: C.H. Beck, 438-444.

Peters, F.E., 1977: "The Nabateans in the Hawran." _Journal of the American Oriental Society_ 97, no. 3:263-277.

_____, 1978: "Romans and Bedouin in Southern Syria." _Journal of Near Eastern Studies_ 37, no. 4:315-326.

_____, 1980: "Regional Development in the Roman Empire: The Lava Lands of Syria." _Thought_ 55, no. 216:110-121.

_____, 1983: "City Planning in Greco-Roman Syria: Some New Considerations." _Damaszener Mitteilungen_ I.

Pflaum, H.G., 1952: "La fortification de la ville d'Adraha d'Arabie." *Syria* 29:307-330.

Price, M. and Trell, Bluma., 1977: *Coins and their Cities, Architecture on the Ancient Coins of Greece, Rome and Palestine.* Detroit.

Raswan, Carl, 1930: "Tribal Areas and Migration Lines of the North Arabian Bedouin." *Geographical Review* 20:494-502.

Rey-Coquais, Jean Paul, 1965: "Nouvelles inscriptions grecques et latines de Bosra." *Les annales archéologiques de Syrie* 15, nos. 1-2:65-86.

Rostovtzeff, M., 1932: *Caravan Cities.* Oxford: The Clarendon Press.

Sartre, Maurice, 1973: "Inscriptions inédites de l'Arabie romaine." *Syria* 50:223-233.

_____, 1976: "Bostra: capitale de l'Arabie romaine." *Archaeologia* 94:38-47.

Sauvaget, Jean, 1941: *Alep. Essai sur le développement d'une grand ville syrienne des origines au milieu du xixe siecle.* Paris.

Schürer, Emil, 1973: *The History of the Jewish People in the Age of Jesus Christ* I. Rev. and ed. by G. Vermes and F. Millar. Edinburgh: T. and T. Clark Lts.

Seyrig, Henri, 1941: "Les inscriptions de Bostra." *Syria* 22:44-48.

Sourdel, Dominique, 1952: *Les cultes du Hauran, à l'epoque romaine.* Paris.

Speidel, M.P., 1977: "The Roman Army in Arabia." In *Aufstieg und Niedergang der romischen Welt* II, 8, edited by H. Temporini and W. Haase, Berlin: De Gruyter, 688-730.

Starcky, J., 1964: "Petra et la Nabatene." *Supplement au Dictionnaire de la Bible,* fasc. 39, cols. 886-1017.

Strabo, 1930: *Geography.* Tr. by H.L. Jones. Vol. VII. New York (Loeb Classical Library).

Syria: Publications of the Princeton University Archaeological Expeditions to Syria in 1904-1905 and 1909: H.C. Butler, *Architecture, Southern Syria,* 1919; E. Littmann, R. Magie and R. Stuart. *Greek and Latin Inscriptions, Southern Syria.* 1907-1921; and E. Littman, *Semitic Inscriptions. Nabataean Inscriptions from the Southern Hauran.* 1914, Leiden.

Thomsen, P., 1917: "Die römischen Meilensteine der Provinzen Syria, Arabia, und Palestina." *Zeitschrift des Deutschen Palästina-Vereins* 40:1-103.

Voûte, Pauline, 1971-1972: "Chronique des fouilles et prospections en Syrie de 1965 a 1970." _Anatolica_ 4:83-131.

Ward-Perkins, J.B., 1974: _Cities of Ancient Greece and Italy: Planning in Classical Antiquity._ New York.

Waddington, W.H., 1870: _Inscriptions grecques et latines de la Syrie: Recueillies et expliquées._ Paris: Librairie de Firmin Didot Freres, Fils, etc.

Winnett, F.V. and Reed, W., 1970: _Ancient Records from North Arabia._ London.

Wirth, Eugen, 1971: _Syrien._ _Eine geographische Landeskunde._ Darmstadt: Wissenschaftliche Buchgesellschaft.

Wycherley, R.E., 1962: _How the Greeks Built Cities._ New York: Doubleday & Co.

Zouhdi, B., 1977-1978: "Les monnaies de Bosra au Musée National de Damas." (In Arabic.) _Les annales archéologiques arabes syriennes, Revue d'archéologie et d'histoire_ XXVII-XXVIII, Damascus:85-109.

Plan 1. Streets and Lanes of Bosra eski Sham

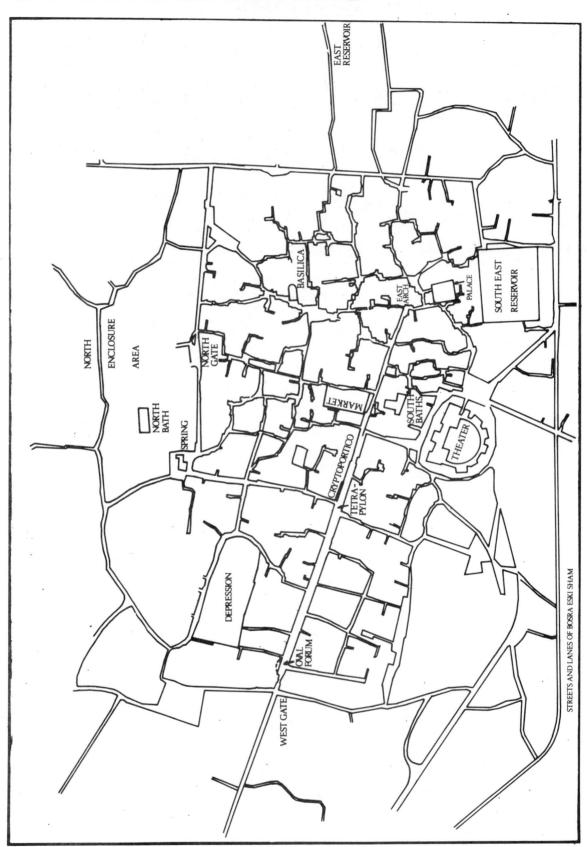

STREETS AND LANES OF BOSRA ESKI SHAM

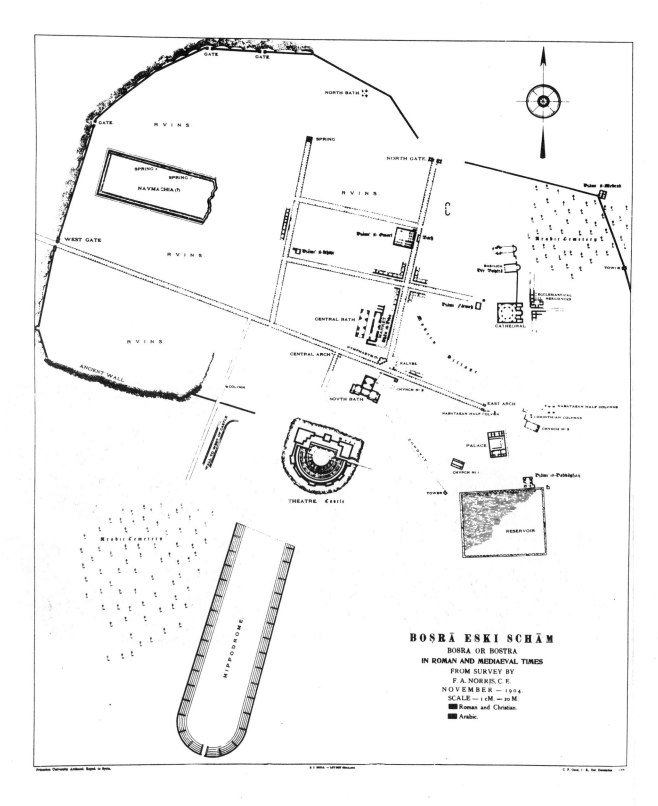

Plan 2. Princeton University Archaeological Expedition to Syria. From
Survey by F.A. Norris, Nov. 1904.

129

Figure 1.   Panorama of Busra eski Sham with Jebel Hawran in the
            background.

Figure 2. The East Arch

Figure 3. The Main Roman Street looking East. Roman shop fronts and Cryptoportico vents on north side of street.

D.S.Miller

Figure 4. The Roman Theater

F. E. Peters

Figure 5. The Southeast Reservoir

D.S.Miller

Figure 6. The Roman Street leading to the Theater.

D.S. Miller

Figure 7. Threshing Floor, Busra eski Sham

D.S. Miller

Roman Empire in Late Antiquity.

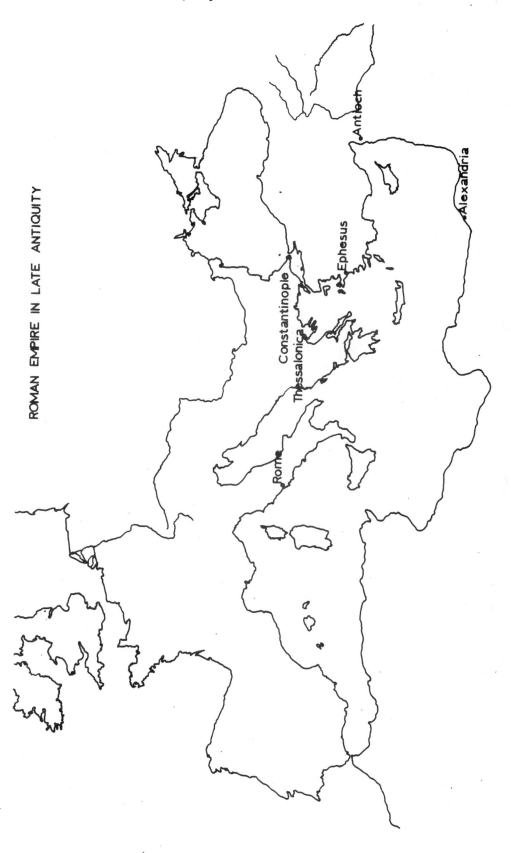

Urban Violence in Late Antiquity

Timothy E. Gregory

Violence takes its place, along with filth, disease, fire, and earthquake, as one of the less attractive aspects of urban society. Cities bring people close together and this both exacerbates social tensions and intensifies the effects of violence by involving large numbers of people simply by their proximity. Urban violence, therefore, must be considered when weighing the benefits and disadvantages of city life throughout history; moralists of every age have realized this and the contrast between the allegedly peaceful countryside and the violent city is a common topos in moralistic literature.[1]

Violence, of course, can be defined in a variety of ways and it may have a number of characteristics and manifestations. War and crime, for example, are both violent, and many observers regard certain economic and social structures as violent, and many observers regard certain economic and social structures as violent by their very nature. Likewise, both emotional and psychological violence exist, and many domestic situations are characterized by violence of one kind of another. Obviously, a study such as this cannot hope to deal with violence in all of its possible aspects, and I will here be concerned only with a reasonable well-defined phenomenon: rioting and popular demonstrations on the one hand and state or other institutional violence which was either the cause of the popular reaction or a response to it.

Thus, this study will focus almost exclusively on actions that affected the urban crowd.[2] It is appropriate, therefore, to begin with a definition of what is meant by the term "crowd." Actually, a negative delineation is much easier in the present instance: to say what is not, rather than what is, meant by the term. First, I will not assume that any specific social or economic make-up characterized the urban crowd of late antiquity. Obviously, because the poor will always have been relatively numerous in an ancient city, any given crowd is likely to have contained many poor individuals, but there is no reason to equate the crowd with the poor or with their particular interests, unless we have specific evidence to that effect.

The crowd, in fact, is likely to have been a continuously shifting entity whose composition changed with changing issues. Indeed, it is certain that on many occasions there was more than one specific "crowd," and crowd rivalry, whether it be called gang warfare or social strife, is one of the common characteristics of urban violence in many periods. I would argue that there was no such things as the crowd in an ancient city -- except in the sense that everyone other than the actual wielders of institutionalized power were potential members of the individual crowds that came into existence as a response to specific events. It is unreasonable, therefore, to expect fixed characteristics to represent typical crowd behavior or to expect the crowd regularly to take a particular social or political position (Seybarth 1963 and 1969).

Urban violence existed in all periods of antiquity,[3] but it appears to have been particularly prevalent during the later Roman empire (here defined ca. A.D. 300-600), when public order frequently broke down and events such as the Nika Revolt (A.D. 532) shook the very foundations of the state.[4] Lacking any statistical information, it is difficult to quantify something such as violence and to whether rioting and other acts of public disorder were actually more common in the years after Constantine than they had been before. The sources for this period were obviously very interested in such phenomena and they report them remarkably frequently, but this very interest is likely to have distorted the historical record and we cannot, in the end, be certain that public disorder was any more common in the fifth century than it had been in the second. The bloodshed, however, was certainly considerable: even allowing for certain exaggeration, it is significant that the sources list the number of dead in the Nika Revolt at 40,000 and those massacred in Thessalonica in 390 as 7,000, while a dispute between rival Christian groups in Constantinople led to such slaughter that the atrium of the church was filled with blood, which overflowed into the portico and out into the street.[5] Whether or not urban violence was unusually common under the later empire must remain a moot point; it was, however, a serious problem and one that appears to have been particularly characteristic of the age.

To the degree that they have considered the issue of urban violence (which is surprisingly little), most historians of the period have explained the phenomenon by some vague reference to the deterioration of the character of the people, the decline of civic patriotism, or simply the collapse of the empire. Paraphrasing ancient thought, for example, William Lecky viewed the people of the cities of late antiquity as "immersed in sensuality and the most frivolous pleasures." "(They) only emerged from their listlessness when some theological subtilty, or some rivalry in the chariot races, stimulated them into frantic riots" (1891:13). Observations such as these are hardly enlightening and they betray a condescention and general dislike of lower class urban-dwellers that may be understandable in the scholarship of the last century but is hardly acceptable in our own. Little better, however, are simplistic views of the crowd as using violence consciously to further some specific political, social, or economic program (Jarry 1960 and 1968). Observations such as these show simply that previous generations have not given urban violence the attention it deserves as a serious object of study.

Because urban violence was such a widespread phenomenon, the historian is first faced with the task of organizing his material into some managable scheme. One means of doing this is to group events together according to the motives assigned to the rioters in the primary sources; in other words, to examine specific events according to the type of violence they seem to represent. This has the obvious disadvantage of accepting at the outset the motivation assigned to the rioters by the sources, but this is something that can be questioned in the course of the study and it does have the advantage of separating out for individual attention events that seem to represent similar phenomena.

One of the most common of these classes of riots was connected with hunger or the critical shortage of foodstuffs and supplies (Kohns 1961; and MacMullen). Cities in all periods are by necessity dependent on regular and adequate provisioning from the countryside, and the situation in this regard was particularly serious given the very large population concentrations in many Roman cities and the still relatively primitive mechanisms for procurement and transport (Teall 1959; Kohns 1961:63-77; and Tegstrom 1974). The failure of a crop or the interference of pirates or unfavorable winds could cause sudden disaster.

The late Roman emperors realized these problems and the effect that shortages might have on public order and they took strong measures to minimize the difficulties (Jones 1940:251-258; and Jones 1964:687-705, 734-737). These included the virtual conscription of shipowners and haulers to bring foodstuffs to the urban centers, the fixing of prices on many staple commodities (and the free distribution of others), and the regularization and control of guilds (e.g. bakers) responsible for the preparation and sale of foodstuffs. Nevertheless, even such stringent measures as these did not always work and shortages frequently occurred, often accompanied by violence.

We are particularly well informed about such phenomena in Rome because the records of the prefects of the city, the official primarily responsible for the maintenance of public order, were used by a number of authors whose works have survived (Chastagnol 1960). One of the authors who apparently had access to these official records was Ammianus Marcellinus, a Greek from Syria who wrote in Rome toward the end of the fourth century (Syme 1968; Thompson 1969; and Blockby 1975). Ammianus had a critical view of the inhabitants of the Imperial City and he records a number of disturbances. He noted, for example, that in A.D. 359 storms and adverse winds blew the grain transport ships off their course and kept them in sheltered harbors while the food supplies in Rome diminished rapidly (19.10.1-4). The people of the city learned of this and, although the warehouses were apparently not completely empty, they feared famine as the worst of all ills (ultimum malorum omnium). The result was violence (viguae minacissimae plebis).

A certain Tertullus was perfect of the city at the time (Kohns 1961: 123-128) and Ammianus reports that riots (seditiones) earlier in his prefecture had completely shattered his resolve. As a result Tertullus dispaired of his own life and did nothing about the violence other than offer his young sons to the rioters. The prefect confronted the crowd and pointed out that his children would share the common fate in case of a famine. Further, he offered to turn his sons over to the fury of the mob. Remarkably, this action apparently calmed the people and they patiently awaited the future without further disturbance. In the event, the weather changed, providentially just as Tertullus was sacrificing in the temple of Castor and Pollux at Ostia, and the grain ships arrived, averting the famine.

This event reveals several interesting aspects of the hunger riot, or, in this case, the riot over anticipated hunger. First, we see how easily such riots might occur: here the violence apparently errupted

140

before the actual crisis became serious. Secondly, the violence was clearly directed against the prefect, as the person responsible either for the difficulty or its resolution (Mathews 1974:20). Ammianus objected that this was unreasonable since it was through no fault of Tertullus that the grain ships had not arrived. The Roman state, however, had clearly laid itself open to such difficulties by undertaking to insure the supply of the city in the first place: the state was responsible for arranging the arrival of the grain and its officials were to be blamed in case that system broke down. It is difficult to see what the state could have done differently, but it is notable that the government virtually asked for trouble in this way, although, of course, the emperor was careful that the difficulty fell on the head of the prefect and not on his own.

Further, it is significant that the prefect had virtually no force of his own with which to oppose the rioters: we do not even hear of the prefect's staff and he was apparently left to deal with the difficulty himself. We shall have occasion to mention this phenomenon later, but it is certainly no wonder that Tertullus despaired when faced with violence from the crowd. On another occasion a different prefect could do nothing other than flee the city and seek safety in his suburban estate (Ammianus 27.3.11-13).

Finally, we must seriously wonder why Tertullus' action was successful in calming the angry crowd. A cynical modern observer might suggest that this merely reflects the rioters' lack of a considered motive: just as the people unreasonably blamed the prefect for the expected shortage, so they ended their protest when he made an emotional appeal. Ammianus, in a rare statement of approval of the urban plebs, noted that they were by nature inclined toward mercy (clementiam suapte natura proclive) and that they were simply appeased by the prefect's action and the difficulty of his situation. Such an explanation is at first sight unlikely, given the obviously violent fear which the people felt toward the prospect of famine. A closer examination, however, suggests some support for Ammianus' view. The people, as we remember, held Tertullus personally responsible for the non-arrival of the grain shipment. By his action he not only accepted the responsibility but actually pledged hostages, as it were, for the proper fulfillment of that responsibility. This is not, of course, exactly what Ammianus says, but the effect of Tertullus' plea must have been much the same. The people had clearly come to look to the imperial officials for salvation from hunger and Tertullus at least took that responsibility seriously, even to the point of offering his sons as victims should the projected famine occur. Fortunately for him it did not and he never had to make good on his promise.

Hunger riots, of course, were not always so easily calmed, and much more serious violence frequently occurred. One such event took place in Antioch in 353. There was an expected shortage of grain and the Caesar Gallus, who happened to be present in the city, attempted to calm the people by telling them that no one would go hungry as long as Theophilus, the consular governor of Syria, did not wish it.[6] This, by the way, was another example of the emperor using a lower official as a popular scapegoat in a difficult situation. Gallus could not deal with the shortage, so he put the responsibility squarely on the local governor.

When the shortage was not resolved but grew worse, the crowd first attacked the pretentious (*ambitiosa*) house of Eubulus, a certain rich man, and set it on fire. We do not know what role, if any, Eubulus played in the shortage, but it is not unreasonable to suggest that he was a merchant or someone involved in the grain transport to the city; alternatively, the crowd may have singled him out simply because of his wealth and conspicuous consumption. The rioters then turned their attention to the governor, taking Gallus' statement as license to do whatever they wanted. Perhaps led by five men from the imperial arms works (Libanius *Or*.19.47; and Liebescheutz 1972:58), the angry crowd seized the unfortunate Theophilus and kicked and beat him; when he was half-dead they tore him limb from limb. With the focus of their anger removed, the demonstrators considered the enormity of their action and the revolt apparently collapsed. There was no imperial intervention and the difficulty was ultimately resolved only by the resumption of regular supply to the city. The horrible end of the governor, however, had an impact on contemporary writers, pagan and Christian alike, and most viewed it as a singular condemnation of the violence of the mob. Ammianus, for example, tells us that Theophilus was innocent of any wrong-doing but was simply caught in an impossible position between the desparation of the rioters and the majesty of the imperial throne.

In Rome again, the first prefecture of Orfitus (A.D. 353-355) witnessed serious riots (*seditiones graves*) over the scarcity of wine, a commodity perhaps less essential than bread but one obviously important enough to arouse the popular wrath (Ammianus 14.6.1). Similar disturbances occurred over the scarcity of wine during the prefecture of Leontius (A.D. 355-356). Leontius was, however, made of sterner stuff than most other imperial officials of the period and he took the situation resolutely in hand. Although deserted by his staff (*officium*), Leontius rode his carriage right into the midst of the angry crowd. Scanning the rioters, Leontius identified a certain prominent individual as the ringleader and had him arrested and immediately flogged in the sight of everyone. Cowed by this direct and forceful action, the crowd immediately dispersed and the revolt collapsed (Ammianus 15.7.1-10).[7]

Other examples of hunger (or supply) riots are easy to find, but perhaps these mentioned will suffice to characterize the type. Projected famine seems always to have been as great a danger as actual shortage, and the reaction of the crowd appears always to have been, first, a kind of vocal petition to the responsible authorities to remedy the situation; later, as the crisis became more imminent or more severe, the reaction frequently turned vindictive and personal, usually directed at the imperial official responsible for the supply of foodstuffs to the city, but occasionally involving rich urban-dwellers, whose consumption and way of life might have been expected to excite the envy and wrath of poorer people in a time of economic crisis. Only rarely is there evidence of the violent suppression of a hunger riot. Either the crisis was resolved by the arrival of the expected foodstuffs or the riot died away as the result of the obvious inability of the crowd to secure its demands by violent means. A riot could force officials to lower prices or look harder for scarce supplies, but it obviously could not hasten the arrival of weather-delayed ships or completely counter the effects of a poor harvest.

Riots in the hippodrome make up a special class of disturbance that was particularly characteristic of the late Roman city (Cameron 1973 and 1976). The hippodrome and the theatre were particularly common places for rioting both because of the passions which the spectacles excited and because the emperor and his officials frequently used these sites as a place to confront the crowd or to make, sometimes unpopular, announcements and proclamations (MacMullen 1966:178-179; and Cameron 1976:161-183). In the present instance one can distinguish among these kinds of riots, and here I would like to examine those riots which arose specifically from the sporting aspect of the hippodrome rather than its position as a political forum; more clearly political riots will be considered in a later section.

Chariot racing was unquestionably the most popular pasttime in a late Roman city, "the favorite among all amusements, from sunrise until evening, in sunshine and in rain. (The people) stand open-mouthed, examining minutely the good points or the defects of the charioteers and their horses. And it is quite a thing to see an innumerable crowd of people, their mind filled with a kind of ardor, hanging on the outcome of the chariot races" (Ammianus 14.6.25-26). Everyone seems to have had a favorite chariotter, and these were adored and pampered like professional football players or rock music stars of today. Wagers were high and much emotion was spent over the outcome of individual races; rival charioteers were frequently accused of using poison or even magic to assure their victory. In such a highly charged situation it is not surprising that tempers often rose and the result was violence.

Frequently the direct cause of the rioting was the arrest of a popular chariotter. Such an incident took place during the prefecture of Leontius, already mentioned above. Leontius had arrested a certain Philoromus, a charioteer, and he was the people's darling (proprium pignus). "All of the people" (plebs omnis) rose to defend Philoromus and they set upon Leontius, hoping to intimidate him and force him to release the charioteer (Ammiamus 15.7.2). Leontius, however, as we have seen, was a formidable opponent. He sent his police agents (apparitores) among the crowd and had some of them summarily tortured and exiled -- the sources do not say whether these were the ringleaders or simply rioters seized at random. This effectively put down the revolt, although the wine riot mentioned above followed only a few days later. Probably the two difficulties were closely connected, and dissatisfaction over the affair of the charioteer must certainly have contributed to the second outbreak of violence.

The famous Nika Revolt of A.D. 532 began in a similar way, when a vocal crowd demanded the release of condemned faction members (Stein 1949:2, 449-456). The circus factions were originally companies which supplied the equipment and the charioteers for the celebration of the games in Rome and throughout the empire (Cameron 1976:5-23). In late of people associated themselves with one another of the colors, primarily the Blues and the Greens. From the fifth century onward the factions were intimately connected with much of the violence in the cities, and until quite recently this was thought to represent the expression of social, religious, or economic unrest (Manojlovic 1936; Jarry 1968; and Cameron 1976:74-153). Thus, the factions were seen almost like political parties representing certain ideological positions and fighting for them with all the force at their disposal: the Greens were said to be the poorer elements of society, generally "democratic," eastern in orientation, and Monphsite in religious sentiment, while the Blues were wealthier, aristocratic or monarchist, oriented toward the West, and orthodox in their religious beliefs. Work by Alan Cameron, however, has put all this in a very different light. One may perhaps disagree with some of the details of his studies, but the general conclusions remain sound: the circus factions were what they appear to have been, nuclear sporting clubs which were used by the imperial court for the organization of ceremonial. Faction violence, then, was primarily hooliganism, carried out particularly by the young devotees of the sport. Most simply, faction riots were the escalation of circus rivalry and the shift of scene from hippodrome to the streets of the cities.

A case in point is a riot of this kind that took place in Constantinople in A.D. 560. Our informant is the chronicler Malalas, who took a particularly keen interest in factional violence:

> After the enjoyment of the hippodrome, the Greens were
> withdrawing by the Stoa of Moschianos with a watch
> posted. Suddenly the Greens were insulted by some
> people from the so-called Palace of Appion. The Blues
> set upon the Greens and there was an engagement in
> various places. Passing from Sykai the Blues began
> to set fires and to burn the seaside warehouses. If
> someone attempted to put the fire out he was shot by
> the Blues, for they had various exchanges with the
> workers. Locked in battle, they burned the so-called
> Palace of Andrew in the Neorion. Similarly they fell
> upon the Mese (the central street) and from there they
> set fire to the so-called Palace of Barsumios, which
> was built while he held the office of prefect. And
> the burning continued up to the Bronze Tetrapylon and
> the stoa opposite it. The battle lasted two days.
> Marinos, the Count of the Excubitors, and Justin, the
> most honorable Kuropalatis, came out with a considerable
> military force and they barely put down the two factions
> (Malalas 490-491).[8]

What took place is easily explained. The occasion was the celebration of the Genethliaka, games held every May to celebrate the founding of the city of Constantinople.[9] The Greens left the hippodrome, either in a spirit of exhultation after impressive victories or despondent after defeat, and the Blues set upon them. The result was a general rampage of apparently wanton destruction in which the Blues took the lead. The violence began as a continuation of the rivalry in the hippodrome, but this was soon forgotten and the factions began to burn whole areas of the city. There is no evidence that they were selective in their destruction but that all parties suffered alike. Cameron is surely correct in calling this hooliganism and drawing the closest parallel with the aftermath of modern football rivalries where whole business districts are occasionally destroyed by over-enthusiastic fans. This, of course, is not to say that hippodrome violence was never connected with political or religious issues: the Nika Revolt and the burning of a synagogue by the Athiochene factions in 507 are cases in point. But the connection appears always to have been post facto; the violence began as simple hippodrome mania or support for individuals, later escalated as a result of pre-existing hatreds or the exploitation of ambitious leaders.

We come now to political violence and find, surprisingly, that this was actually rather rare in the later empire, despite the supposed oppression that characterized the period. If the urban dwellers of late antiquity felt themselves politically oppressed they did not apparently express that feeling by rioting. One of the few examples of an apparently political riot was the famous "revolt of the statues" in Antioch in 387. This was instigated by the announcement of an imperial edict raising taxes.[10] Members of the city council assembled in front of the governor's palace and asked for a reduction of the tax. A crowd gathered and, led by members of the theatre claque, they began to complain about government exactions. Receiving no satisfaction from the governor, the people went off to find Flavian, the bishop of the city, but he was away so they returned to the governor's palace. There the crowd pulled down the painted pictures and the bronze statues of the imperial family and dragged them through the streets (Libanius Or.22.7). These images were official representations of the imperial presence and a law had recently decreed that those seeking asylum could do so at such an imperial image: desecration of the images was an act of treason and an open indication of rebellion. The crowd then vented its anger by burning the house of a prominent citizen. Only then did a force of local police (toxotai) arrive and dispersed the crowd. Shortly afterwards an imperial general (the comes Orientis) appeared in Antioch and arrested those accused of arson, but the riot had ended and people anxiously awaited the reaction of the emporor to the violence.

We are fairly well informed about this event, for it was the subject of several orations written by Libanius and John Chrysostom, both of whom were eye-witnesses. Apparently the theatre claque was largely responsible for the organization and direction of the violence and both Libanius and Chrysostom claim that outside troublemakers stirred up the crowd. It is interesting that, although the crowd had a fairly specific demand, this demand was apparently quickly forgotten in the rapid escalation of the violence. As a result the revolt ceased to be a demand for redress and became a futile and frustrated protest. On a positive note, however, the emperor sent imperial commissioners to investigate the incident. They ordered some punishment, but Theodosius himself ultimately pardoned the city, which might have suffered a much worse fate.

This is emphasized with singular clarity by a series of events that happened shortly thereafter in Thessalonica. The difficulty began in the hippodrome, as a certain charioteer had been arrested for propositioning Butheric, an important military commander, perhaps the magister militum per Illyricum. At a subsequent celebration of games in the hippodrome that people called out for the release of the charioteer and when this was refused they rose up and killed Butheric.[11] Theodosius was then resident in Milan and when he learned of the deed, he determined to make an example of the people of Thessalonica. Accordingly, he ordered for more games to be held and when all the people were assembled in the hippodrome he ordered soldiers to attack them, and according to one source some seven thousand people were slain. According to another source the massacre was more systematic and therefore all the more hideous, since those to be killed were apparently selected in some way and then notified. Strangers who had not been in the city at the time of the murder of Butheric were included, and selfless attempts of fathers to spare their sons and slaves their masters were met with cold steel. This, of course, is the action for which Ambrose, bishop of Milan, excommunicated Theodosius and made him do proper penance before he would allow him to enter the church (Palanque 1933:227-244).

At first sight this riot and the subsequent massacre look like simple hippodrome violence, but they may also be considered an example of something with political consequences. The riot occurred in A.D. 390 and the victim was Butheric, certainly a Goth who held a very high post in the imperial military service. It was just at this time that anti-Germanic feeling was beginning to rise in the East, a movement that was to find a spokesman in Synesius and, even more to the point, be violently actualized in the massacre of Gainas and his Germanic soldiers in Constantinople in A.D. 400.[12] There is no certain evidence to support this hypothesis, and there can be no question but that the violence began simply as the sources describe it, as a response to action taken against a popular charioteer. But that Butheric was a German must not have made him especially welcome in Thessalonica, a city whose region had been particularly disturbed since the Gothic victory at the Battle of Adrianople in 378. What Butheric was doing in the city is another matter of interest, since it was normally not imperial policy to station troops in urban centers.

The massacre in Thessalonica took place shortly after the usurpation of Eugenius when Theodosius had moved large numbers of soldiers from East to West, so Butheric might have been either on his way back to Italy or he might have been in Thessalonica especially to ensure the loyalty of that important city. In either case, Theodosius was particularly angry at the murder of his lieutenant, coming as it did on the heels of the riot in Antioch and the revolt in Italy. He determined to make a signal point about the loyalty of the populace to imperial rule and his point was certainly felt. Later historical tradition has reasonably focused on the confrontation between Ambrose and the emperor and the inability of the latter to resist the moral authority of the church. This may well have been one of the lessons of the massacre, but the other was certainly not lost on contemporaries, not least the inhabitants of Thessalonica: when the emperor intervened directly with

146

force the effect was terrible and overwhelming. The terror that struck the people of Antioch after the riot of the statues is an indication that the power of the state was understood, at least in some circles. The emperor rarely intervened decisively to put down an insurrection; this was normally left to subordinates with insufficient military force. But when he did act the result was rarely in doubt and the bloodshed frequently staggering.

A final category of violence that was common in the cities of late antiquity was motivated by religious differences. This should not be surprising since religion was one of the most important concerns of the age, and toleration was normally not seen as a virtue: to allow one's religious opponent freedom of worship meant only his damnation and the endangering of one's own salvation. Religious violence broke out frequently, but it will be useful to make a distinction between conflict between pagans and Christians and that between rival Christian groups.

Christianity ultimately triumphed in the struggle with paganism and most of our information about the accompanying violence not only comes from Christian writers but shows the Christians as victors.[13] This is not to say that pagans did not sometimes manage successful attacks on their Christian enemies, but that the contest was unevenly matched even from an early date. Toward the end of the fourth century the violence intensified between pagans and Christians and many pagan temples were destroyed. The emperors only rarely ordered the destruction of pagan shrines, but a kind of guerilla warfare was frequently carried out by local bishops and monks, especially in areas outside the great urban centers of the empire. Many Christians thought that the destruction of the temples was the most effective way to bring about the conversion of pagans to the new religion.[14]

One of the most zealous in this undertaking was Theophilus, the powerful bishop of Alexandria, and perhaps the most famous confrontation took place over the temple of Serapis in that city.[15] The difficulty began in A.D. 391 when Theophilus, with the expressed authority of the emperor, deconsecrated the temple of Dionysus and turned it into a church. Not content with this, Theophilus made a public spectacle of cult objects - particularly phallic representations -- hoping to bring discredit on the pagan practices which made use of such articles. The pagans were outraged by this insult and they attacked the Christians, killing some and wounding others. They then seized the great temple of Serapis and converted it into a fortress from which they sallied forth and captured unfortunate Christians. These they forced to sacrifice under torture; those who refused were crucified or otherwise cruelly put to death.

The insurrection continued for some time without any official intervention. Finally, the military commander Romanus and the praefectus Augustalis (the governor of Egypt) Evagrius appeared on the scene and exhorted the pagans to lay down their weapons and surrender the Serapeum. As might be expected, this appeal had no effect and the officials could do no more than to send off a report to the emperor. Meanwhile, the pagans shut up inside the temple were dismayed by the ability of the Christians to destroy the cult statues without suffering

147

any apparent harm: this was certainly a strong argument in the Christians' favor. This was countered by the philosopher Olympius[16] who was among the defenders of the Serapeum. He assured the pagans that they should pay no attention to the destruction of the images since these were merely corruptable reflections of the gods, whose real powers (dynameis) had flown off to heaven. Olympius was apparently successful in his argument, and the pagan resistance remained firm, but the conviction of the pagans may have been shaken.

This disturbance took place the year after the massacre in Thessalonica and Theodosius hesitated to use the same kind of force again. Instead, he ordered the demolition of the temples of Alexandria as responsible for the riots in the first place. He further declared that those Christians killed by the pagans should be regarded as martyrs for their faith and their murderers pardoned, since they had helped them win the crown of immortality. Sozomen, our main informant for this event, says that the emperor pardoned the pagans in hopes that this would induce them to become Christians, but it is more likely that he hoped that such action would help put an end to the insurrection by causing the pagans to desert the Serapeum. We have no way of knowing what Romanus and Evagrius wrote in their official report to the emperor, but they may have mentioned the growing disillusionment of the pagans and Theodosius perhaps hoped to capitalize on that.

If this was the emperor's intent, events proved him right. When the edict was read aloud in public the Christians gave a shout of joy which, Sozomen says, so frightened the pagans that they immediately fled from the temple, which was quickly seized by their opponents and converted into a church. The discomfiture of the pagans may have been furthered by a strange event, which Sozomen reports only as hearsay: on the night preceding the end of the revolt Olympius supposedly heard the singing of an alleluia in the temple, signalling its soon-to-be-realized conversion into a church. Whether or not this event actually took place, it probably represents the uneasiness of the pagans shut up in the temple and their fear of impending doom. The emperor's decision to pardon the murderers must have seemed like an unexpected opportunity to put an end to their own difficulties.

Noteworthy in this riot was the general inability of the government to maintain order. Imperial officials did not step in until the insurrection was well under way and many lives had already been lost. Then, when they did intervene, their actions were ineffective and they could do no more than inform the emperor about the course of events. Even Theodosius himself found it more prudent to act in a conciliatory way, and the rebellion collapsed more on its own accord than through its suppression by the state. Indeed, the publication of the emperor's blanket pardon was probably the largest single factor in ending the difficulty.

Alexandria was notorious in antiquity for the violence of its inhabitants, and another violent conflict involving religious differences took place during the episcopacy of Cyril, Theophilus' nephew and his successor as bishop of Alexandria. The original cause of the difficulty was the enmity between Cyril and the Augustal prefect

Orestes, who resented the growing power of the bishop and his encroachment on governmental prerogatives (Socrates 7.15; and Phitostorgius 8.9). One day Orestes was speaking in the theatre, which was the normal place for proclamations and the interchange between government and the people and, according to our Christian sources, a particularly favorite place of the Alexandrian Jews. At one point a well-known supporter of Cyril appeared and a cry went out that he had come to stir up trouble among the Jews. Ready to believe the worst about Cyril, Orestes had the man seized and beaten.

Cyril blamed the Jews for this outrage and warned them of severe repercussions should any repetition occur. The Jews then apparently formed a plot whereby they cried out that there was a fire in one of the churches and, when the Christians ran to put it out, they set upon them and slit their throats. Cyril needed no further excuse and he brought together a great crowd of people, took possession of the synagogues, and drove the Jews from the city, allowing his followers free right to plunder their goods. Orestes was powerless to intervene in either of these incidents and he could do nothing more than write a letter of complaint to the emperor.

In the end the people of Alexandria grew weary of the hostility between their bishop and the prefect and they importuned Cyril to make his peace with Orestes. This the bishop was willing to do, not surprisingly, since he had gotten what he wanted from the situation, but Orestes refused to be reconciled. The result was nearly disastrous for the prefect since Cyril summoned the monks from the Nitrian desert to his defense. Such bands of monks, hardened by their austere life and driven to a nearly fanatic zeal by their conviction of the truth, were the very mainstay of Christian violence in this period, and their use by unscrupulous bishops became a threat to the very church itself until it was limited by order of the Council of Chalcedon in 451 (Bacht 1953; and Dragron 1970). Five hundred of these monks left their desert retreats and flocked to Alexandria to support the bishop. They found the prefect in the streets and they insulted him, calling him a sacrificer and a pagan: the obvious point was that anyone who opposed the bishop of Alexandria must have been a pagan. Orestes replied that he was a good Christian and had been baptized by the bishop of Constantinople. This apparently did not carry much weight with the Egyptian clergy, which had for some time regarded their Constantinopolitan counterparts with some suspicion, and the monks began to throw stones at the prefect; one of them hit Orestes in the head, seriously wounding him. Instead of defending the prefect, most of his staff withdrew in fear of sharing a similar fate, and the people of Alexandria had to intervene to save the luckless official's life. Members of the crowd seized the monk who had wounded Orestes and he was tortured and later died, giving Cyril the opportunity to try to have him regarded as a martyr.

The difficulties, however, were by no means over and the continuation of the violence involved the famous female pagan philosopher Hypatia, a figure who has enjoyed much sympathy in succeeding generations (Rist 1965; and Suda 4.644-646). Hypatia was the daughter of the mathematician Theon and, although a woman, she became head of the Platonic Academy in Alexandria. She was outstanding as a philosopher and counted Synesios among her students. Hypatia was apparently beautiful but her modesty and unreproachable character allowed her to keep company openly with men without the least trace of scandal, something that was unusual in all periods of the ancient world.

The prefect Orestes was particularly fond of Hypatia's company and they frequently met for conversation. This gave some people the idea that Hypatia's influence lay behind the prefect's enmity toward Cyril: if Orestes was himself a Christian, some other sinister influence must have been responsible for his opposition to the bishop. Accordingly, a plot was formed, led by a certain Peter the Reader; Cyril himself was probably ignorant of their plans, although his own violent activities must certainly have formed a precedent for the conspirators' actions. The group found Hypatia in the streets of Alexandria and seizing her they took her to the Caesarian church. There they stripped her and stabbed and scraped her skin until she was dead; the perpetrators then tore the body limb from limb and burned it. As the contemporary church historian Socrates said, this was "a particular crime which left a foul stain on Cyril and his church," (7.15) and which has given to this day an unfortunate reputation to the Christian attempt to convert the pagans.

These events, a mere twenty-five years after the seizure of the Serapeum, show how thoroughly Christian Alexandria had become and how the bishop was now clearly the most important authority, rivalling and generally outstripping the power of the Augustal prefect. The bishop used that authority (among other things) to overwhelm all opposition, whether pagan, Jewish, or even Christian. Paganism had obviously become a dangerous persuasion and an erudite pagan philosopher was as anachronistic -- and as dangerous as a functioning pagan temple. The rhetoric of the age was perhaps simplistic and occasionally inflamatory in nature, and people who believe firmly in the absolute correctness of their position do not always act with moderation or circumspection. This is naturally not to condone the barbarous action of the mob led by Peter the Reader, but it is perhaps to put it in the proper historical context. Further, when the bishop of Alexandria openly used violence in his own behalf, it is not surprising that other people would do so as well.

If Christians were willing to use violence against pagans, it is no wonder that they began to use it against other Christians who differed in matters of belief or practice (Brown, 1963 and 1964; Joannou 1972; and Gregory 1979). For if a pagan might be brought to see the error of his ways, if necessary through violence, how much more might the same means be used with Christians who had experienced divine truth but turned against it? In most cases violence against Christian dissidents was controlled by the government, but occasionally it found its way into the streets of the great cities of the empire in much the same way as we have discussed above. Some of the great Christian riots, like those involving paganism, took place in Alexandria: witness the fate of the Arian bishop George in the fourth century and his unfortunate successor Proterius in the fifth century, both of them brutally murdered by the multitudes they were supposed to govern (Socrates 5.7; and Evagrius

2.8). But similar violence errupted periodically in all the great cities of the empire (Gregory 1979).

On some occasions the issue was essentially administrative or personal (as opposed to theological): often a dispute over the removal of a popular bishop. Perhaps the most famous case of this kind was the deposition of John Chrysostom in Constantinople in A.D. 403.[17] Chrysostom, a tremendously popular preacher from Antioch, earned for himself important enemies because of his criticism of the rich and powerful, including the empress Eudocia. Among his enemies, interestingly enough, was Theophilus of Alexandria, who did not hesitate to intervene directly in the affairs of Constantinople. John was accused of consorting with heretics and of improper actions as bishop and, when he did not answer the summons of a local council, he was deposed and sent into exile.

John's enemies, however, had failed to take account of his popularity with the people of Constantinople and they were caught by surprise at the massive popular outcry:

> When he had gone into exile, the faithful rose in violent
> revolt. And they heaped abuse on the emperor, the synod,
> and especially on Theophilus and Severianus, whom they re-
> garded as the instigators of the plot (Socrates 6.16).

This Severianus, bishop of Gabala in Syria, happened to be giving a sermon when the disturbance broke out. He took the occasion to praise the sentence against John, saying that at least he had been guilty of the sin of pride. This set off the final episode. In the account of Sozomen:

> These words angered the people and the disturbance became
> completely uncontrollable. They could not be kept quiet
> in the churches and market places, and they carried their
> lamentation and complaint for the return of John even to
> the palace of the emperor (Sozomen 8.18).

The petitions of the people had their effect and the emperor (or the empress, the sources are unclear) immediately ordered the recall of the popular bishop. Chrysostom arrived in Constantinople some time later and the sea was filled with small boats carrying the faithful who had come to welcome their bishop back to his city. Despite Chrysostom's wish to wait until the sentence against him had been lifted, the populace forced him to enter the city and to resume his episocapacy.

As events were to show, Chrysostom's enemies had not exhausted their machinations and they began planning once again for the bishop's downfall. This time they took account of popular feeling and acted to neutralize it, in part by acting covertly and in part by overwhelming the populace with military force. In A.D. 404 Chrysostom was deposed a second time and he ultimately died in exile. Nevertheless, the popular outcry was again considerable and in the confusion following the second exile the great Constantinian church of Aghia Sophia, the cathedral of the city, was devoured by fire, along with a substantial part of the capital. Despite official repression, most of John's followers remained faithful to him and refused to hold communion with his successors. This became such a scandal that John's memory was ultimately restored, his remains brought back to Constantinople, and a popular festival initiated in his honor.[18]

The violence surrounding the deposition of John Chrysostom was caused exclusively by personal and administrative difficulties; John's enemies attempted to introduce doctrinal questions but they were unsuccessful in this and they themselves ultimately abandoned the issue. Other difficulties among Christian groups were, by contrast, more clearly doctrinal in origin. One of these events took place in Ephesus, the metropolitan city of Asia, at the time of the so-called Robber Synod in A.D. 449 (Gregory 1979:143-161). The dispute concerned the theological position of Flavian, the bishop of Constantinople, and his opponent Dioscorus, the bishop of Alexandria (the successor of Cyril). Flavian had held a local council in Constantinople in 448 and this condemned the teachings of Eutyches, a volitile and outspoken monastic leader. Eutyches gained the support of Dioscorus, and a general council was called to judge the issue.

Ecclesiastical councils were important events, and bishops arrived for the deliberations armed not only with their theological arguments, but frequently with less subtle means of persuasion. Dioscorus, in fact, appeared at Ephesus at the head of a veritable army, including soldiers (some of them put at his disposal by the emperor), Egyptian monks, and the notorious parabalani, Egyptian monastic hospital attendants whose job among the sick and dying made them absolutely fearless and thus a formidable weapon in a violent confrontation.

When they arrived in Ephesus, the followers of Dioscorus first went to the residence of Stephen, bishop of the city, and secured his support by the application of suitable intimidation. In the words of Stephen:

> Elpidius and Eulogius, soldiers, and the monks of Eutyches --
> about three hundred in number -- came upon me in the episcopal
> residence. And they were about to kill me . . . and thus
> everything happened through force and necessity.[19]

But the real confrontation came during the council itself, which was presided over by Dioscorus himself. After engineering the reversal of the council of Constantinople the year before and the restoration of Eutyches, Dioscorus surprised the assembled bishops by calling for the deposition of Flavian. The emissaries of Pope Leo forgot their need for a Greek translator and shouted out "contradicitur." Other bishops also protested this summary action in strong words. This gave Dioscorus the opportunity he wanted. In the words of an eyewitness, the bishop of Alexandria

> rose from his throne and, standing on his footstool, said,
> "Do you threaten me with violence? Bring in the counts."[20]

Soldiers rushed into the church and overawed all opposition, "and thus fearing we all signed." Along with the soldiers were monks, including the Egyptian _parabalani_ and the followers of Barsumas, a Syrian archimandrite famous for his opposition to pagans and Jews and popularly believed to have "destroyed all Syria." In addition, the sources mention the people of Ephesus, won largely over to the side of Dioscorus, who thronged into the conciliar church to add their weight to the confrontation.

Several of the bishops were injured in the disturbance and Flavian was among them. He was deposed as a result of this terrorism and within a few days he died, perhaps as a result of the treatment he had received at the council. And the violence did not end there but continued while any supporters of the deposed bishop were still at large. Monks and members of the crowd instituted a virtual reign of terror:

> And they were carrying off men, some from the ships, some from the streets and houses, and others while they were praying from the churches. They pursued those who fled. And all zeal they sought out and dug up those who were hiding in caves and in holes in the earth. And it was a matter of great fear and danger for a man to speak with the adherents of Flavian on account of those who were dwelling in the neighbor-hood and keeping watch as spies to see who entered unto them (Nestorius 352-353).

It is doubtful that much of this violence was spontaneous; Dioscorus and his supporters were clearly manipulating the entire scene.

The theological differences between Flavian and Dioscorus were serious, but to most modern non-specialists the points at issue are difficult to distinguish.[21] How much of the theological debate did the ordinary urban-dweller actually understand -- for example, the distinction between the prosopic and the hypostatic union in the person of Christ? Obviously we cannot say, but in the end it probably didn't matter what was actually understood, as long as the individual realized that he had to make a choice and that his salvation ultimately depended on that choice.

Another example of how strongly theological positions were held is the riot that followed the additions to the Trisagion proposed by the emperor Anastasius in Constantinople in A.D. 512 (Charamis 1974:78-79; Malalas 406-407; and Evagrius 3.44). The issue was theological but it involved liturgical change, directly affecting the way people communicated with God. The Trisagion itself was a very popular petition: "Holy God, Holy Strong One, Holy Immortal One, Have mercy on us." Anastasius added to this prayer the formula, "Who was crucified for us." The importance of this addition was that it attributed the human sufferings of Christ to God himself, something which Anastasius (and the Monophysites) accepted, but which the (mainly Chalcedonian) people of Constantinople strongly rejected. The result was predictable:

> The people were uncontrollably violent and people of rank and station were seriously endangered, and many of the important parts of the city were set on fire. The people found in the house of Marinus the Syrian, a monk from the

country. They cut off his head, alleging that the clause had been added at his instigation, and having fixed it on a pole they jeeringly exclaimed: "See the plotter against the Trinity" (Evagrius 3.44).

The church historian Evagrius, our principal informant, says that all of Constantinople was filled with tumult and there was no means to control it. Anastasius, realizing that his policy was the cause of the difficulty, appeared in the hippodrome, dressed poorly and without his crown. He announced that he was ready to resign as emperor, but reminded the assembled crowd that monarchy was the only possible form of government and that someone would have to succeed him in any case. Surprisingly, "as by some divine impulse," the mood of the populace was changed and the revolt collapsed.

This is the simple explanation of Evagrius, but the real reason for the end of the disturbance was apparently that the crowd got its way. Whether immediately or shortly thereafter the addition to the Trisagion was abandoned, representing another significant case where the popular will ultimately prevailed. The emperor was clearly responsible for the liturgical change and he couldn't shift the blame to a subordinate official. As in the case of John Chrysostom (but this time over a theological issue), the emperor found it difficult, even impossible, to oppose firmly held popular opinion.[22]

From the examination of these few examples it should be possible to make some observations about the nature of violence in the cities of late antiquity. In the first place, it is clear that the violence was not totally wanton or senseless but that, even in the most questionable cases, some grievance or problem actually set off the disturbance. When frustrated, excited, fearful, or angry, the late Roman urban dweller, like his counterpart in most ages, was likely to resort to violence. The specific issues that led to the violence, however, are those that dominated the period, and of these religion was certainly the most important. Probably second to this came the excitement of the hippodrome, with all the passion that the races unleashed, while hunger riots were undoubtedly rarer, although particularly serious since the state could often do little to appease the rioters' demands. Governmental collapse, financial oppression, and the barbarian invasions were some of the most pressing concerns of late antiquity, but these seemed to have played little role in urban violence, which was only rarely concerned with political issues. Riots occasionally touched on these themes, but this was normally only on a secondary level, frequently after some more pressing issue -- for example, the release of prisoners -- set the violence in motion.

Like similar phenomena elsewhere, urban riots in late antiquity assumed rather than denied the existing social structure: they were certainly not designed to overthrow the system, and more often than not they were directed at minor officials while leaving the emperor unassailed. The reason for this was probably the generally integrated nature of late Roman society and the crowd's determination to secure a single concession from the government. The rioters were not concerned to overthrow the state but to get a governor to lower prices, release an imprisoned charioteer, or support a popular bishop.

Overall, the success of the rioters appears to have been directly related to the nature of the issue: when the concern was ideological and popular opinion was clearly fixed, the government could do very little and the rioters got what they wanted remarkably frequently. When the issue was more practical and limited, the government was more likely to hold out and await the collapse of the movement, which always seems to have come soon enough.

Finally, it is necessary to say a word about the apparent hesitation of the government to intervene in a disturbance until the very last moment. In part this was undoubtedly a matter of policy, but it was also because the institutional structure of the state was not designed for the maintenance of public order. The cities had virtually no policy force and responsible officials had to face the angry crowd unarmed and alone. The only resort was the army, which was almost never stationed in or near the great cities and thus required considerable time for its deployment. Further, the army was a weapon which could not be used with any delicacy or finesse, and military intervention generally led to massive bloodshed. Thus, there appears to have been little in the way of middle-range response and this must have been one of the reasons for the frequency of urban violence and the willingness of the state to allow riots to run their course.

1. See, for example, the thoughtful comments by Highet 1954:65-68.

2. See the important definitions and caveats of Rude 1959, 1961, and compare with the older views of, for example, Le Bon 1909.

3. For violence in earlier Roman history see Heaton 1939, Brunt 1966, Lintott 1968, Yavetz 1969, and Africa 1971.

4. For violence in the later empire see Martindale 1960, Kohns 1961, and MacMullen 1966.

5. The Nika Revolt and violence in Thessaloniki are discussed below; for the incident in Constantinople, Socrates 2.38.

6. See Gregory Nazianzus *Vita Basilii* 1.57, Ammianus 14.7.5-6, Libanius *Oratio* 19.47-49, Julian *Misopogon* 363C, 370C, and Downey 1961:366.

7. Leontius was also responsible for the arrest of the popular bishop Liberius and his exile from Rome.

8. For the identification of the places mentioned see Janin 1964.

9. See the interesting comments of Cameron 1976:277.

10. See Libanius *Orationes* 19-23, John Chrysostom *Homiliae de statuis ad populum Antiochenum*, Browning 1952, and Downey 1961:426-433.

11. See Sozomen 7.25, Rufinus 11.18, Paulinus *vita Ambrosii* 24, Theodoret 5.17.

12. See Socrates 5.6, Sozomen 8.7, Zosimus 5.12-18, cf. Cameron 1970: 124-155.

13. For various aspects of this struggle see Momigliano 1963.

14. For a specific example of this see Sozomen 8.15.

15. See Sozomen 7.15. Socrates 5.16-17, has a slightly different account.

16. For philosophers similar to Olympius see Eunapius' *Lives of the Philosophers* and the mention of the destruction of the Serapeum, 420-422.

17. For a more detailed examination of these events see Gregory 1979: 41-79.

18. Socrates 7.25, 7.45. A remarkably similar case of the removal of a popular bishop has recently been in the news from Crete, where Bishop Irenaeus returned to Crete for a visit, however, he was taken by force by enthusiastic supporters who declared that they would go

to any length to keep him on the island. Thousands of Cretans went on strike and many left their homes to maintain a vigil in front of Irenaeus' residence. Throughout the confrontation the Cretans made clear their willingness to resort to violence. Sakellariou 1980.

19. See Acta Conciliorum Oecumenicorum II.i.1, p. 75.

20. See Acta Conciliorum Oecumenicorum II.i.1, p. 180.

21. See, for example, Anastos 1962.

22. This study has not concerned itself with the interesting but very different phenomenon of rural violence in the West during late antiquity. On this see Frend 1952 and Liebescheutz 1963.

Bibliography

Primary Sources

Acta Conciliorum Cocumunicorum, 1914-1974: Ed. Eduard Schwartz. Berlin.

Armianus Marcellinus, 1978: (1935-39) *Res Gestae*. Ed. Wolfgang Seyfarth, 2 vols. Trans. J.C. Rolfe, 3 vols. London, 1935-39.

John Chrysostom *Homiliae de Statuis ad populum Antiochenum*. Migne,
Patriologia graeca 49, 15-222.

Eunapius, 1922: *Lives of the Philosophers and Sophists*. Ed. W.C.
Wright. London.

Evagrius, 1964: *Historia ecclesiastica*. Ed. J. Bidez and L.
Parmentier. London.

Gregory of Nazianzus *Vita S. Basilii*. Migne, *Patrologia graeca* 35-37.

Julian, 1932-64: *Oeuvres completes*. Ed. J. Bidez, G. Rochefort, and C.
Lacombrade, 4 vols. Paris.

Libanius, 1903-1922: *Opera*. Ed. R. Roerster, 12 vols. Leipzig.

Malalas, 1831: *Chronographia*. Ed. L. Dindorf. Bonn.

Nestorius, 1925: *The Bazaar of Herakleides*. Ed. and trans. C.R. Driver
and Leonard Hodgson. Oxford.

Paulinus of Milan *Vita S. Ambrosii*. Migne, *Patriologia latina* 14, 27-46.

Philostorgius, 1972: *Historia ecclesiastica*. Ed. J. Bidez. Berlin.

Rufinus, 1908: *Historia ecclesiastica*. Ed. Th. Mommsen. Berlin.

Socrates *Historia ecclesiastica*. Migne, *Patrologia graeca* 67, 33-841.

Sozomen, 1960: *Historia ecclesiastica*. Ed. J. Bidez. Berlin.

Suda, 1928-38: *Lexicon*. Ed. Ada Adler, 5 vols. Leipzig.

Theodoret, 1954: *Historia ecclesiastica*. Ed. L. Parmentier. Berlin.

Zosimus, 1887: *Historia nova*. Ed. L. Mendelssohn. Leipzig.

Secondary Sources

Africa, T.W., 1971: "Urban Violence in Imperial Rome," *The Journal of
Interdisciplinary History* 2:3-21.

Anastos, M., 1962: "Nestorius Was Orthodox," _Dumbarton Oaks Papers_ 16:119-140.

Bacht, H., 1953: "Bie Rolle des orientalischen Monchtums in den kirchenpolitischen Auseinandersetzungen um Chalkendon," In _Das Konzil von Chalkedon_, ed. A. Grillmeier and H. Bacht, 2:193-314. Wurzburg.

Blockley, R., 1975: _Ammianus Marcellinus. A Study of his Historical and Political Thought_. Collectio Latomus 141, Brussels.

Brown, P., 1964: "St. Augustine's Attitude to Religious Coercion," _Journal of Roman Studies_ 54:107-116.

_____, 1963: "Religious Coercion in the Later Roman Empire: the Case of North Africa," _History_ 47:283-305.

Brunt, P.A., 1966: "The Roman Mob." _Past and Present_ 35:3-27.

Cameron, A., 1976: _Circus Factions. Blues and Greens at Rome and Byzantium_, Oxford.

_____, 1973: _Porphyrius the Charioteer_, Oxford.

_____, 1970: _Claudian: Poetry and Propaganda at the Court of Honorius_, Oxford.

Charanis, P., 1974: _Church and State in the Later Roman Empire. The Religious Policy of Anastasius the First, 491-528_, Thessaloniki.

Chastagnol, A., 1960: _La Prefecture urbaine a Rome sous le Bas-Empire_, Paris.

Dagron, G., 1970: Les moines et la ville. _Travaux et Memoires_ 4:229-276.

Downey, G., 1961: _A History of Antioch in Syria_, Princeton.

Frend, W.H.C., 1952: _The Donatist Church_, Oxford.

Gregory, T.E., 1979: "Vox Populi," _Violence and Popular Involvement in the Religious Controversies of the Fifth Century A.D._ Columbus.

Heaton, J.W., 1939: _Mob Violence in the Late Roman Republic_, Urbana.

Highet, G., 1954: _Juvenal the Satirist_, Oxford.

Janin, R., 1964: _Constantinople byzantine_, Paris.

Jarry, J., 1968: _Heresies et factions dans l'Empire byzantine du IVe au VIIe siecle_, Cairo.

_____, 1960: "Heresies et factions a Constantinople du Ve au VIIe siecle," _Syria_ 37:348-371.

Joannou, P., 1972: *La legislation imperiale et la christianisation de l'empire romain, 311-476.* Orientalia Christiana analecta 192, Rome.

Jones, A.H.M., 1964: *The Later Roman Empire, 284-602: A Social, Economic and Administrative Survey.* 3 vols., Oxford.

_____, 1940: *The Greek City from Alexander to Justinian*, Oxford.

Kohns, H.P., 1961: *Versorgungskrisen und Hungerrevolten im spatantiken Rom.* Antiquitas 6, Bonn.

LeBon, G., 1909: *The Crowd in History*, London.

Lecky, W., 1891: *A History of European Morals*, London.

Liebescheutz, W., 1963: "Did the Pelagian Movement Have Social Aims?," *Historia* 12:227-241.

Liebescheutz, J.H.W.G., 1972: *Antioch. City and Imperial Administration in the Later Roman Empire*, Oxford.

Lintott, A.W., 1968: *Violence in Republican Rome*, Oxford.

MacMullen, R., 1966: *Enemies of the Roman Order*, Cambridge, Mass.

Manojlovic, G., 1936: "Le Peuple de Constantinople," Trans. by H. Gregoire. *Byzantion* 11:617-716.

Martindale, J.R., 1960: Public Disorders in the Late Roman Empire, Their Causes and Character," BA Thesis, Oxford.

Matthews, J., 1975: *Western Aristocracies and Imperial Court, A.D. 364-425.* Oxford.

Momigliano, A., ed., 1963: *The Conflict between Paganism and Christianity in the Fourth Century*, Oxford.

Palanque, J.R., 1933: *Saint Ambroise et L'empire romain*, Paris.

Rist, J.M., 1965: "Hypatia," *Phoenix* 19:214-225.

Rude, G., 1964: *The Crowd in History*, New York.

_____, 1959: *The Crowd in the French Revolution*, New York.

Sakellariou, K., 1980: "And they Removed him from his Pastorate (in modern Greek)," *To Vima*, 7 September: 2-3.

Seyfarth, W., 1969: "Von der Bedeutung der Plebs in der Spatantike," In *Die Rolle der Plebs im spatromischen Reich*, eds. V. Besevliev and W. Seyfarth, pp. 7-18. Berlin.

_____, 1963: *Soziale Fragen der spatromischen Kaiserzeit im Spiegel des Theodosianus*, Berlin.

Stein, E., 1949: *Histoire du Bas-Empire*, vol. 2. Ed. and trans. J.R.
   Palanque, Paris.

Syme, R., 1968: *Ammianus and the Historia Augusta*, Oxford.

Thompson, E.A., 1969: *The Historical World of Ammianus Marcellinus*,
   Groningen.

Teall, J.L., 1959: "The Grain Supply of the Byzantine Empire,
   330-1204," *Dumbarton Oaks Papers* 13:87-139.

Tengstrom, E., 1974: *Bread for the People. Studies of the Corn-supply
   of Rome during the Late Empire*, Stockholm.

Yavetz, Z., 1969: *Plebs and Princeps*, Oxford.